CHURCH
KINGDOM
WORLD

CHURCH
KINGDOM
WORLD

THE CHURCH AS MYSTERY
AND PROPHETIC SIGN

Edited by Gennadios Limouris

Faith and Order Paper No. 130
World Council of Churches, Geneva

Cover: The ceiling of the baptistry of St Mark's Basilica, Venice: Christ and the apostles.

The WCC Language Service translated the papers by Staniloae (first translated from Romanian into French by Dan-Ilie Ciobotea), Lochman and Boné.

ISBN 2-8254-0847-6

© 1986 World Council of Churches, 150 route de Ferney, 1211 Geneva 20, Switzerland

Typeset by Macmillan India Ltd

Printed in Switzerland

CONTENTS

PREFACE: A NEW BEGINNING

Since the emergence of the modern ecumenical movement there has been a constant concern for a proper inter-relation between its three main emphases and forms of expression: theological efforts seeking to prepare the way towards visible unity, endeavours to bring Christians and churches together in common mission and evangelism, and the concern for common Christian witness and service in the world. Following the formation of the World Council of Churches, the task of holding together these three streams of ecumenical commitment has become even more urgent; the integrity and coherence of the Council are here at stake.

The movement, and later the Commission, on Faith and Order of the World Council of Churches, representing the first of these three emphases, has sought from the beginning to keep in mind the broader perspective of unity for mission, witness and service. Some of its former studies have dealt quite explicitly with aspects of this wider dimension and a more comprehensive attempt was made through the study on "Unity of the Church — Unity of Humankind".[1] This study led to important clarifications, although not to a concluding report which could be presented to the churches.

A new attempt had to be made, therefore, especially since over the last years an increasingly strong desire has been voiced in ecumenical circles to eliminate the impression that within the WCC the struggle for church unity and the commitment to common witness and service are parallel and not clearly interconnected tasks. Accordingly, the Vancouver Assembly emphatically welcomed the proposal of the Faith and Order Commission to undertake a new study on "The Unity of the Church and the Renewal of Human Community". Vancouver emphasized that this study should have a clear ecclesiological focus through highlighting the concept of the church as *sign*. This approach, which was then widened by the Standing Commission on Faith and Order in terms of "The Church as Mystery and Prophetic Sign", is of great significance. It does not aim at a comprehensive ecclesiology in ecumenical perspective. It seeks to develop the conviction that the inter-relation between church and human community is not merely a matter of external relationships, of functions and of activities of the Christian community. Rather, the relation between church and human community should be conceived as basically rooted in the nature, place and calling of the church in the Triune God's saving plan for the whole of humanity.

The attempt to show forth at a deeper theological level the inter-relation between the unity of the church and the renewal of human community was the basis for the first consultation within the framework of the new study. Meeting 3 – 10 January 1985 at the Roman Catholic Conference Centre in Chantilly, near Paris, France, the thirty participants of the international consultation heard a number of presentations and responses to them. They discussed in groups and endeavoured to develop various clarifications and perspectives. From the reports of the groups emerged a first draft text on "The Church as Mystery and Prophetic Sign". It is a preliminary outline and provides a basis for further work.

At Chantilly Faith and Order for the first time held two consultations simultaneously. The second was part of the other major Faith and Order study programme "Towards the Common Expression of the Apostolic Faith Today" and dealt with a contemporary interpretation of the third article of the Nicene-Constantinopolitan Creed (381). Holding these two consultations together — at the same time and in the same place — proved to be an enriching experience in terms of common worship, theological exchange and contacts with the various churches of the Paris region. The two groups also met over lunch with Cardinal Jean-Marie Lustiger, Roman Catholic Archbishop of Paris.

The draft report from Chantilly on "The Church as Mystery and Prophetic Sign" was further discussed and revised at the plenary meeting of the Faith and Order Commission at Stavanger, Norway, in August 1985. It will undoubtedly need more revision and expansion as the study proceeds. At the same time, the study on unity and renewal is now focusing on two areas of human brokenness and renewal with a view to their ecclesiological implications: the community of women and men in church and society, and the struggles for justice and peace. A number of consultations on these two issues, reflecting on concrete cases and examples, will provide further insights which need to be seen in relation to the reflections on the church as mystery and prophetic sign.

Even though the study on "The Unity of the Church and the Renewal of Human Community" is still in its initial stages and will require a number of years before completion, we would like to document this initial stage by way of the present publication. Its purpose is threefold: to make the study better known, to invite wider participation, and to present some highly interesting reflections by theologians from different

Christian traditions. The book brings together the papers and responses given at Chantilly and the first draft of the report, which is presently under further revision. It may however serve as an interesting example of how a first step may be undertaken in the course of a short consultation in order to lay a basis for future work.

My colleague the Rev. Dr Gennadios Limouris carried special responsibility for organizing the Chantilly consultation. I am grateful to him and to all who helped him in preparing this book.

Geneva, April 1986   Günther Gassmann
                                          Director
                                          Faith and Order Commission

NOTE

1. Cf. Geiko Müller-Fahrenholz, "Unity in Today's World", *Faith and Order Paper No. 88*, Geneva, WCC, 1978.

NOTES FROM A DIARY

Arctic weather, the coldest for two centuries. Wintry white surroundings at Chateau "Les Fontaines" at Chantilly, near Paris, a former seminary and a historic spot for the Jesuit community, with a rich scientific and theological library, one of the best in France. The consultation marks a new beginning of the Faith and Order programme on "The Unity of the Church and the Renewal of Human Community" — a new beginning which will perhaps give rise to several years of study.

Our friends from France are with us to participate in *two* consultations, in fact — one on the apostolic faith, and the other on unity and renewal.

Highlight of the opening service is a homily by the moderator of the Faith and Order Commission, Prof. John Deschner, underlining the importance of apostolic faith — in the sense of truth — as primordial for each Christian and church to advance together towards visible unity.

Then a warm welcome to the participants, including our friends from the Paris area: Rev. Jacques Blanc, president of the Council of Lutheran and Reformed Churches in France; Rev. Marc Chambron of the Lutheran Church of the Holy Trinity, Paris; Rev. Daniel Atger of the Reformed Church of the Annunciation; Rev. Michel Freychet, in charge of ecumenical affairs at the Protestant Federation of France; Armenian Bishop Nakashian, Paris; Rev. Jacques Fischer of the Lutheran Church of Paris, and many others.

General introductions by the moderator and the director of the Commission on the programmes and the appropriateness of holding the two consultations together, and a communal meal, conclude the first day of this new beginning.

But we are just at the beginning, and there is still a long way to go — a series of papers, working groups, discussions and theological debates will follow, sometimes going on until midnight.

What really marks this new style of "cohabitation" at the two consultations is the communal worship — morning and evening — coupled with the warm relationship that exists between the participants. Prayers, hymns, experiences and different customs vary each day's worship and illustrate that it is possible to praise the Lord in a diversity of ways where gospel and culture join in faith and prayer from the heart.

The sixth of January — Sunday — is Epiphany, which commemorates the baptism of our Lord in the Jordan. Our friends attend different services in Paris: at Nôtre-Dame, where Cardinal J. M. Lustiger celebrates mass; at St Etienne where Metropolitan Meletios of the Greek Orthodox Archdiocese of France, co-celebrating with our Orthodox participants, blesses the waters; at the American, Lutheran and Reformed Churches. All these congregations welcome their Sunday visitors.

At mid-day, we rejoice in the presence of the Cardinal of Paris at our meal with the Community of Sisters of the Immaculate Conception. With simplicity, kindness and warm humour, this pastor leaves with us a confession of faith: "I am a pastor, the carrier of the crosses of my sheep, and for that one must be simple-hearted, seen and unseen, realistic and in continual prayer." During the two hours together questions, ideas and opinions are exchanged. This visit gives us strength and courage for the new beginning.

In the afternoon a pilgrimage to a sacred spot — we climb the hill to the Orthodox Institute of St Sergius on the outskirts of Paris. More than sixty years old, the Institute — like a Russian village, right in the heart of this secular city — still bears witness to the past which has so marked Orthodox theology of the nineteenth century and ecumenism in the West. Prominent theologians, thinkers and philosophers in exile have found refuge and taught in this "Russian monastery".

We visit the church, a former Protestant place of worship, now one of the most beautiful Russian Orthodox churches of the diaspora with its icons from Russia and other liturgical objects. Candles, incense, vigil lamps — expressions of Russian piety which awaken us to the reality of the mystery of the church.

Fr Alexis Kniazev is rector of the Institute. Born in Russia before the Revolution, a man of two worlds and two cultures, and of prayer and courage, he welcomes us with cordiality and kindness.

The evenings are long, and there is much discussion and debate. Is the church a *mystery* or a prophetic *sign* for the world today? We fall into the pattern of our meetings. One day we break the rhythm of our life to visit the famous stables and castle of Chantilly; as Camus says, "la culture enracine la tradition".

The day before the end of the meeting, French television, for their programme "Présence orthodoxe", comes to film our consultation. Participants are interviewed on different topics, ranging from reception of the Lima document (BEM) to diakonia and pastoral care in suffering Lebanon — they share their many-sided interconfessional perspectives. This is the first time Faith and Order goes on French television. And image is followed by sound — France Culture's programme visits us for a round-table discussion on church unity and this consultation, and on Faith and Order's programmes in general.

During our stay at "Les Fontaines", several friends from the ecclesiastical world of Paris come to greet us: Mgr Jérémie, assistant bishop of the Greek Orthodox Archdiocese of France, the Rev. Jacques Maury, president of the Protestant Federation, and others.

On the evening of 9 January, the consultation comes to an end — a report is "born" which will undergo correction and revision and must be presented to the Plenary Commission in August in Stavanger, Norway, for further discussion.

Our friends take the road home, with the hope and conviction that the church is a mystery in the communion with Christ, but also a prophetic sign which reconciles and serves for and in the world.

In thanking all those who have helped us to make this new beginning, I would like to express particular appreciation to my colleagues, Dr Thomas Best, Mrs Eileen Chapman and Mrs Renate Sbeghen. I should also like to record my warm thanks to colleagues in the WCC Publications Department for their cordial cooperation. I hope that this publication will be a useful contribution to our common goals and tasks towards the visible unity of the church.

Orthodox Easter, May 1986   Gennadios Limouris

THE CHURCH AS SACRAMENT, SIGN AND INSTRUMENT

The Reception of this Ecclesiological Understanding in Ecumenical Debate

Günther Gassmann

I. Introduction: terminological and theological background

The designation of the church as "sacrament" is ambiguous and conceals a wide range of different ecclesiologies. Moreover, does not the extension of the concept of sacrament to include the church serve to confuse rather than clarify? Is not the application of this concept to the church an expression of an inappropriate triumphalistic ecclesiology? Those are only some of the criticisms levelled against it. It is also a fact that certain ecclesiastical and theological traditions have defined the idea of sacrament narrowly, and in essence limited it to the sacraments of baptism and the Lord's Supper. That has led to reservations against a wider use of the concept of sacrament.

Against this background it is all the more remarkable that during the last fifteen years a reception of the idea of the church as sacrament has taken place in ecumenical debate. Certainly, at the same time, preference has been expressed for the complementary concepts of "sign" and "instrument", which perhaps indicates a certain reluctance to use the concept of sacrament in this wider sense. Such reluctance springs, on the one hand, from the desire to avoid a proliferation of different understandings of what a sacrament is, and, on the other, from a sense that the concepts of sign and instrument are less open to misunderstanding and less patient of a triumphalistic ecclesiology. When applied to the church, these concepts stress its nature as servant and indicate that the church is not grounded in itself and is, at the same time, directed to something beyond itself. That certainly is also true of the concept of sacrament, but it is not so immediately apparent.

This certain hesitation in view of the idea of the sacramental nature of the church on the one hand and on the other a parallel explanatory,

•The Rev. Dr Günther Gassmann, a Lutheran pastor, director of the Secretariat of the WCC's Faith and Order Commission.

complementary use of "sign" or "instrument" either in addition to it or instead of it, seems to me to be also perceptible in the way in which one of the key texts for our subject has been formulated:

> By her relationship with Christ, the Church is *a kind of* sacrament *or* sign of intimate union with God, and of the unity of all mankind. She is also an instrument for the achievement of such union and unity. [1]

The church is "sacrament" by its relationship with Christ, not in itself. "Sacrament" is interpreted by "sign" and "instrument" as a means to communion with God and the unity of all humankind. For a closer understanding of what it means for the church to be "a kind of" sacrament, reference must be made to the total context in which the term is being used. In view of its ambiguity, the same applies, too, to the examples of its reception in the course of ecumenical debate.

What reasons lie behind this entry of the idea of the church as sacrament, sign and instrument into ecumenical debate? It can, for example, be shown that the ecclesiological deliberations and statements in the theological work of the Faith and Order movement and now of the WCC Commission on Faith and Order have gradually drawn closer to an understanding of the church as sacrament as a visible sign of grace. There has been a close link from the beginning between this development and a tendency which also leads to this new terminology: the basic concern in all ecumenical discussion of the church and its unity to understand both as not having their meaning and their goal in themselves. The church and its unity (or our striving to make its unity visible) point beyond themselves to the world into which the church is sent as an instrument of salvation and the love of God, and also to the fulfilment in the kingdom of God.

This orientation of the ecumenical debate on ecclesiology converges with what can be indicated by the formula "church as sacrament, sign and instrument". Hence, at a certain stage of development in ecumenical debate, its "reception" became possible. In the course of that process, the reception of the formula in various texts of the Second Vatican Council has, of course, exerted a powerful and often explicitly acknowledged influence. Moreover, the fact that it is an open formula has meant that different approaches within the ecumenical movement have been able to make use of it. How it is meant to be understood can only be gathered from the context in which the formula is used.

If we review the ecumenical documents relevant to our present survey (and this review is, of course, incomplete), we realize that we can use the word "reception" only with certain qualifications. It indicates no more — but no less either — than that from about 1968 onwards the expression "church as sacrament, sign and instrument" and its individual terms have increasingly been used in various ecumenical documents, but of course not in all of them. In some cases it has been in the context of an explicit discussion of these terms and of their appropriateness and interpretation. In other documents, the terms are abruptly introduced and then the context may provide some indication as to what they are intended to express. We shall now trace that process of reception, understood in that sense.

II. The reception of the concept of the church as sacrament, sign and instrument

1. The early use of the concept

In the development of ecumenical theological thought we observe the same phenomenon as we see more generally in the history of theology: long before a new theological proposition or perspective finds wide acceptance, we find reflections and statements in which it is indicated or expressed in rudimentary outline. Concerning our theme, we read already in the report of the First World Conference on Faith and Order in Lausanne (1927) that "the Church is God's chosen instrument by which Christ, through the Holy Spirit, reconciles men to God through faith. . ."[2] In the report of the Second World Conference on Faith and Order in Edinburgh (1937), the church is described as "the realisation of God's gracious purposes in creation and redemption, and the continuous organ (sc. instrument) of God's grace in Christ by the Holy Spirit".[3] Our theme can be seen taking on clearer shape in the report of the advisory commission on the main theme to the Second Assembly of the World Council of Churches at Evanston in 1954. There the church is designated as "the bearer of hope, the sign and witness of God's mighty acts, the means (sc. instrument) of His working", as "the sign of that which He is doing and will yet do" and as "the means through which God is carrying His purpose to effect". The question is already being raised at this stage whether the church in its human weakness can live up to this high calling. Because the church has God as its foundation and lives in his strength, "it remains witness, instrument and field of action for Him while history lasts. . ."[4]

2. The explicit reception in the study "Unity of the Church — Unity of Mankind"*

A continually broadening reception in ecumenical debate of the concept of the church as sacrament, sign and instrument began in 1968 at the *Fourth Assembly of the World Council of Churches at Uppsala*. As at the Second Vatican Council — and certainly influenced by its statements on

---

*Later "The Unity of the Church and the Unity of Humankind".

the subject — this happened by means of a particular sentence, which was later frequently quoted as a key reference: "The Church is bold in speaking of itself as the sign of the coming unity of mankind."[5] This sentence from the report of Section One was formulated in the context of an assembly which had running through it the particular theme of the church's relation to the world within a comprehensive historical and theological perspective. On that background the Faith and Order Commission had already asked one year before Uppsala at its meeting in Bristol in 1967: "What is the function of the Church in relation to the unifying purpose of God for the world?. . . What. . . is the relation of the churches' quest for unity among themselves to the hope for the unity of mankind?"[6] Those words set the basic agenda for the Faith and Order study "Unity of the Church — Unity of Mankind", which was decided on in 1968 and in the course of which the key sentence from Section One at Uppsala, and with it the idea of the church as sacrament, sign and instrument, was first taken up and further developed in greater detail. We can examine only that specific aspect of that study here.[7]

In the first outline for the study in 1969 there is a section on "The Church as a Sign of True Community". In it we read: "The Church is a sign that, in all their diversity, men belong together. It must therefore prove itself the Church by its ability to really embrace the diverse forms of human life and to relate them to one another."[8] This initial understanding of "sign" as purely exemplary and applied to the inner life of the church was widened in the reaction by a Dutch study group to the outline: "The Church should regard itself as an instrument and sign of God's unique unifying activity among all people. The Church should serve as an example of unity to the world."[9]

In a preparatory paper for the *Faith and Order Commission meeting in Louvain in 1971* we find for the first time a direct comment on the concept of the church as sign (with reference being made to Uppsala 1968 and *Lumen Gentium*): the church "is the sign by which God's all-embracing love is visible in this world. It is not only a symbolic image. It is a sign, because the living Christ wishes to be, and is, present in its midst. It *is* a sign. But it is also no more than a sign. The mystery of the love of God is not exhausted through this sign, but, at best, just hinted from afar. So just as the church can be understood in this way as a sacrament or sign, its oneness can also be understood as a sign." Here several differentiations are already implied. The church is sign not only as an example but also as an instrument. It is a sign because the living Christ is present and at work in his church. But this quality of the church is limited. Both the church as such and its oneness can be understood as signs, but in the case of its oneness the claim is then qualified: "This sign of oneness is broken by the tensions and divisions in which the churches are living. . ."[10] The Louvain meeting transformed this qualification into the question as to how the church and the churches can, nevertheless, be signs of the presence of Christ, of reconciliation and of the coming unity of humankind.[11]

In a review (1972/73) of the development so far of the study "Unity of the Church — Unity of Mankind" the first differentiating interpretations made in 1971 are further developed. References to the key sentences from Uppsala and *Lumen Gentium* are followed by an attempt at a definition of "sign": "Signs point to a reality, an event, a meaning with which they are not identical but whose presence they make real and effective. Being intimately linked with the reality they represent, they remain signs only as long as this presence is effective and recognized as such." Both the real effectiveness of the sign and its connection with and subordination to what it is intended to mediate are emphasized here. At the same time, the question posed at Louvain is taken up and answered Christologically: with its weaknesses and divisions, the church can dare to make the claim to be a sign "or even sacrament" of the coming unity of mankind "only by virtue of her relationship with Christ". "In his life, death and resurrection Jesus Christ has become the sign of the unity of all men. In him the expected unity in the kingdom of God has become manifest in human history. . . The Church as the fellowship of those who follow him in faith, love and hope participates in his power to be a sign of the unity of all men. . . As witness to this coming unity it is called to take up its cross and become, like the crucified Lord, the sign of God's judgment and mercy. But in thus following Christ and being guided by his Spirit it lives under the promise that God who has raised him from the dead will also vindicate it as a sign of the coming unity."[12]

The paper proposes further considerations and differentiations in an attempt to incorporate the concept of the church as sign or sacrament into the whole saving work of the Triune God from the incarnation to its consummation in the kingdom of God. It is thus stressed that the church is not a sign by its own choice. "God himself has chosen it to be in Christ the sign or sacrament of the unity in his kingdom." But its calling is worked out in its involvement in humankind's struggles, hopes and fears. Participating in Christ's signifying power, the church cannot be "less concrete, less human, less demanding, less contradictory". "The unity of all men" can also be expressed as "the salvation of all mankind", of which the church is the sign, in that it "proclaims Christ as the source of peace, freedom and fellowship". Thus the church is intended to be a sign not only in its proclamation but in its whole existence. And it is not only a sign of salvation but also of judgment: "Following the crucified Christ it cannot expect less than its Master who on the cross has been made the sign of mankind's ultimate judgment." An idea from the preparatory paper for Louvain 1971 is again taken up in the words: "In all this the Church is more than a sign: It is God alone who in Christ through the Spirit unites mankind unto himself. But it is also no less than a sign: God makes true his promise as proclaimed by his servants. God makes the Church a sign almost against its own desires and in spite of human sin which renders the sign obscure. To be and to live as this sign is its whole reason for being."[13]

This already relatively full development of the concept of the church as sign was eventually presented in systematic form in a preparatory paper for the meeting of the *Faith and Order Working Committee in Zagorsk in 1973*. After a short introduction justifying the use of the concepts of "sacrament" and "sign" as applying also to the church, a series of short paragraphs follow giving the reasons why the church is a sign and in what respects. The church is a sign:

a) because it points towards Christ, who is the true sign or sacrament chosen by God;

b) because Christ is truly present in it;

c) because it points to the future, making present that which is to come;

d) because it lives under the promise that Christ will be present wherever his word is proclaimed and the sacraments, baptism and eucharist, are being celebrated.

The document continues by spelling out how the church fulfills its calling to be a sign:

a) God has sent the church in Christ to be a sign of his salvation and judgment. This sign becomes visible only where it is confronted with the particular conditions of human life in one place.

b) Living as a sign means to put no limits to what God may intend to work through his church and even outside its limits and boundaries.

c) As a sign of the kingdom and lordship of God, the church will have to be a prophetic sign calling to repentance. It must be a sign of reconciliation as well as binding together those who are separated by human sin.

d) As a sign the church is called to show forth Christ as he becomes alive in a particular situation: as consolation in view of ultimate limits, as liberation and militant courage in view of oppressive powers, as prophetic challenge to any identity based on self-assertion, as acceptance where an identity is in danger of being destroyed.[14]

The Faith and Order Working Committee discussed this paper in Zagorsk in 1973. There was not yet full unanimity on the use or the meaning of the word "sign" as applied to the church, but the concept as such was positively received. It was however also decided to omit references to the church as "sacrament", since they were not theologically essential to the general thrust of the argument.[15]

The study "Unity of the Church — Unity of Mankind" came to an end in its then form at the meeting of the *Faith and Order Commission at Accra in 1974*. Because of the very different positions between the churches and often within churches on this issue, no conclusions of the study in the form of a detailed report could be formulated or accepted. Nothing more than a brief statement based on the study was approved at Accra. Its last section is headed "The Church as 'Sign'". The paragraph in this section relevant to our present subject is but a pale reflection of the wealth of thought on the subject that we have met with in the course of this review: "The Church is called to be a visible sign of the presence of Christ, who is both hidden and revealed to faith, reconciling and healing human alienation in the worshipping community. The Church's calling to be such a sign includes struggle and conflict for the sake of the just interdependence of mankind."[16]

I have drawn on the texts produced in the course of the study "Unity of the Church — Unity of Mankind" in some detail here, because they are little known and some of them are not easily accessible and particularly because they represent the most thorough theological examination to date of the concept of the church as sacrament, sign and instrument in ecumenical debate. It is truly remarkable that, in the course of a difficult and controversial study, which produced no conclusive results, a new ecclesiological perspective should have been investigated so intensively and continually new descriptions of it reached. In it the study made a significant contribution to the ecumenical debate.[17] Whenever the concept of the church as sacrament, sign and instrument appears in various ecumenical texts after Accra 1974, it can basically be traced back to that study.

3. Reception in other WCC texts

While the idea of the church as sacrament, sign and instrument was treated in depth in the study on "The Unity of the Church and the Unity of Mankind", it also appeared in two other areas of the WCC's work prior to 1975, in one case even before the concept made its "breakthrough" at Uppsala in 1968. In 1967 and 1968 the Working Group between the Roman Catholic Church and the World Council of Churches carried out a study on "Catholicity and Apostolicity". In one of the contributions to this study, the Catholic theologican J. L. Witte presented "Some Theses on the Sacramental Nature of the Church"[18] but his attempt to have this new perspective — based on Vatican II — included in the study was only partially taken up in the final report. Appendix IV of this report examines "The Sacramental Aspect of Apostolicity" without, however, describing the church itself in these terms. Since this whole study influenced the work and the report of Section One in Uppsala, "The Holy Spirit and the Catholicity of the Church", it no doubt also helped to prepare the ground for the more far-reaching statement about the church as sign of the coming unity of mankind.

The second area in which the idea of the church as sacrament, sign and instrument was dealt with directly was the study on "Concepts of Unity and Models of Union". The work on this was done in close inter-relation with the study on "The Unity of the Church and the Unity of Humankind" since both were carried out under the auspices of Faith and Order and there is some overlap in their subject matter. In his introductory address on this theme at a consultation in Salamanca in 1973, Lukas Vischer noted that the concept of the church as a "sign" deserved special attention in the efforts to describe our common goal in the search for unity. [19] This was done first of all in a presentation by Ernst Käsemann on "The Ecclesiological Use of the Keywords 'Sacrament' and 'Sign'", which is reproduced in the German report of the meeting. Because of the danger that these ambiguous terms might blur the distinction between Christ and the church and because, given the divisions of Christendom, no church could surely presume such a high claim, Käsemann strongly recommends "that these dangerous key phrases which do nothing to advance dialogue be avoided". If it is possible at all to speak of a "sign", he said, then the cross is the true sign of the church. Where the church succeeds in showing forth the truth of God and human beings and world in the sign of the cross, then "it is, like its Lord Himself, a sign in the perspective of the resurrection of the dead and the dawn of a new creation". Although this use of the term "sign" is ecclesiologically possible, Käsemann nevertheless pleads for another designation to be used. [20]

The Salamanca report itself, on the other hand, sees the terms "sacrament", "sign" and "instrument" as a possible means of arriving at a description of the unity of the church. Although the terms "sacrament" and "sign" refer in the first place to the mystery of God's revelation in Jesus Christ, they have in the course of history also been used for the community of those who believe in him. "Because this community is an integral part of the mystery of God's action in bringing about his kingdom, it is, in a derivative sense, 'sacrament' and 'sign' in history, reflecting God's purpose and promise to all people. As the Church communicates the gospel, it is 'sign' in the sense of instrument. It contributes to the salvation and communion of people with God in Jesus Christ." In describing the church in this way, the report continues, there can be no thought of identifying the church and the kingdom of God. The church is no more than a sign indicating the reality of God's purpose for the world. Given the disobedience of Christians to their calling and the divisions among the churches this sign is often hidden. The church is, therefore, a sign which constantly needs to be made visible. This section of the report concludes with the suggestion that further attention be given to the terms "sign" and "sacrament" in the ecumenical movement. [21]

After the very thorough examination of the ecclesiological use of "sacrament" and "sign" in the study on "The Unity of the Church and the Unity of Humankind" and the ready reception of the terms in the Salamanca report, it is all the more surprising to find them being used with such reticence and in such weakened form in the report of the WCC *Fifth Assembly in Nairobi* — at least when one is aware of all the discussions that had gone before. In the report to the Assembly, *From Uppsala to Nairobi*, we still find the very true statement that: "In the course of the study (i.e. 'The Unity of the Church and the Unity of Humankind') the designation of the Church as sacrament became more and more important." Renewed emphasis is also put on the nature of the sign as calling and task (as in the Salamanca report): "The divided churches will grow together as they aim to become the sign they are called to be."[22] The report of Section II at Nairobi takes up the key sentence from Uppsala and spells it out in concrete terms, stating that "the Church must be open to women and men of every nation and culture, of every time and place, of every sort and disability". What is lost here is the wealth of theological meaning contained in the idea of the church as sign. An echo of it can be heard, however, at two points further on in the same report: "It is as a community which is itself being healed that the Church can be God's instrument for the healing of the nations." Elsewhere there is mention of two tendencies in the search for unity, one of which "places primary stress upon faithfulness to the calling of the Church to be sign, instrument and foretaste of Christ's purpose to draw all people to himself".[23] Section IV, in its report, describes the church's task as that of being "a sign of God's liberating power" and "a sign of hope" for the society in which it is placed and to which it belongs.[24] Such statements no doubt disarm the criticism that, in this understanding, the church is seen as "a kind of 'spiritual' sign of coming unity".[25] Here too, however, the deeper theological dimension of the sign concept has been lost from view. Even though one cannot expect a conference report to contain subtle theological argument, Nairobi could nonetheless have been more explicit in its reception of the process of reflection which had preceded it.

After Nairobi the idea of the church as sacrament, sign and instrument appeared in a number of ecumenical contexts, with the original reticence vis-à-vis the term "sacrament" apparently having receded considerably. The gradual broadening acceptance of this terminology evident here does not, however, go hand in hand with a common understanding of the terms used, as the following four examples clearly show.

In an essay by the general secretary of the WCC, extracts of which are included in the preparatory material for the 1983 Assembly in Vancouver, we read: "Just as the divisions and conflicts of the churches are signs and reflections of the divisions in our world, so the unity of the Church is a sign and sacrament of God's purpose to unite all into Christ as the head of a new humanity and a new creation."[26] This sentence in a sense condenses and summarizes the insights of the study on the unity of the church and the unity of humankind with the Christological and eschatological dimension being indicated as clearly as the nature of sign and sacrament as gift and task.

The "Common Account of Hope" worked out at the meeting of the *Faith and Order Commission at Bangalore in 1978* says of the communion of the churches that, however much it has been obscured by our disobedience and divisions, it can still, in God and through the power of the Holy Spirit at work today, "become a sign of hope for others".[27] As regards the form to be taken by church unity, the conference at Bangalore has this to say: "The Church is a sign and instrument of Christ's mission to all humankind. The sign is obscured by the present divisions." The churches must, therefore, "seek to be a reliable, trustworthy sign as a people constantly uniting in mutual forgiveness and reconciliation". Commenting on the church as sign, the report adds that "in affirming the sign-character of the Church two dangers can be avoided. The one would be to imagine that the Church could be called to bring about the Kingdom of Christ and to take into its own hands what Christ alone can fulfil. The other would be to be oblivious to the calling, visibly and tangibly to manifest our oneness in faith and hope in history. To be a sign and instrument is one way of expressing that Christians are called to be faithful stewards of God's gifts, 'in full accord and of one mind' (Phil. 2 : 2)."[28]

The eschatological dimension which echoes in all references to the church as sign emerges very strongly in the report of the *World Conference on Mission and Evangelism in Melbourne in 1980*. In the conference's message to the churches we read: "The good news of the Kingdom must be presented to the world by the Church, the Body of Christ, the sacrament of the Kingdom in every place and time."[29] Elsewhere in the report of the conference some explanation of this is given: "The world-wide Church is itself a sign of the Kingdom of God because it is the body of Christ on earth. It is called to be an instrument of the Kingdom by continuing Christ's mission to the world in a struggle for the growth of all human beings into fullness of life."[30] Clearly the conference saw the ecclesiological use of sacrament, sign and instrument as a possible means of reaching an adequate description of the relation between the church and the kingdom of God. Another of the section reports explains: "The whole Church of God, in every place and time, is a sacrament of the Kingdom which came in the person of Jesus Christ and will come in its fullness when he returns in glory." Here too, however, it is repeatedly stressed that the sacramental sign-character of the church can only be made authentic, credible and effective through the way in which the church lives and works in and for the world.[31] Lastly, it emerges from the Melbourne report that Ernst Käsemann has clearly modified his position on the ecclesiological use of the term "sign" (though continuing to emphasize the *theologia crucis*). In his address in Melbourne he says: "Our place on earth is to stand under the cross. God's rule in this our time cannot be separated from the crucified Christ. All believers and churches are at best signs and instruments for the dawning of the end and for that fulfilment in which God alone will rule over the world and will destroy all enemies and rivals. Yet we are indeed to be signs and instruments of that end, if God is not to be blasphemed as untrustworthy."[32]

In *Lima in 1982 the Commission of Faith and Order* decided to resume the earlier study ' on "The Unity of the Church and the Unity of Humankind", altering its theme and orientation to "The Unity of the Church and the Renewal of Human Community". This change was introduced in an attempt "to avoid a misunderstanding that the unity of the church be just an instrument of general cosmopolitan or generally humanitarian unity. The unity of the church is a gift of the Spirit. It has doxological and sacramental integrity which cannot be measured in terms of its secular efficacity for other goals only."[33] In his report to the Commission, William Lazareth urged that the sacramental and socio-ethical dimension implied in the sign concept should be held together. The steps by which the churches give expression to their growing community with one another are, he said, "internal" signs for Christians. Only if the churches are united in their efforts and at the same time together face the needs and problems affecting the human community will their unity also become a sign for the human community.[34]

Following this orientation it was the *Sixth Assembly of the WCC at Vancouver 1983* which proposed "that the Faith and Order Commission make a theological exploration of the Church as 'sign' a central part of its programme on the Unity of the Church and the Renewal of Human Community."[35] This provided the basis for the present reflection on "The Church as Mystery and Prophetic Sign" in the framework of this study.

4. The church as sacrament, sign and instrument in bilateral discussions

However, it is not only in WCC texts that the reception by the ecumenical community of the concept of the church as sacrament, sign and instrument is reflected. As long ago as 1968, the year of the Uppsala Assembly, the *Lambeth Conference* of the Anglican Communion declared that the church must seek to resemble its Lord in his servant humility. "Only in this way can it be an effective sign of the presence in the world of the servant Christ." And in another statement from this conference there are clear echoes of the *Lumen Gentium* and the Uppsala formulations: "So the Church is called to be the foretaste of a redeemed creation, a sign of the coming unity of mankind, a pointer to the time when God shall be all in all."[36] A year later (1969) the theological commission of the *Lutheran World Federation* ended a preparatory paper for the LWF Assembly in Evian in 1970 with a sentence which sounds like an echo of the Lambeth Conference statements: "Ecumenical endeavour which finds its life in the given unity, and which at the same time reaches out to the promised unity, will never seek church unity for its own sake, but will seek it rather as a tool for the reconciliation of all men and as a sign of the new creation which God himself brings about in judgment and in grace."[37]

To round off this survey of the reception of the idea of the church as sacrament, sign and instrument in ecumenical debate, it may be useful to mention a few examples from the reports of bilateral conversations. One place where our theme is taken up and formulated as very concise theses is in the ecclesiological introduction to the final report of the *Anglican/Roman Catholic International Commission*: "The Church as *koinonia* requires visible expression because it is intended to be the 'sacrament' of God's saving work. A sacrament is both sign and instrument. *Koinonia* is a sign that God's purpose in Christ is being realized in the world through grace. It is also an instrument for the accomplishment of this purpose inasmuch as it proclaims the truth of the gospel and witnesses to it by its life, thus entering more deeply into the mystery of the Kingdom. The community thus announces what it is called to become."[38]

The report of the official dialogue between the *World Alliance of Reformed Churches and the Roman Catholic Church* says of the church that it is called in what it is, says and does, "to be the visible witness and sign of the liberating will of God, of the redemption granted in Jesus Christ, and of the Kingdom of peace that is to come. . ." Further on we read: "By living as a new people persuaded of God's acceptance in Christ, the Church is a persuasive sign of God's love for all his creation and of his liberating purpose for all men."[39] Jacques Desseaux believes the idea of the church as sacrament is closer to the Reformed tradition than the Lutheran and adduces the two above-mentioned references in support of this contention.[40] But in the report of the official conversations between the *Lutheran World Federation and the Anglican Communion*, the church is defined as "an instrument for proclaiming and manifesting God's sovereign rule and saving grace".[41] And a sentence in the report of the *Lutheran/Roman Catholic conversations in the USA* is reminiscent of the statement from the Lambeth Conference in 1968: "The members of the Church, wherever they are found, are part of a single people, the one body of Christ, whose mission is to be an anticipatory and efficacious sign of the final unification of all things when God will be all in all."[42] The *Joint Roman Catholic/Lutheran Commission* for its part again affirms: "The Holy Spirit enables and obliges the Church to be an effective sign in the world of the salvation obtained through Christ." The sentence which precedes this statement in the report gives an explanation of it: "The Church is the community in which by faith the new life, reconciliation, justification and peace are received, lived, attested and thus communicated to humanity."[43]

The similar lines of thought which come to expression in these various bilateral reports are somehow summarized in the report of the *Anglican-Reformed International Commission* when it states: "The Church is a sign and the first-fruits of the ultimate order which transcends history. In so far as it is a true sign and the true first-fruits, it will also have an instrumental value in promoting justice and freedom in the transcient social order of history. . ."[44]

This brings us to the end of our voyage of discovery through the ecumenical discussion, and discovery it certainly has been, for the wide and rich diversity of the ecumenical debate has not yet been explored from the point of view of its reception of the concept of the church as sacrament, sign and instrument. This is why I have largely confined myself to presenting the main points of reference. But even this has in a sense been a voyage of discovery which has yielded much richer results than I had expected. As regards our understanding of "reception", however, this suggests that much more is happening in the reception of certain theological concepts in ecumenical debate than might be supposed if one looks only at certain eye-catching formal acts of reception.

III. Summary and conclusions

The remarkably wide reception of the ecclesiological use of the terms sacrament, sign and instrument in ecumenical debate suggests that this terminology is found to be helpful in describing the place and vocation of the church and its unity in God's plan of salvation. In some cases the adoption of these terms is justified on the grounds that they help to avert precisely that erroneous understanding of the church which critics of this terminology see as being implicit in its use, namely, the total identification of the church with Jesus Christ, the fullness of his grace and the presence of his rule and kingdom. Clearly, and this must be stressed here, what is intended through the reception of this terminology in ecumenical discussion is anything but a triumphalistic understanding of the church.

Obviously, we cannot expect to find a uniform understanding of the ecclesiological use of sacrament, sign and instrument in the various ecumenical texts from the past fifteen years. Nevertheless, it is, I think, clear from the references I have given that there has been a development towards a deeper and, in some cases, more differentiated theological interpretation of this newly adopted ecclesiological terminology. This is apparent even where these terms are employed only in a passing reference and in very different contexts.

Since this concerns a process of reception in ecumenical debate it is only logical that not only the church as such but also, specifically, the unity of the church should be described in terms of sacrament, sign and instrument. This could equally apply to the other marks of the church, its holiness, catholicity and apostolicity. And whatever the particular emphasis at any time may be, it always refers to the church as a whole. The character of the church as sign always includes its unity, holiness, catholicity and apostolicity. Thus, the definition of the unity of the church as sign is an expression of the sign-character of the church as a whole.

As can be seen from the references presented above, tracing the reception of the idea of the church as sacrament, sign and instrument, the most frequently used term "sign" is actually the least unambiguous of the three. "Sign" is used, on the one hand, in the sense of pointer, symbol, example and model, and on the other, in the sense of an effective means, a tool or instrument. Both are legitimate, though clearly the latter understanding is the more common, in many cases being given added force by the inclusion of the word "effective". "Sacrament" seems always to be used in the sense of effective mediation, representation or anticipation.

The sign-character of the church is either assumed as given, or else understood as participation in the one true, fundamental sign, Jesus Christ, or as God's gift to his church or, again, as a calling either yet to be fulfilled or else to be fulfilled constantly anew. There are clear differences of emphasis here, as there are, too, over the question of whether the sign-character of the church is obscured or even destroyed by human sin, disobedience to God's will and the divisions of Christianity. The church's effectiveness as a sign, therefore, is either affirmed as basically unimpaired, or else its presence and effectiveness are challenged and seen as something yet to be realized. Common to both positions, however, is the view that the sign-character of the church is not purely "spiritual" but, according to an incarnational understanding of the church, needs to be set in relationship to the conflicts, needs and hopes of our world.

What emerges very clearly from the description of the church as sacrament, sign and instrument is that the church and its unity do not exist for their own sake. The church is sign, sacrament and instrument of God's love, of his rule, his universal plan of salvation for all humankind in Jesus Christ. Following in the discipleship of the suffering and crucified Jesus Christ it is also, as we read elsewhere, the sign of God's judgment and grace. Finally, and this is the idea which is expressed most frequently, it is the sign of the coming union of all human beings in God's kingdom, the redemption of creation and the fulfilment of all things. The "coming unity of humankind" initially understood as something to be realized in history, has been more and more often placed in this eschatological perspective. This is not to say that the church's mission to be an effective sign of reconciliation and hope here and now for the contemporary world and for humanity is in any way separated from the eschatological perspective. The phrase "anticipatory sign" shows clearly that the two belong inseparably together.

The church can be a sign in this way because, and this is emphasized repeatedly, the living Lord Jesus Christ is present and at work in it. It is a sign as, in the power of the Holy Spirit, it allows Jesus Christ and his truth to be effective through its witness, its proclamation and its life. It is a sign and no more than that, however, serving him who is using it for the salvation and reconciliation of his people.

This, then, is a summary of the different ways in which the idea of the church as sacrament, sign and instrument has been interpreted and of the basic common line of thinking which is emerging in the process of the reception of this idea in ecumenical debate. A clearer linking of the sacraments in the church and the sacramental nature of the church itself has yet to be worked out. On the other hand, some one-sidedness has been corrected in the process of reception and certain approaches have been taken up and developed theologically. "Finished" or polished concepts cannot be expected from a process as dynamic and complex as this. Though still provisional and exploratory, it has furnished new means of expressing certain concepts, which has in turn had repercussions on the content of the concepts themselves. Not only this, but it has helped to bring different ecclesiological understandings closer to one another. This in itself is surely reason enough to earn it more concentrated attention in on going ecumenical reflection, especially in the context of the study on "The Unity of the Church and the Renewal of Human Community".

NOTES

1. Second Vatican Council, *Lumen Gentium*, 1.1.
2. L. Vischer, *A Documentary History of the Faith and Order Movement 1927—1963*, St Louis, The Bethany Press, 1963, p. 31.
3. *Ibid.*, p.42.
4. In *Christ—the Hope of the World*, documents on the main theme of the Second Assembly, Geneva, WCC, 1954, pp.15—16.
5. *The Uppsala Report 1968*, Geneva, WCC, 1968, p.17.
6. *New Directions in Faith and Order*, Bristol 1967, Geneva, WCC, 1968, pp.131—32.
7. On the development of this study cf. G. Müller-Fahrenholz, *Unity in Today's World: the Faith and Order Studies on "Unity of the Church — Unity of Humankind"*, Geneva, WCC, 1978; K. Pathil, *Models in Ecumenical Dialogue*, Bangalore, Dhamaram Publications, 1981, pp.370—78.
8. Study document on "Unity of the Church—Unity of Mankind", in Müller-Fahrenholz, *op. cit.*, p.43.
9. *Study Encounter*, Vol. VII, No. 2, Geneva, WCC, 1971, SE/06, p.11.

10. "Unity of the Church — Unity of Mankind", mimeographed, Geneva, WCC, 1971, FO/71:11, p.4.
11. *Faith and Order — Louvain 1971*, Geneva, WCC, 1971, p.207 (L. Vischer) and 240 (Conspectus of Studies).
12. "Unity of the Church — Unity of Mankind", mimeographed, Geneva, WCC, 1973, FO/72:10(R), pp.14—16.
13. *Ibid.*, pp.16—17.
14. "Unity of the Church — Unity of Mankind", mimeographed, Geneva, WCC, 1973, FO/73:28, pp.11—14; also in *What Unity Requires*, Geneva, WCC, 1976, pp.4—7.
15. Minutes, Meeting of the Working Committee in Zagorsk, Geneva, WCC, 1973, pp.12—13 and 44.
16. *Uniting in Hope*, Commission on Faith and Order, Accra 1974, Geneva, WCC, 1974, p.93.
17. Cf. also Pathil, *op. cit.*, p.376: "The most important contribution of the study is the understanding of this 'sign-character' of the Church."
18. In *One in Christ*, VI, No. 3, 1970, pp.390—409.
19. R. Groscurth, Hrsg., *Wandernde Horizonte auf dem Weg zu kirchlicher Einheit*, Frankfurt, Lembeck Verlag 1974, p.38.
20. *Ibid.*, pp.125—27 and 130—32.
21. *Ibid.*, pp.163—64.
22. *Uppsala to Nairobi 1968—1975*, Report of the Central Committee to the Fifth Assembly of the World Council of Churches, New York/London, Friendship Press/SPCK, 1975, pp.78—79.
23. *Breaking Barriers: Nairobi 1975*, ed. D. M. Paton, London/Grand Rapids, SPCK/Wm. B. Eerdmans, 1975, pp.61 and 65.
24. *Ibid.*, pp.90—91 and 94—95.
25. Cf. P. W. Fuerth, *The Concept of Catholicity in the Documents of the World Council of Churches 1948—1968*, Rome, Editrice Anselmiana, 1973, p.251: He continues by saying: "Only when the Churches in the WCC become more conscious of the Church's sacramentality can their consciousness of catholicity grow."
26. P. Potter, "The Unity of the Church: What is to be done?", in *Lausanne 77: Fifty Years of Faith and Order*, Geneva, WCC, 1977, p.79.
27. *Sharing in One Hope*, Faith and Order Commission, Bangalore 1978, Geneva, WCC, 1978, p.6.
28. *Ibid.*, p.239.
29. *Your Kingdom Come*, report on the World Conference on Mission and Evangelism, Melbourne 1980, Geneva, WCC, 1980, pp.235—36.
30. *Ibid.*, p.184.
31. *Ibid.*, pp.180—82 and 193.
32. *Ibid.*, p.69.
33. *Minutes*, Standing Commission 1981, Geneva, WCC, 1981, p.35.
34. *Towards Visible Unity*, Comission on Faith and Order, Lima 1982, Vol.I: Minutes and Addresses, ed. M. Kinnamon, Geneva, WCC, 1982, p.19.
35. *Gathered for Life*, report of the Sixth Assembly of the World Council of Churches, Geneva, WCC, 1983, p.50.
36. *The Lambeth Conference 1968*, resolutions and reports, London, SPCK, 1968, p.122.
37. *Lutheran World*, XVII, No. 1, 1970, p.50.
38. Anglican-Roman Catholic International Commission, *Final Report*, London, SPCK, 1982, pp.7—8.
39. *The Presence of Christ in Church and World*, Geneva/Rome, WARC/SPCU, 1977, pp.18—19.
40. *Dialogues théologiques et accords oecuméniques*, Paris, Les Éditions du Cerf, 1982, pp.124—25.

41. *Growth in Agreement*, reports and agreed statements of ecumenical conversations on a world level, ed. H. Meyer and L. Vischer, New York/Geneva, Paulist Press/WCC, 1984, p.21.
42. *Papal Primacy and the Universal Church: Lutherans and Catholics in Dialogue V*, ed. P. C. Empie and T. A. Murphy, Minneapolis, Augsburg Publishing House, 1974, p.10.
43. *Growth in Agreement, op. cit.*, pp.250−51.
44. *God's Reign and Our Unity*, report of the Anglican-Reformed International Commission 1984, London/Edinburgh, SPCK/Saint Andrews Press, 1984, pp.21 and also 19.

THE CHURCH AS MYSTERY AND SIGN IN RELATION TO THE HOLY TRINITY — IN ECCLESIOLOGICAL PERSPECTIVES

Gennadios Limouris

A significant development in the ecumenical movement of this century has been the challenge related to the crucial topic of ecclesiology, emerging from the Christian church's bilateral and multilateral dialogues. It is the "century of the ecclesiology".[1] The Christian world's quest for unity is one with its quest for the church. All who work for this reality must ask themselves therefore what kind of unity this is to be or, in other words, what nature the church has so that it might correspond to God's plan and will for it. Of course, there are conflicting assessments concerning the nature of the church's unity, the role of the church and its ecclesiastical inner structure and tradition. However, there are some common features that are particular to the theology that has come from the one holy, catholic and apostolic church—a common historic framework, sometimes a continuity in tradition, an overall influence of Greek-Roman philosophy — particularly in Europe — sometimes a similarity in worship and a common consciousness in the preserving, nurturing and developing of the theological tradition of the church. Therefore, unity debates become the focus of ecclesiological discussions in the ecumenical arena today. But diversity on the ecclesiological foundations of unity today remains the main obstacle for doctrinal agreement between the churches.

The movement for church unity has grown and diversified in an impressive way since Nairobi 1975. Contrary to what many say, we are in the midst of a resurgence of concern for church unity; in that *aggiornamento* the World Council of Churches is playing a crucial and significant role.

• Rev. Dr Gennadios Limouris, Secretariat of the WCC's Faith and Order Commission. This paper has been expanded in light of the discussions at Chantilly.

From the beginning of the ecumenical movement, the Faith and Order Commission had envisaged working for unity in Christ as a necessary presupposition to contribute to the need of a common witness (μαρτυρία) of Christians and Christian churches. Thus the Faith and Order movement focused its attention on the doctrinal issues of disunity and unity.

The *aim* of the Faith and Order Commission "to proclaim the oneness of the church of Jesus Christ and to call the churches to the visible unity of the one faith and eucharistic fellowship, expressed in worship and in common life in Christ, in order that the world may believe" was never regarded as being a goal in itself. It was always seen in the framework of God's all-encompassing purpose for his church and his world. One aspect of this broader perspective is envisaged in the first of the seven *functions* of the Commission: "To study such questions of faith, order and worship as bear on this task and to examine such social, cultural, political, racial and other factors as affect the unity of the church."

God in relation to the tri-personal Trinity

God in himself is a mystery. Of his inner existence nothing can be said. But through his creation, providence and work of salvation ("soteria") God comes down to the level of humankind. He who makes us as thinking and speaking beings has made himself accessible to our thought and our speech. Teaching our spirit, he wakens in us thoughts and words which convey the experience of his encounter with us. But at the same time we realize that our thoughts and our words with regard to him do not adequately describe him as he is in himself.

For us, human beings are flowers grown from the depths of his ineffable mystery. Our words and thoughts of God are both cataphatic and apophatic, that is, they say something and yet at the same time they suggest the ineffable. If we remain shut in within our formulae, they become our idols; if we reject any and every formula, we draw on the undefined chaos of that ocean. Our words and thoughts are a finite opening towards the infinite (ἄπειρος), transparencies for the infinite, and so they are able to foster within us a spiritual life.

We are aware of the infinity of the divine ocean but we do not dissolve in it ourselves. We communicate with it in human fashion, going down into its depths with the diving suit of human nature and human formulae, or sailing on its vast expanse in a boat constructed according to laws based on our experience of the ocean itself and therefore adequate to it, but also adapted to our own human limitations.

Yet we can say that just as the incarnation of the world in the life and works of the historical Christ is a condescension of the divinity towards human obscurity, a condescension through which "mysteries hidden from the foundation of the world" are revealed, so the same word, the

Truth itself, comes down in order to "be incarnate" in our formulae through the labyrinth of confusion and ignorance in which he finds himself. In other words, doctrinal formulations have a twofold aspect. On the one hand, they "reveal" the Truth in terms accessible to human intelligence, and in this sense they have an affirmative or cataphatic aspect and are useful to man both as support in his spiritual grown into maturity, and as safeguard against the mistaken conceptions which human intelligence is always tempted to adopt. But on the other hand, they are not the Truth itself, only expression of the Truth in human terms, and in this sense they have a negative or apophatic aspect. God has revealed himself clearly as Trinity in the work of salvation and hence this salvation is clear only in Christ in whom God has come down among humankind in order to save them.

A personal and saving God is a God simultaneously transcendent and revealed in immanence. In the Old Testament where God still remains only transcendent, even though he acts upon history from a distance, he is not revealed as Trinity.

Therefore, the revelation of the Trinity took place in Christ, for one divine Person became man in order to save humankind, while another divine Person remained above humankind so that He who had become incarnate might raise humankind up to that divine Person who was not incarnate but transcendent.

The Son becomes man but the Father remains the goal of the incarnate Son's striving and that of all humankind whom the Son has united to himself. The incarnate Son could not have been without this goal or else he would not have been able to imprint this striving towards it upon all the faithful.

The Son becomes man in order to be the model and the centre from which a force radiates making humankind like Christ in their striving towards God the Father. This force ($\delta \acute{v} \nu a \mu \iota \varsigma$) which becomes an intimate principle within all who believe, yet at the same time always remains above them, is the third divine Person, the Holy Spirit.

When the God in Trinity reveals himself to us, he reveals himself as a Saviour-God, and a God whom we experience in the saving activity which he exercises upon us and within us. He is revealed to us as an "economic Trinity".

But in this revelation of itself, the Trinity also draws our attention to certain premises about the intrinsic relations between the divine Persons. The theological teaching on the inner reality of the Holy Trinity is based on these indications and on the bond which joins the eternal relations between the divine Persons together with their saving activity.

A God who at the same time is one and three is a mystery beyond our logical grasp; it is the supreme apophatic reality. Fr Boris Bobrinskoy writes: "The divine unity is not merely one of the attributes of God; more exactly it is the profound life of God and the fruit of the love that exists between the divine Persons. This unity is in no way a depersonalizing confusion, nor a structure of monads, nor the sum of the parts of a whole. Only in God does unity assume a complete union which preserves the distinct and absolute qualities of the Persons."[2]

In God the love between "I's" is perfect and therefore the unity between them is surpassing. Even so the distinct "I's" are not abolished within this unity, otherwise the living relationship between them would be impossible.

If love depends essentially on God, then the reciprocal relationship in which love manifests itself also belongs to the divine being. In God there must be a relationship, but from equal to equal, not, as is the case among humankind, from superior to inferior. On the other hand, this relation must not be thought of as referring to something outside God. His world implies that God is in need of something distinct from himself. But the divine relation must take place in God himself.

In order to maintain the definition of love as the essential divine act and the simultaneous definition of this act as a relation while the divine essence remains one, we must see the divine essence at the same time as a relation-unity, or, by conversion, as unity-relation.

Unity must not be destroyed on behalf of relation, nor must relation be abolished in favour of unity. Relation on reciprocal reference is an act, and this act belongs to God's essence. Reference is common in God although each person has his own position in this common act of reference. P. Florensky wrote in this context: "The subject of the truth is a relation of the Three, but a relation which appears as substance, in other words, a substantial relation."[3]

Therefore in the case of the divine reciprocal giving, however, Father and Son preserve their own positions. The Son rejoices in the gift of existence received from the Father, and the Father rejoices in the gift of his own gift received by the Son.

Christians are aware that all humankind are sisters and brothers. But sisters and brothers are born from a common father and mother which means that human beings are sisters and brothers because they come from a common source of being, because they draw their existence from the same common source. In every human being — my brother or my sister — I must see manifested the same source of being which is also revealed in me, but in a different way from my own. Therefore, I must rejoice in all those gifts of God which I do not have, and in all his successes, while he must also extend the benefit of his own gifts and successes to me, because in a certain manner I am in him and he is in me; or, to express it in another way, the same source that is manifested in him is also my own. This is our human consubstantiality. But in this consubstantiality we are different, as the divine Persons are not, and we serve as complement to each other, a fact that derives from a certain separation that exists between us and which we can make larger or smaller since human nature repents itself distinctly in every "I". The separation nevertheless is not total. It is not ontological, as if it were a separation between one nature and another.

In God the consubstantiality of these three Persons is perfect. God is the perfect model of the tri-personal, consubstantial form of human existence of the perfect mutual relationship of three persons.[4]

Perfect consubstantiality can exist only between subjects who do not carry behind them any of the burdens of being "thing" or "subject", that is, between subjects who share a perfect love.

Ekklesia: the gathering of the people of God

Christians gathered together do not constitute a secular "congregatio"; they come not only to meet each other but mainly to meet Christ who sacramentally is there present in the midst of them. He is the very reason for drawing individuals together in order to create an authentic communion of saints. Orthodox ecclesiology differs on this point from other interpretations defining the motivations for fellowship. Two points need clarifying.

1. The very meaning of the term *ekklesia* was originally the calling of individuals into an important gathering. In this connection the emphasis is laid upon the caller and his authority, as well as the act of his calling. Who actually calls, and for what purpose? It is not a person who once appeared, and soon disappeared, or an anthropocentric body inviting out of sentimental reasons. This body has a special authority and power which is entrusted to it from above. The call is made because something happened in history, an event which turned the tide of history. Humankind, therefore, is invited to turn its attention towards this event (Christ Resurrected) and receive redemption and salvation. These tidings of redemption and salvation are the motives for calling all, the people throughout the ages and in all corners of the world. If the apostles could not resist spreading this invitation, even though they were often threatened by death, their secret must be attributed to the fact that they knew from personal experience the height and the depth of the blessings accompanying this calling. *Ekklesia* was in fact the place in time where one human person met the Risen Lord and enjoyed the offerings of the Redeemer. In this sense Cyril of Jerusalem, addressing the catechumens, describes the size of this institution beyond geographical restrictions. "If you are in a town, do not ask only where is this particular church, but where is the Catholic church because this is the proper name of this holy Mother of all of us; Spouse of our Christ."[5]

2. While the gathering of people is highly important, it is not they who determine the legitimacy, the validity and the authority of such a

gathering. Of course, the church must be seen in its double aspect, sociological and sacramental, spiritual and temporal. Human presence is necessary, but it is not this element which gives weight to and determines the authenticity of the church. There have been moments in history when heretics, such as the Arians, were numerically greater than the Orthodox. And yet this difference could not substantiate the heresy.

It is not just the assembled people who constitute the church, but the people with the sacramental presence of Christ. In short, it is Christ with his people who create the church — head and body — the first-born Son and the after-born brethren. There have been, however, different views on this. The assembled congregation has been seen as constituting the church and as conferring the power of the ministry to a minister because they designate him by their testimony and unanimous voice.

Without underestimating the human factor, and the mandating factors, we must avoid the error of regarding the Christological vertical factor as subordinate or secondary. There is no doubt that the church is objectively *congregatio generis humani*,[6] an assembly resulting from a gathering of people, or that it is *ecclesia ex circumcisione, ecclesia ex gentibus*. But it is also the invitor who is able to offer blessings already prepared from the very beginning of creation to those who come *ex qua credunt homines*.

Continuously from the early centuries there has always been a stable criterion for distinguishing the true church from pseudo-assemblies held by schismatics or heretics, i. e. mere groups of "Christians" worshipping and confessing Christ. If we endeavour to apply the principle of the participants as determining the nature of the church, then we are in danger of plunging ourselves into complete confusion. What was important in the old days and still is, is not who and how many are gathered, but under what conditions they are gathered, to what kind of altar and to what bishop or authority they are joined. The fight of St Augustine against the Donatists was based exactly on this argument. Being deprived of the Holy Spirit they were no more authorized to offer real sacraments and to have anything to do with the effective grace. He maintained that the Holy Spirit cannot exist everywhere in fragments. Its existence is only with the real church. Only by such clear-cut beliefs did early Christianity succeed in saving the Catholic faith and preserve the unbroken unity of the *una sancta*.

Israel was treated in all kinds of ways by God so that she might become the true people, the chosen of God, the "laos tou Theou". But on the contrary Israel made every possible effort to become one nation among the other nations. Similarly new directives had to be given again and again to remind the new Israel of her vocation. All the pronouncements of Christ concerning his kingdom must be understood in this context. The church of Christ gives us the means of truly presenting Christ's memory. The church becomes the historical locus, the embodiment of God's saving action in the temporal order. The church knows that the word (logos) becomes flesh in its own existence. The reconciliation is not to be remembered as one particular event and moment in the past. Redemption is a continual process, the divine work of redemption (καταλλαγή) that takes place in and through the church.

All the great events of Christ's sufferings and triumphs are happening again in a mysterious way, through the sacramental life of the church. Calvary and the resurrection are the church's daily experience. This is why in every liturgy we refer to these events not only as belonging to the past but as taking place really now, before us. "Now, today is the crown of our salvation and the manifestation of the eternal mystery. The Son of God becomes the Son of the Virgin, and during the holy week the church sings: 'Let all mortal flesh keep silence and stand with fear and trembling . . . for the King of Kings and the Lord of Lords comes forth to be sacrificed and to be given for food to the faithful . . .' "[7] Or: "Thou hast appeared today to the world, and Thy Light, O Lord, has been shown to us . . . . The Lord of all endures circumcision and his righteousness circumcises the sins of mortals and today gives salvation to the world . . . . The Virgin today brings forth the Omnipotent, and the earth offers a cave to the Unapproachable."[8]

All these expressions must not be taken as poetic hyperboles in the Orthodox church hymnography. In fact they reflect the existential experience of the church's worship and belief in the resurrection and the presence of the Spirit in its midst. The church becomes the risen, living body of Christ through its reception of the Spirit and the sacramental presence of Christ. In this way, then, the believer shares in the reality of Christ when he shares in the spiritual reality of the church.

The greatest miracle of Christ's deeds in the New Testament is the creation of the church on the day of Pentecost. Anything miraculous about Jesus is superfluous and irrelevant in the light of the far greater miracle of the rise of the church as the continuous saving event and institution in history. One can say that liberal Western theology suffers from a certain docetism on ecclesiological matters. It cannot see the difference between the memory and the affirmation of a past event and the occurrence of that past event. The church, in its visible form, does not exist only to affirm in all seriousness that an event took place, prior to anyone's experiencing of it. It is the continuation of his redemptive work; for this purpose it was given apostles, empowered with the Holy Spirit. The reality of Christ must not be isolated in one particular moment of history by dissociating him from the church. In doing this we dichotomize the fundamental affirmation of the doctrine of the mystical body, the head from the rest of the organism. The church has an ontological presence on Christological grounds.

Again, all the faithful in Christ, although alive in an eschatological perspective, have to live on an institutional basis, since they are social beings. This is the external side, impossible to be separated from the mystical. The mystical communion is expressed in a visible communion. Concerning the paramount affirmation, Dionysius the Areopagite in his ecclesiastical hierarchy relates the close connection between the priestly liturgical function and the celestical function of the angels. In a similar way, John Damascene underlines the hylomorphic structure of the sacraments, as bread and wine for the eucharist. The church acts for its members. Since they are in space and time they need elementary organization. They are not an amorphous body. This is why, from early times, bishops were warned by St Ignatius and St Polycarp that they are servants (διάκονοι) in the diakonia of Christ for the people of God. The church has always protested against deviations, against clericalism and secularism, and the ministry must be kept in its spiritual and heavenly frame.

The unity of the church in the Pentecostal vision

Reflecting on the church in an ecclesiological sense reveals three particular images — all of them scriptural — which are of special value. The first is negative — a picture of what the church is not — while the second and third are positive.

The first image is found in an incident during our Lord's last journey to Jerusalem. There had been an argument among the twelve apostles about precedence, about who should be the first in the kingdom, and Christ put an end to it by saying: "You know that the rulers of the Gentiles lord it over them, and their great men exercise authority over them. It shall not be so among you" (Matt. 20: 25 – 26).

Here, then, is a negative picture, indicating what the church is not. "It shall not be so among you." The statement means that the community which Jesus came to establish is radically different from any other type of community. The church is not to be understood in terms of human worldly power of earthly authority and jurisdiction. In ecclesiology, then, we must be exceedingly careful not to take as a "model" some political or cultural forms existing in the secular pluralistic society around us. We must not assimilate the church to monarchist structures like those of the Roman Empire, or hierarchies like those of medieval feudalism, or even to the patterns like those of modern democracy. The bishop (the leader of the historic church), for example, is to be thought of neither as a feudal overlord nor as a democratically appointed "representative". The chief bishop or primate is neither an absolute monarch nor a constitutional president nor the chairman of a board of directors. To interpret the church's leadership, and by implication the church, by such analogies as these is to overlook its uniqueness. It is to forget Christ's warning: "It shall not be so among you."

At his temptation, Christ deliberately rejected the offer of worldly power; and Christ's church must likewise resist the same temptation. "My kingship is not of this world" (John 18: 36).

Let us turn to our second image, that of the church gathered for worship and celebration of the divine eucharist. In this context the church is to be understood eucharistically. The church is essentially the body of Christ. It is a reality revealed in the act of the eucharist, even fulfilling itself visibly in time through the constant celebration of the Lord's mystical supper. In the words of St Paul: "The bread which we break, is it not a participation in the body of Christ? Because there is one loaf, we who are many are one body, for we all partake of the same loaf" (1 Cor. 10: 16–17). The faithful become members of Christ's mystical body, the church, by communicating together in his sacramental body at the eucharist. It is the eucharist that manifests the church and its unity. The church is held together, not just by outward apostolic jurisdiction, but by the eucharist which is celebrated by Christ and in his name until the end of history. Unity is not imposed arbitrarily by any external authority, but offered from within by common participation in the one loaf. The historical ministerial organs of church government, the discipline of canon law, of ecclesiastical courts and the rest, are certainly indispensable, but they entirely rely on the charisma of Christ in the Spirit. What is primary is the "charisma" of the eucharist. When the church celebrates the eucharist, then and only then is it empowered to become on earth what it truly is in heaven.

To appreciate fully the understanding of the church and its unity in the perspective of the eucharist, we need to keep in view the relationship between baptism (including chrismation or confirmation) and eucharist which are the revelatory and saving acts of God by which the church in history is constituted. By considering these sacramental acts in isolation, theologians often create inadmissable dichotomies between the real presence of the divine grace and its dynamic ecclesiological effects, revelation and creativity. It is through these sacraments that human history becomes ecclesiological and bears divine qualities, so that it transforms history having itself been transformed into a reality which is "Spirit-bearer", "Christ-bearer", "God-bearer".

A careful study of this sacramental activity will confirm the supernatural effect of the operating grace which constitutes the church in history and leads it to the eternal kingdom of God. Liturgy shows us clearly and in an experimental way what the church receives and how it becomes an instrument of the holy paraclete sharing in his activities for the establishment of the kingdom of God. This experience in fact shows us that the church is a kind of Christ's epiphany in and through his people in history. In sacramental celebrations the same Christ reappears again and again as the bearer of the kingdom of God upon all flesh. It is the same Christ, who by love — that same love which was fully shown at Calvary — transfuses to the partakers of the sacraments, his perfections and moral attributes, that is, deification (θέωσις). The Greek fathers of the church insisted strongly on this sacramental deification, underlining at the same time that this operation is not at all restricted to the person involved, but is an action which is stimulating, creative, challenging, promoting and existential.

Through a study of the primitive church, we can understand this point even better and see the wider effects of the sacramental and eucharistic activity of the church. In the liturgical prayers of the officiating bishop — who virtually represents Christ — the congregation, the people of God offers and receives the sacrifice as a spiritual oblation under the power of the Holy Spirit. This corporate offertory has two sides — one ontological and another eschatological. Its immediate aim is sanctification, but it prepares equally for the expansion of the kingdom of God. Such has been the place and influence of the liturgy on the life of the Orthodox people that Orthodox spirituality has been rightly described in liturgical as well as missionary terms.

This means that in Orthodoxy church and liturgy go together. In dealing with the action of the dedicated widows and the virgins, St Paul does nothing else than to reflect faithfully on the Old Testament thought about sacrifices. In the same way as the people of Israel chose a special animal to represent them at the offering of the sacrifice, so these devout women belonged to a special category and were offered, as it were, on behalf of the whole congregation. It is important to note that the liturgical framework supported them in this difficult task. In order to understand this better, we need to explore the Christian conception of the "victim" as used in Pauline theology (Rom. 13).

The *anamnesis* of the Holy Supper is not only a representation of a past historical event, but also a challenge and a binding force for missionary activities for the glory of Christ. This aspect is liturgically manifested, making the eucharistic action a "theophany", i.e. a continuous revelation of God with repercussions for religious life.

In the West St Augustine's eucharistic theology has often puzzled historians of dogma, in as much as he was able to speak of the eucharist both in terms of the body and blood of Christ and also (for the first time) in terms of "figure" and "sign". The use of these apparently contradictory terms seems strange today, when it is assumed that one cannot logically hold both views, but only one or the other.

I doubt whether Augustine ever realized the existence of such a dilemma, given that both streams of thought were present in the ecclesiastical tradition which he had inherited. Thus from Tertullian he would have learned of the bread "by which He makes manifest His own body"[9] and which is "a figure of His body".[10] From Cyprian he would have learned that the eucharist is a true sacrifice which the priest "offers to God the Father in the Church" when he celebrates the eucharist on Christ's behalf. Yet Cyprian can nevertheless talk of the blood of Christ being "shewn forth" in the chalice.[11] Again, in Optatus of Milevis, his predecessor in the controversy with the Donatists, Augustine would have read that the altar is "the seat of the body and blood of Christ [. . .] where they (His body and blood) used to dwell for certain moments of time". For Optatus the chalice is a "container of the blood of Christ".[12] Again, in Ambrose of Milan, whom he so greatly admired, Augustine would have found a realism parallel to that of Optatus, but also the statement that the oblation is the "figure of the body and the blood of our Lord Jesus Christ".[13] In fact, the Western eucharistic tradition, which Augustine had inherited, combined both realistic and figurative elements, and Augustine accepted them both, since both derived from the teaching of Orthodox theologians.

Frederick van der Meer has expressed the matter very well: "Augustine wrote at an epoch when the worship of the body and blood of Christ consisted simply in reverent reception, handling and consumption: at such time men had not yet adverted to the idea of looking for the factual presence, which can be continually worshipped, behind the signs which they grasped and the means of grace of which they availed themselves. And in consequence the words *figura* and *signicum corporis Christi* sound otherwise in their ears than they do now."[14]

Therefore, in discussing Augustine's theology of the church and the eucharist, we have to take into account a number of very different factors: ecclesiastical and liturgical tradition, popular religion — in which Augustine came increasingly to share as he grew older — religious controversy, both with the Donatists, who differed from the Catholics on the doctrine of the church, and with pagans, who differed from the Christians on the nature of worship, and finally Augustine's own thought, with its strongly platonic bent, combined with a steadily-increasing biblicism, and steadily-increasing sense of man's utter dependence on the grace of God. Of these elements, it is the first and the last — ecclesiastical tradition and the Bible and the doctrine of grace — which were, in the long run, the most powerful in shaping Augustine's thought, but not exclusively so. It is clear that, to the end of his life, however much he might have found it necessary to attack them, Augustine retained an admiration for the thought of the neoplatonists, who had helped him to come to a decision to seek baptism at Milan in 386; and however much he might have deplored the separation of the Donatists, there is in Augustine something of their unyielding temper, and he never concealed his debt to their greatest theologian, Tyconius.[15]

Such then, must be our "icon" of the church: the whole people of God, gathered around the Lord's table — bishop, priests, deacons and laity — all together performing the single action of the eucharist.

But while thinking of the church Christologically as the body of Christ, we need also to keep in mind another "icon" to complete and balance our ecclesiology — a pneumatological "icon" of the church as the kingdom of the Holy Spirit. St Irenaeus spoke of the Son and the Spirit as the "two hands of God" which always work together. If the church is eucharistic, it is at the same time pentecostal: it is an extension of the incarnation and of Pentecost. After the upper room of Maundy Thursday there comes the upper room of Whitsunday, and both upper rooms are normative for a just appreciation of the nature of the church. "When the day of Pentecost had come, they were all together in one place. And suddenly a sound came from heaven like the rush of a mighty wind, and it filled all the house where they were sitting. And there appeared to them tongues as of fire, distributed and resting on each one of them. And they were all filled with the Holy Spirit . . . " (Acts 2: 1−4).

In this gift of the Spirit at Pentecost, there are three elements of special importance. First, the Spirit is not conferred solely upon a particular hierarchical order, but is a gift to the whole people of God: "They were all filled with the Holy Spirit" (Acts 2:4). It is helpful to recall the distinction, emphasized by Vladimir Lossky, between the two givings of the Spirit. The first occurs on Easter Sunday, when Jesus — risen but not yet ascended — breathes upon the disciples and says to them: "Receive the Holy Spirit. If you forgive the sins of any, they are forgiven; if you retain the sins of any, they are retained" (John 20: 22−23). At this moment the apostles represent the hierarchy of the church: the gift of the Spirit is specifically linked with the authority to bind and loose, and this particular power is not conferred upon the whole body of Christ, but is transmitted through the apostolic college to the episcopate. In the second giving of the Spirit, recorded in Acts 2ff, on the other hand, the apostles no longer represent the hierarchy, but rather they constitute the entire body of the church as it then existed. The Spirit descends at Pentecost upon each and every member of the redeemed community, and this universality of the pentecostal gift continues in the church throughout all the ages. Therefore we are all of us Spirit-bearers: "You have been anointed by the Holy One, and you all know"(1 John 2: 20).

In the second place, the gift of the Spirit at Pentecost is a gift of unity; in the words of Acts 2:1 "they were all together in one place". It is the special task of the Spirit to draw humankind together. This aspect of the Spirit's work is vividly emphasized in Greek hymnography, when it contrasts God's descent at Pentecost with his descent at the building of the tower of Babel (Gen. 11:7). The God of old came down in order to divide humanity, but at Pentecost He came down in order to unite it. As the hymn of the feast of Pentecost expresses it: "When the Most High descended and confused the tongues, He divided the nations; but when He distributed the tongues of fire, He called all to unity."

Unity and differentiation: such are the two aspects — contrasted but not opposed — of the gift of the Spirit to the church. The church is a mystery of unity in diversity and of diversity in unity. In the church a multitude of persons are united in one, and yet each of them preserves his/her personal integrity unimpaired. In any association on the purely human level there will always exist a tension between individual liberty and the demands of corporate solidarity. Only within the church, and through the gift of the Spirit, is the conflict between these two things resolved. In the kingdom of the Holy Spirit there is neither totalitarianism nor individualism, neither dictatorship nor anarchy, but harmony and unanimity.

According to Orthodox ecclesiology, this free unanimity through the indwelling of the Spirit is realized above all in the assembling of a church *council*. Pentecost was in a sense the first ecumenical council, and every subsequent council is a re-enactment of Pentecost. At every true council the gift of the Holy Spirit — at the same time a gift of freedom and differentiation, and a gift of unity — is to be seen as expressing itself in action. At a true council no single member arbitrarily imposes his will upon the rest, but each consults with the others and in this way, through the guidance of the Spirit, together they freely discuss and confess a "common mind". The final decision which emerges from their consultations is far more than a compromise between their varying viewpoints, far more than the sum total of the opinions which individual members brought with them into the council hall. Something extraordinary becomes apparent at the council itself; and this "something extra" is precisely the presence and action of the Spirit of God. "For it has seemed good to the Holy Spirit and to us . . . " (Acts 15: 28).

The pentecostal "icon" of the church and, together with it, our eucharistic "icon" form a salutary corrective to the first and inexact image, the image of earthly power and jurisdiction. "It shall not be so among you" because the church is not a kingdom of this world, but the kingdom of the Holy Spirit; and therefore its rules and principles are not those of human government.

Earlier we asked: what holds the church together? And we answered: not outward power of jurisdiction, but communion in the holy mysteries. We may ask further: what constitutes the final authority in the church? According to their different traditions, Christians tend to reply: the Bible, or the ecumenical council or the pope. Yet none of these things can truly constitute final authority. Just as it is wrong to externalize our notion of unity, making the oneness of the church depend on outward power of jurisdiction, so it is wrong to externalize our notion of authority, identifying it with the letter of scripture, the institution of the council, or the persons, etc. The final authority in the church is the indwelling presence of the Holy Spirit. It is the Spirit who is the true author and interpreter of the inspired word of God, who directs councils, who guides bishops, patriarchs and popes. When challenged about our doctrine of authority, surely we cannot do better than reply with the promise of our Lord: "When the Spirit of truth comes, he will guide you into all the truth" (John 16: 13).

The oneness of the church and the eucharistic community

The church's oneness cannot be understood apart from its other attributes — holy, catholic and apostolic — as it has been expressed and confessed in the Nicene-Constantinopolitan Creed (381) and which are equally essential to the confession of its mystery. In recent theological discussions there has been a constant temptation to discuss unity in isolation, without making any reference to the other attributes. Even if a church proved to be one — in whatever sense — it may not be the authentic church of Christ if it does not also have the other necessary attributes of holiness, catholicity and apostolicity. Therefore a real criterion for the understanding of the history of church is this synthesis of fundamental attributes without any attempt at isolating any one of them from the rest.

This leads us to begin our enquiry into the essence and specific characteristics of unity — when and how the church is one, and not one out of many. We know that in the apostolic and post-apostolic period evangelists and teachers went around preaching the good tidings of Christ. Preaching was not their only profession. It was preaching within the church, on behalf of the church, and before an audience seeking to enter into the ranks of the church. Of course, certain pseudo-teachers who claimed to preach the truth were easily found out and dismissed. Our concern is precisely this: Why did the Catholic church say openly to them that they did not belong to the true church, and what factors assured them that this church was the true one?

The argument put forward was that the church can only be one and undivided because Christ is One and because it maintains the same faith of the apostles down through the ages. Ignatius of Antioch states that the bishops to whom he sent his letters were not the simple presidents of communities, but successors of the apostles.[16] Later on the historian Eusebius praises the importance of "these pillars of faith who were the immediate successors of the Apostles, laid the foundations of the faith in foreign countries, established pastors, and became the pastors and evangelists of different churches of the world".[17]

Belief in the unity of the church presents an obvious dilemma for today. Since the church consists of a variety of people from different races, colours, cultural aspirations and ways of thinking, how then can they manifest their faith unanimously? We have to make a distinction between unanimity and conformity. Unity can exist in diversity and plurality without necessarily implying uniformity.

But is there not today a great reluctance in the ecumenical movement and discussions to accept different forms of church life, worship and doctrinal expression? We tend to use our differences as defence against other churches, instead of accepting them as external signs of the inner riches of the infinite and unbounded grace of the Holy Spirit. But we cannot and should not impose on others our own forms of church life. Perhaps in this respect we have to experience the fact that the road to reunion may involve a kind of death in order that we may receive the new life of the Holy Spirit which flows deep within the differing forms of church life. The unity we seek to restore must necessarily have room for a multiplicity of different forms. It is not to be established through the acceptance of one central human authority or of one programme of action on social and political issues. Nor can it be based on using the Bible as a kind of Koran, that is as a source of inflexible rules applicable under all conditions.

The unity we seek is neither that of church discipline under a centralized authoritarian institution, nor is it based only on the kerygmatic message of the gospel to the world; but it is primarily based on and maintained by the charisms received from the Holy Spirit by the people of God in the historic church. It is therefore a charismatic and eucharistic unity, expressed through and for the communion with the grace of God the Holy Trinity. These words are not to be interpreted as introducing a relativization of the importance of the confessions for re-establishing unity. On the contrary they intend to situate the confessional statements in their right place and function as pointing to the same fundamental event of the unbroken unity realized in the event of the revelation of the life of the Holy Trinity in the church, whose only verbal witness a church confession has always to be. A confession should never be used as a separating force but as a uniting one pointing towards the one central event of the church: its oneness, realized by the Trinitarian God in his historical church.[18]

In the same way discipline is necessary to protect liberty of expression since the church is a divine-human society. True and supreme liberty respects and defends all legitimate liberties. Thus liberty with discipline must be found in the church, as well as unity with diversity. If the church is one, it is also catholic — it embraces all the world. In order that a man may express himself in a catholic way and be free and easy in his thinking, he must also conform to certain prescribed rules laid down by a guardian authority responsible for this common treasure. His spirit must be great and he must be unwilling to impose his personal tastes, preferences and esthetic opinions on others. Without such a discipline there will be chaos — a battlefield of antagonisms.

The charter of oneness in the catholic church is that of symphony in polyphony. The balance of the various instruments is preserved by the conductor of this orchestra. While all together contribute to a harmonious performance, nevertheless each instrument guards its speciality and its proper character. Only from this multitude of instruments and performers are discords and false notes excluded. Respect for the diversity of the instruments in the harmony of the assembly is what makes the unity of this mystical orchestra. *In concordi caritate vestra Jesus Christus canitur* — this is the formula of the authentic spirit of oneness and of catholicity that was outlined in the early second century by Ignatius of Antioch[19] (Rom. 4: 1).

Instead of trying to "adjust" the truth to measure up to our own ideas, we must adjust our own ideas to the infinite idea of the truth. We cannot apply the bed of Procrustes onto doctrinal issues. The best guide and interpreter of the essential thinking of the church is the life of the church itself on all vital issues, *Regulae ad sentiendum cum Ecclesia*. In order to think exactly as the church does, one must live the life of the church, pray with the church and offer oneself in the way it teaches and practises. This follow-up is the way to prevent a ritualistic or spiritual tyranny in the life of the church as it tries to maintain its catholicity.

In contrast to the ancient Greek-Roman philosophy which was unable to conceive of a universal unity of humanity, Christ came to call all humankind to become one — regardless of sex, race and social class. There was to be diversity in one place, unity in another. Not only did Christians stress this point, but St Paul, in writing to gentile Christians, expounds this essential character of the church — the oneness of the people of God.

Human infidelity to the divine Image opens the way to separation from God and to disruption of the unity in human life. This results in damage to the spiritual unity which above all ought to remain untouched. The great Origen rightly said: *Ubi peccata ibi multitudo* . . . .[20] Following the same line of thought, Maximus the Confessor considered original sin to be a separation or fragmentation, or even an individualization. While God tries by all means to bring all into unity, our nature — because of sin — is broken into a thousand pieces. While humankind ought to constitute a harmonious entity where the "I" and "you" are not in opposition, instead it tends to become a warehouse of explosives where individuals learn how to advance in violent disagreement.[21]

The only remedy for this catastrophic disorder, especially in the religious and spiritual field, is an operation which aims at re-establishing this lost unity. A double reconstruction — a unity with God and a unity among human beings. St Augustine summarized this divine action in an excellent statement: "The divine goodness has reassembled fragments from everywhere and puts them into the foundry of its love, and here it reconstructs their broken unity. This is how God has remade what He had previously created and has reformed that which He had formed."[22]

St Gregory Nazianzenus, describing the great miracle of Calvary in one of his sermons, strikingly exalted its manifold blessings: "There were, on that day, all kind of miracles: God on the cross, the sun obscured, the veil of the temple torn, blood and water pouring from his side, the earth trembling, stones crumbling to pieces, the dead coming again into life . . . Who shall celebrate in dignity these wonderful events? But none is comparable to the miracle of our salvation; these precious drops of blood renewing the entire world and refreshing all men as with the juice of fig-trees or clotted milk, by uniting us and clasping us in one."[23]

Unity copies the divine unity of the Holy Trinity. A complete unanimity reigns among the three Triune persons, and provides the pattern according to which we also can be one. The manifested unity is seen not only in faith, but also in all the aspects of church life — the same ecclesiastical authority, the same sacraments, the same liturgical unity. What makes the church one, Irenaeus of Lyons says, is that we hold the same baptism, the same Tradition, the same government, the same episcopacy.

St Paul, conscious in his day of this unity, warns the Galatians to test pseudo-missionaries and suspect evangelists because they go around teaching "another gospel" ($\H{\epsilon}\tau\epsilon\rho o\nu\; E\mathring{\upsilon}\alpha\gamma\gamma\acute{\epsilon}\lambda\iota o\nu$) (Gal. 1:7). Now what differentiates the kerygma of these false evangelists from that of the true church is that they are outside the church, having left it deliberately, while St Paul and his disciples are within.

To sum up, unity is the church itself and all its life resides in this unity and this union with Christ. This continuous union with its mystical head makes it both eternal and earthly, following the theandric union of its Master. On this basis St Paul develops his arguments on unity (1 Cor. 12:12–27).

A guarantee that the church is united with its Master is that the Spirit dwells within it. The classic argument used by Ignatius, St Cyprian, St Augustine and others is that the Holy Spirit can be found only in the Catholic Church. The Donatists cannot claim that they possess efficacious sacraments because they are deprived of the Spirit. The Spirit vivifies only living organisms and members — those who are found in the church and not outside. Those who have cut themselves off from the tree of life, the church, live no longer with Christ and are destitute of the Spirit.

Opposition to this unity of the church is an unpardonable sin. We feel the presence of the Spirit in the performance of the sacraments, especially in the power to bind and loose sins. Heretics and schismatics may have received the Spirit, but not for their salvation but for their condemnation.[24] In the eucharist we take not only the body and the blood of our Lord, but also the Spirit. The Pauline analogy (Eph. 5:30) shows the ethical implications of this inner unity between a married couple with Christ. In this case the married couple constitutes a microcosm of the wider cosmos of the faithful — their union with Christ dictates high responsibilities. Respect, therefore, your bodies, says Paul.

Unity was given to us on the very day of Pentecost.[25] We become partakers of this unity through the same Spirit which indwells for ever in the church. This unity is manifested not only through baptism but also through our membership of the church which constitutes a visible sign and promise of remaining in this unity. Thus it is an ontological, existential and organic unity. In this unity again all members of local churches and communities bear the same distinguishing marks of churchmanship (*notae ecclesiae*). Each has the plenitude of the truth and the faith. This does not mean that one has a certain portion of the faith and the next another portion, so that to fill the gap makes a complementary pattern.

The church is not only an expression of this unity given by Christ, but at the same time it helps the Christian to receive and appropriate the gifts of unity by his response and faithfulness. In other words, both these movements from God and from humankind are seen through and are subject to human experience. Therefore they originate from Christ's incarnation. If "the Word became flesh and dwelt among us" (John 1:14) this is because man could not otherwise attain the invisible mysteries. The whole economy of our salvation is a historical and temporal event, but perpetuated through the eternal love of the first-born ($\pi\rho\omega\tau\acute{o}\tau o\kappa o\varsigma$) Saviour.

Since unity was given to us through the divine incarnation, we respond and accept it through visible signs, such as from the very beginning, obedience to the presbyters, acceptance of the Tradition, and close relationship with the liturgical and sacramental life.

Baptism is a mystery which unites and incorporates a member with Christ and with the community, while the eucharist nourishes and strengthens what once belonged to God. Ecclesiology is nothing more than a theology of this union begun by baptism and afterwards continuing in faithful membership of and living with the church.

The increasing actualization of the whole redemption of humankind was accomplished once for all by Christ's atonement. This "once for all" ($\grave{\epsilon}\phi$' $\ddot{\alpha}\pi\alpha\xi$) is continually operative in the church. This is why dogma and worship in the Orthodox church constantly repeat the great events of Christ's resurrection and victory over death and sin, as if they are actually happening again at every given moment, for dogma states the fact that the church is an unbroken unity and continuation of what happened at the resurrection.

It is quite a different thing to inherit a certain faith than to invent a new one of your own and set up another denomination. The question of deciding whether the separated confessional bodies possess elements of the *una sancta* and are churches in the proper sense, is determined in two ways.

A vigorous answer comes from St Augustine, repeated later by Albert the Great. St Augustine often said of the Donatists: "The evil of their dissension, schism and heresy is their own. The good things, however, which we acknowledge in them are not theirs: they have the good things that belong to our Lord, and to the church." "The sacraments are the nests of the church but these nests do not belong to the heretics; thus, when they lay down their little ones, they do not lay them down outside the church, but within her."[26]

In the Nicene-Constantinopolitan Creed (381) we do not find simple characteristics of the church — one, holy, catholic, apostolic. . . . We are told that the church on earth, regardless of its divisions and frictions, remains in fact one. Its unity is not lost at all. There might exist "churches", a divided Christendom; but nevertheless its unity with the apostolic faith is not interrupted or broken. Again this church composed of sinners is holy. Holiness is visible — is manifested. The same can be said about the means of holiness; they too are visible sacraments — ascesis and so on. There is no question here of the celestial church but of the empirical one, seen and felt in our daily lives. The life of the church is a historical reality. Its saints are its members. To become holy is not an easy task, it implies constant mortifications, spiritual fights, but above all, synchronization and identification with its Head — its Chief. Its Chief is indeed holy, the Holy One of the holy people.

Naturally, this consideration leads to another essential element, which is the aim and the dimension of our endeavours towards perfection and is called ($\theta\acute{\epsilon}\omega\sigma\iota\varsigma$) deification — so familiar to Orthodox spirituality. To give one example we may recall the great ascetic Nilus of Sinai's startling statement which maintains that a spiritual man sees his neighbour as "another God after our God".[27]

The church in relation to the Holy Trinity

The oneness of the church and its unity follow of necessity from the unity of God. Yet the Orthodox idea of the church is certainly spiritual and mystical in this sense that Orthodox theology never treats the earthly aspect of the church in isolation, but thinks always of the church in Christ and the Holy Spirit.

Therefore, the church begins with the special relationship existing between church and God. Three terms can be used to describe this relation: (1) the church is the *image* of the Holy Trinity, (2) the *body* of Christ, (3) *a continued Pentecost*. Consequently the doctrine of the church

is Trinitarian, Christological and pneumatological. The patristic ecclesiology is linked with the patristic Christology and soteriology. Because in
the mystery of the incarnation of the Son and logos of God is included
also the mystery of the church.[28]

1. As an "icon"

As each human being is created according to the image of the Trinitarian
God (Gen. 1:26), so the church as a whole is an *icon* of God the Trinity,
reproducing on earth the mystery of the unity in diversity. In the Holy
Trinity the three Persons are one God, yet each is fully personal; in the
church a multitude of human beings are united in one, yet each preserves
his/her personal diversity unimpaired. The mutual indwelling of the
persons of the Holy Trinity is paralleled by the coinherence of the
members of the church. In the church there is no conflict between
freedom and authority; there is *only* unity, but not totalitarianism. This
conception of the church as an "icon" of the Holy Trinity has many
further applications. "Unity in diversity" — just as each person of the
Trinity is completely autonomous. The unity of the church is linked
more particularly with the person of the church, its diversity with the
person of the Holy Spirit.

2. As the body of Christ

"We, who are many, are one body in Christ" (Rom. 12:5). Between
Christ and the church there is the closest possible bond which we find in
the famous words of Ignatius, "where Christ is, there is the Catholic
church".[29] The church is the extension of the incarnation, the place
where the incarnation perpetuates itself. The church, wrote the Greek
theologian Ch. Androutsos, is "the centre and organ of Christ's
redeeming work; . . . it is nothing else than the continuation and
extension of his prophetic, priestly and kingly power . . . the church and
its founder are inextricably bound together . . . the church is Christ with
us."[30] Christ did not leave the church when He ascended into heaven:
"Lo, I am with you always, to the close of the age" (Matt. 28:20) "for
where two or three are gathered in my name, there am I in the midst of
them" (Matt. 18:20).

The unity between Christ and his church is effected above all through
the sacraments. In baptism the new Christian is buried and raised with
Christ, and in the eucharist the members of Christ's body, the church,
receive his body in the sacraments.

So the eucharist, uniting the members of the church to Christ, at the
same time unites them to one another: "We who are many are one body,
for we all partake of the same loaf" (1 Cor. 10:17). Therefore, the
eucharist creates the unity of the church; as Ignatius said, it is a eucharistic

community, a sacramental organism which exists — and exists in its fullness — wherever the eucharist is celebrated.

The well-known Russian Orthodox emigré theologian, Fr Sergius Bulgakov, put it this way in the opening words of his book *The Orthodox Church*: "The Church of Christ is not an institution; it is new life with Christ and in Christ, guided by the Holy Spirit. Christ, the Son of God, came to earth, was made man, uniting His divine life with that of humanity. The Church, in her quality of Body of Christ, which lives with the life of Christ, is by that fact the domain where the Holy Spirit lives and works. More: the Church is life by the Holy Spirit because it is the body of Christ. This is why the Church may be considered as a blessed life in the Holy Spirit, or the life of the Holy Spirit in humanity."[31]

This is also why St Cyprian of Carthage could write centuries earlier that "he is not a Christian who is not in the Church of Christ", and "he cannot have God as Father who has not the Church as mother", and most bluntly, "without the Church there is no salvation". For as Fr Georges Florovsky has said, commenting on this text which he labelled a tautology, "Salvation is the Church."[32]

Salvation is the church, and the church is the salvation, the gift of eternal life in the knowledge of God through communion with him in his Son and his Spirit.

It is no coincidence that the term "body of Christ" should mean both the church and the sacrament; and that the phrase *communio sanctorum* in the Apostles' Creed should mean both "the communion of the holy people" (communion of saints) and "the communion of the holy things" (communion in the sacraments). Thus, the church must be thought of primarily in sacramental terms. Ph. Maury, speaking of the great importance of the history of the church representing a permanent reality throughout time, concludes: "We cannot live, believe and stay together as Christians outside of the communion of saints . . . a knowledge of Church history compels us to believe . . ."[33]

3. As a continued Pentecost

Such an emphasis that we confess the church as the body of Christ and the role of the Holy Spirit is sometimes forgotten in our theological discussions, particularly in the ecumenical movement. But in their work among humankind, Son and Spirit are complementary to each other and this is a reality in the doctrine of the church as it is elsewhere.

While Ignatius said: "Where Christ is, there is the catholic church", Irenaeus wrote with equal truth: "Where the church is, there is the Spirit, and where the Spirit is, there is the church".[34] The church, precisely because it is the body of Christ, is also the temple and dwelling place of the Spirit.

The Holy Spirit is a spirit of freedom. While Christ unites us, the Holy

Spirit ensures our infinite diversity in the church: at Pentecost the tongues of fire were "cloven" or divided, descending *separately* upon each of those present. Therefore, during Pentecost the "genesis" of the church is taking place and the church experiences being a continued Pentecost, a "new eon"[35] which is expressed and lived by the believers, through the life of the sacraments, participating and confessing their belief in the church.

The gift of the Spirit is a gift to the church, and for the whole church, but at the same time it is a personal gift, appropriated by each in his/her own way. "There are varieties of gifts, but the same Spirit" (1 Cor. 12:4). Life in the church does not mean the ironing out of human variety nor the imposition of rigid and uniform patterns upon all alike but the exact opposite. The saints, so far from displaying a drab monotony, have developed the most vivid and distinctive personalities. It is not holiness but evil which is dull.

Therefore, the church as the "icon" of the Trinity, the body of Christ, the fullness of the Spirit is both *visible* and *invisible*, both *divine* and *human*. It is *visible* for it is imposed of concrete congregations, worshipping here on earth; it is *invisible* for it also includes the saints. It is *human* for its earthly members are sinners; it is *divine* for it is the body of Christ. There is no separation between the visible and the invisible, between the church militant and church triumphant because the two make up one single and continuous reality. The Russian philosopher Khomiakov said: "The church visible, upon earth, lives in complete communion and unity with the whole body of the Church, of which Christ is the Head". It stands at a point of intersection between the present age and the age to come, and it lives in both ages at once.

Therefore, while using the phrase "the church visible and invisible", we insist always that there are not two churches, but *only* one. As the Russian philosopher Khomiakov said: "It is only in relation to man that it is possible to recognize a division of the Church into visible and invisible; its unity is, in reality, true and absolute. Those who are alive on earth, those who have finished their earthly course, those who, like the angels, were not created for a life on earth, those in future generations, who have not yet begun their earthly course, are all united together in one Church, in one and the same grace of God . . . The Church, the Body of Christ, manifests forth and fulfils itself in time, without changing its essential unity or inward life of grace. And therefore, when we speak of 'the Church visible and invisible' we so speak only in relation to man . . .".[36] This is a cardinal point in Orthodox teaching. Orthodoxy does not believe merely in an ideal church, invisible and heavenly. This "ideal church" exists visibly on earth as a concrete reality. Yet Orthodox thinking does not forget that there is a human element in the church as well as a divine one. According to G. Florovsky, the church is "the living image of eternity within time".[37]

The dogma of Chalcedon must be applied to the church as well as to Christ. Just as Christ the God-Man has two natures — divine and human — so in the church there is a *synergia* or cooperation between the two that the one is perfect and sinless, while the other is not yet fully so. Only a part of the humanity of the church — the saints, in heaven — has attained perfection, while here on earth the church's members often misuse their human freedom. The church on earth exists in a state of tension: it is already the body of Christ, and thus perfect and sinless, and yet, since its members are imperfect and sinful, it must continually become what it is.[38]

Thus the sin of humankind cannot affect the essential nature of the church. We must not say that because Christians on earth sin and are imperfect, the church therefore sins and is imperfect, too; for the church, even on earth, is a thing of heaven and cannot sin.[39] St Ephraim of Syria rightly spoke of the "church of the penitent, the Church of those who perish", but this church is at the same time the "icon" of the Trinity.[40] The mystery of the church consists in the very fact that *together* sinners become something different from what they are as individuals; this "something different" is the body of Christ.[41]

Such is the way in which Orthodox theology must approach the mystery of the church. The church is integrally linked with God. It is a new life according to the image of the Holy Trinity, a life in Christ and in the Holy Spirit, a life realized by participation in the sacraments.

The unity of the church is the unity in Christ, by the Spirit, with the Triune God. The church is Christ's body, and there is only one body, as there is one Christ and one Spirit. The church then is that great mystery in which Christ unites himself with all those whom God has chosen by the Holy Spirit. This includes all those from Adam and Eve till our days and Christians living today form but one segment of that whole reality which spans the ages and unites heaven and earth.

Thus the unity of the church means being united with this great mysterious and transcendent reality. It is this church that manifests itself in its catholic fullness in each local church; the local church is not to be conceived as part of some other reality, the universal church, which is sometimes understood as composed of local churches.

Therefore, the unity of the church is not simply something we confess in the Creed, but also something we experience in the local church, as the eucharistic community presided over by the bishop with his presbyters and deacons.

It is also a unity which is to be consummated and manifested when Christ appears in glory; devoid of all spots and blemishes, freed from sin, perfectly united to the head of the body, Christ, sharing in the life of the Triune God "that they all may be one, even as we are one" (John 17:11). This unity in the Triune God, with Christ in us and we in Christ, Christ in the Father and the Father in Christ by the Spirit, as an eschatological reality, is the standard and norm for the unity of the church today. This church which is the "fullness of Christ" cannot in itself be judged by us, for Christ with his church is the Judge of the world itself.[42]

In this manner St John Chrysostom explains the words of the apostle: "The church is the fulfilment of Christ in the same manner as the head completes the body and the body is completed by the head. Thus we understand why the apostle sees that *Christ*, as the Head, needs *all his members.* Because if many of us were not one the hand, one the foot, one yet another member, *his body would not be complete.* Thus his body is formed of all the members. This means that the head will be complete only when the body is perfect; when we all are most firmly united and strengthened."[43] Bishop Theophanes repeats the explanation of St John Chrysostom: "The church is the fulfilment of Christ in the same manner as the tree is the fulfilment of the grain. All that is contained in the grain in a condensed manner receives its full development in the tree . . . He himself is complete and all-perfect, but not yet has He drawn mankind to himself in final completeness. It is only gradually that mankind enters into communion with him and so gives a new fullness to his work, which thereby attains its full accomplishment."[44]

The church is the image and the abode of God's presence in the world. Through it, says St Symeon the New Theologian, "everything is hidden in the mystery of the human face of God".[45]

The church is completeness itself; it is the continuation and the fulfilment of the theantropic union. The church is transfigured and regenerated mankind. The meaning of this regeneration and transfiguration is that in the church mankind becomes one unity, "in one body" (Eph. 2:16). The life of the church is unity and union. The body is "knit together" and "increaseth" (Col. 2:19)[46] in unity of Spirit, in unity of love. The realm of the church is unity. And of course this unity is no outward one, but is inner, intimate, organic. It is the unity of the living body, the unity of the organism. The church is a unity not only in the sense that it is one and unique; it is a unity, first of all, because its very being consists in reuniting the separated and divided mankind. It is this unity which is called by V. Solovyov "sobornost" or catholicity of the church. In the church humanity passes over into another reality and begins a new manner of existence. A new life becomes possible, a true, whole and complete life, a catholic life, "in the unity of the Spirit, in the bond of peace" (Eph. 4:3). A new existence begins, a new principle of life, "even as Thou, Father, art in me, and I in Thee, that they also may be in us . . . that they may be one even as we are one" (John 17:21−23).[47] This is the mystery of the final reunion in the image of the unity of the Holy Trinity. It is realized in the life and construction of the church, it is the mystery of sobornost, the mystery of catholicity.

St Maximus the Confessor goes further in saying that the church is a *sign*, a prototype of redeemed humanity carrying the whole world in her prayer to the Father through the Son. The whole universe is thus transformed through the church's intercessory prayer into a source of light for the church is the receptacle in which God gives himself to the world making out of the whole of creation a new mystery,[48] the "cosmos of the cosmos".[49] For the believer the church is the body of Christ made up of the human race or, as Bossuet puts it, "le Christ répandu et communiqué" (Christ himself diffused and communicated).

The church as "mystery" and "sign" for the world

We are not better than our world is, that is to say we live in the midst of the prevailing Christian disunity in a world divided by income and wealth, by colour and cultures, by sex and age, as well as being contrary to the will of God and a sin against the very nature of the church. We know that the church is entrusted with a message of reconciliation. This drives us to seek unity amongst ourselves, in order to contribute to the healing of the divisions of humankind, as well as to stand together as Christians who face difficulties and pressures, and who witness to Christ's truth in a hostile or indifferent world. We know the temptation for Christian communities to avoid this challenge. But Christ has poured out his Spirit on his people, to transform them "into his likeness from one degree of glory to another" (2 Cor. 3:18), and to incorporate them in his mission of love and reconciliation to the world (2 Cor. 5:18; John 20:21).

The mystery of the church cannot be defined or fully described. But the steadfast joy of people who discover new life and salvation in Christ through the church reminds us that the church itself is a lived experience. The church is sent into the world as a sign, instrument and first-fruits of the kingdom of God.[50]

The New Testament employs various expressions and speaks about it primarily in images to describe the church in order to show the interdependence and inter-relationship between salvation and commitment, such as the following:

a) The church is "the body of Christ" (1 Cor. 12:27). The head is Christ (Eph. 1:22; Col. 1:18), and his members are those who in faith respond to the gospel (Rom. 10:17), are baptized in the name of the Father, the Son, and the Holy Spirit (Matt. 28:19), and are united with Christ and with each other through participation in the eucharist (1 Cor. 10:16−17). Through this union they are being conformed to his true humanity, filled with his divinity, and made "partakers of the divine nature" (2 Pet. 1:4) ($\theta\acute{\epsilon}\omega\sigma\iota\varsigma$). In its totality the church incorporates both living and departed in the communion of saints.

b) The church is the messianic gathering, the gathering in Christ of all nations into the people of God (Matt. 8:11; Gal. 3:8), and, as the new Israel, completes the special sign of God's grace given in the election of the ancient people of Israel as God's chosen and beloved (Gal. 3:8; Rev. 21:2−3).

c) The church is the holy temple of God, indwelt by his Spirit (1 Cor. 3:16; Eph. 2:22). It is a spiritual house, a royal priesthood appointed to declare to the world the wonderful deeds of him who called them out of darkness into light (1 Pet. 2:5−9).

d) The New Testament also speaks of the church as Christ's bride, whom he presents to himself "without spot or wrinkle or any such thing" (Eph. 5:27; cf. 2 Cor. 11:2). In this connection scripture looks forward to the consummation of history as "the marriage of the Lamb", when the bride will be prepared to meet her bridegroom in glory (Rev. 19:6−8).[51]

These expressions-images of the *mystery* of the church fall into different categories, all forming a coherent synthesis: *ekklesia*, community, God's pilgrim people, the flock of the divine shepherd, the *ekklesia femina*, God's marriage partner, the bride of Christ. They all convey the multiform and multicolour diversity which exists in human nature. The image of the "body" ($\sigma\tilde{\omega}\mu\alpha$) obviously points to the visibility of the mystery, to an earthly body which is visible by its very nature, like Christ as Redeemer, Pantokrator, truly human and truly historical. In this sense, the church is intended to be a "sign" of God in the midst of this world, in its very being and action, in the fact that it is incarnate.

In spite of all human failure and enmity, in spite of apostasy, the mystery of the body of Christ is present as a logos-event. Being in Christ leads also to a process showing this koinonia *in actum*, as a visible witness *in concreto*. Any absence of charity, on the contrary, betrays our calling and consequently God is discredited in the world.

Spiritual life is thus an active participation in the mystery of the cross, that is essentially eschatological. This participation in the mystery makes us understand the balance of glory and poverty, as St Paul describes it in Col. 1:24−27. With an amazing antinomy, the apostle speaks of what is lacking in Christ's afflictions, in his flesh and of the riches of the glory. Thus *teleiosis* is not *eudemonismus*, but involves participation in misery, poverty and suffering, which are synonymous in the Old Testament: "This poor man cried, and the Lord heard him and saved him out of all his troubles" (Ps. 34).

Above all, unity means that churches overcome their differences of doctrine and order which stand between them. This has been the task of the Faith and Order movement from the very beginning. But unity also signifies that the church should be a sign of true communion (κοινωνία) in this divided world.[52] The need to fulfill this task is seen to be particularly urgent today. We are not in fact concerned with a task, but with a different aspect of the same task. The problem of the unity of the church should be raised from the point of view of the present world situation. The church not only draws attention to the promised unity by means of words, it is and should already be a sign[53] of this unity here and now; and it incurs God's judgment in a special way if it fails in this task either through its words or its life. For God, through his revelation in Christ, has laid the foundation for this unity. Christ's humiliation and cross, his resurrection and presence, make true communion possible. It can be experienced and passed on.

The church's common search for unity is to seek the true, one, holy, catholic and apostolic church. The church is called to be a "sign", a pledge, and manifestation of such life in unity. This unity is the quality of the church given to it by God in Jesus Christ through the grace of the Holy Spirit — as an immanent, organic property of its inner nature. But, at the same time, it is something given to the church as a historical community, its permanent vocation to be sought and realized in the life of human society between its foundation by our Lord Jesus Christ and his second and glorious coming: "When he delivers the kingdom to God the Father . . . that God may be everything to everyone" (1 Cor. 15:24–28). This unity, this gift and task in oneness, manifests itself most fully in the church — in the holy eucharist and through the holy eucharist.[54]

The liturgical factor in the life of a community and of each of its members would be unthinkable without the fundamental stimulus from which all is derived, and on which the whole of the liturgy is centred, the eucharist. When we ask where Orthodox spirituality is leading us, we can answer to the goal of human life, the *deificatio*. Through this sharing in the divine nature (2 Pet. 1:4) man is bound up in the life of God. In this state man finds he has attained eternal blessedness, "being made sons of God", as Athanasius of Alexandria said. This is due to the incarnation of Christ since "the flesh has been assumed by the Logos".[55]

In the undivided church, Christian doctrine was never an independent question but was incorporated, or rather sprang from, the full life in the eucharist. All beliefs were gathered in worship. Hence our present difficulties arise when dialogue ignores the inner relationship between dogma and spiritual life in the body of Christ.

In the church each eucharistic offering is not a framework for some momentary lifting up of a relationship with Jesus Christ after which we go home. It is an interwoven beautiful and tragic realization of the creation. It is a symbol of the world transformed into the kingdom. And it is to this that the world objects. One of the weaknesses of contemporary theological thinking is precisely this unbalanced and partial thinking, replacing the major issue in the context of God's universal economy.

What we say or analyze is perhaps justified in itself, but we do not find the right place within space and time.

Therefore, the church is the new creation. It is the experience — here and now in this age, in time and in space — of the kingdom of God, not of this world, the new heaven and the new earth of the new humankind in the new Jerusalem as foretold by the prophets, fulfilled in the Messiah and his Spirit, and beheld in the mystic vision of the apocalypse as the very life of the world to come. And it is not only total newness; it is total fullness as well: the participation in the humanity of Jesus, the incarnate word, in whom dwells the whole "fullness of deity bodily" and in whom human beings come to the "fullness of life" (Col. 2:9). For "from his fullness have we all received, grace upon grace" (John 1:16). It is the church which is Christ's body and his bride, "the fullness of him who fills all in all" (Eph. 1:23). He is the head of the body, the church; He is the beginning, the first-born from the dead, that in everything He might be pre-eminent. For in him all the fullness of God was pleased to dwell, and through him, to unite all things, whether on earth or in heaven . . . (Col. 1:18−20).

For He has made known to us in all wisdom and insight the mystery of his will, according to his purpose which He set forth in Christ as a plan for the fullness of time, to unite all things in him, things in heaven and things on earth . . . and He has put all things under his feet and has made him the head over all things for the church, which is his body, the fullness of him who fills all in all (Eph. 1:9−10, 22−23).

The eucharist actualizes the church for it is the central act of its existence. At each eucharist it is the whole of Christ that is present, not just part of him. Thus in each local eucharistic celebration the catholicity of the church is manifested around its bishop. The continuing mission of the church moves out from the liturgy to bring the Risen Christ of glory to all humankind. The church will manifest itself truly in serving the people of God, in proclaiming the duty of human beings to share in the building of the kingdom of the Holy Trinity. It is the beginning of the cosmic transfiguration in which each communicant is called to share actively. It is the source which inspires all social activities of Christians and it confirms their hope in the ultimate victory of good over evil.

The church of the living God is a sacramental community. It exists as an objective, historical reality in the midst of the earth. It is one with the unity of God. It is holy with his holiness. It is catholic with the boundless fullness of his divine being and life. It is apostolic with his own divine mission. It is eternal life, God's kingdom on earth, salvation itself.[56]

And again the whole church is eschatological because it has no other foundation, content and purpose but to reveal and to communicate the transcendent reality of the kingdom of God. Being in "this world" (*in statu viae*), the church lives by its experience of the "world to come" to which it already belongs and in which it is already "at home" (*in statu patriae*).

Fr A. Schmemann writes that the eschatological "being" of the church explains the Orthodox "ecclesiological silence" during the classical, patristic period in the history of the theology. If, as it has often been noticed, the fathers do not define the church, do not make it into the object of theological reflection, it is because none of such definitions can truly or adequately comprehend and express the essential mystery of the church as *experience* of the kingdom of God, as its epiphany in "this world".[57]

To recommend a return to "Christ alone" in order to promote *unity* is a simplistic attitude. Is this an excuse to escape the other inseparable aspect of the whole issue, namely, a return to the "undivided church"? But the precise purpose of his incarnation was to build up the assembly of his members, the *ekklesia*, the gathering of the redeemed people of God, the new Israel. To emphasize the slogan — so current today — "return to Christ" makes the problem even more sensible for the criterion "return to Christ" is obscure whereas the return to his church clearly indicates the *visibility* of the entrance to him. The oscillation and wavering between Christ and the church is often evident.

An old and a new reality

The unity of the church which we confess in the Nicene-Constantinopolitan Creed has been given by God in Jesus Christ. It is not the result of only human creativity, but the living acceptance of God's will and gift.

God's love has been revealed in and through the life, death and resurrection of Jesus Christ, his Son. He has come to reconcile humankind with God and with one another. He called the disciples, He gave his life for them and his victory over death freed them from the forces of separation and division. Through the power of the Holy Spirit they were made one in him. This koinonia, achieved for the first time in the apostolic community, is at work today as people open their hearts in faith to the gospel of Jesus and participate in the mysteries of the church.

The unity of the church stands in relation to God's promise and purpose for the world. Jesus proclaims that the kingdom of God has drawn near. Sin and its consequences will be overcome. Human self-confidence, rebellion and fear will not come to the end. Brokenness and division will be healed and all things will be gathered up under God's plans and will. The mystery of the kingdom was anticipated in Christ's life, death and resurrection, as it is whenever the believing community participates in him and bears witness to him.

The one church today is the continuation of the apostolic community of the first days. If the churches are to overcome their present stage of division, that original koinonia must be restored among them. They must find the common roots of their faith, the living Tradition, which is experienced in the sacramental life of the one church. By the power of the Holy Spirit the koinonia must be realized anew in each period and time. The church exists under the call to proclaim God's purpose for the world and to live it out in historical contexts and situation.

The mystery of the kingdom is to be announced today and the unity of the church will be achieved only if we, with repentance, humility and discernment, return to our common sources.[58] The church bears witness to the truth not by reminiscence or from the words of others, but from its own living, unceasing experience, from its catholic fullness. Therein lies that "tradition of truth", *traditio veritatis*, about which St Irenaeus spoke. For him it is connected with the "veritable unction of truth", *charisma veritatis certum*,[59] and the "teaching of the apostles" was for him not so much an unchangeable example to be repeated or imitated, as an eternally living and inexhaustible source of life and inspiration.[60]

God's purpose embraces all people. The church is called to discern by faith the signs of God's actions in history, in men and women of other faiths and commitments. Their meaning becomes clear only as they are understood in the perspective of Christ's coming. The church rejoices in these signs and recognizes them as a judgment and bearer of renewal for the church. In particular, it needs to explore, in its search for unity, both what, out of its own experience, it may contribute to the overcoming of human barriers and divisions and also those insights which others may contribute to the life of the church itself.

Is visible unity a possibility at all in this divided world? Nevertheless, God's promise stands. Christ prayed for the unity of his disciples and it is on the ground of his prayer that the search for unity can be pursued with the confidence and expectation that the aim will be realized in ever new ways and with concrete perspectives.

This is really the continuing struggle of the ecumenical movement. It is a "cross" on a long way, a cross with obstacles and theological differences. Unity surpasses the capacity of the mind. All that reason could do would be to understand it once it had been accomplished, but it could not grasp beforehand how it would be accomplished: "The kingdom of God is not coming with signs to be observed" (Luke 17:20).

NOTES

1. Cf. O. Dibelius, *Das Jahrhundert der Kirche*, Berlin, 1927; see also J. R. Nelson and K. D. Schmidt, in T. Rendtorff, *Kirche und Theologie*, Gütersloh, 1966, p.11: "Die Kirche bildet eines der Hauptanliegen der Theologie des 20. Jahrhunderts"; J. Karmiris, *Orthodox Ecclesiology*, Vol. V, Athens, 1973, p.7 (in Greek).
2. "The Continuity of the Church and Orthodoxy", in *Sobornost* 5, 1965, p.18.

48   Church, Kingdom, World

3. "Der Pfeiler und die Grundfeste der Wahrheit", in *Östliches Christentum, II. Philosophie*, München, 1925, p.47. Florensky here follows Pseudo-Dionisius who defines the divine being as goodness.
4. D. Staniloae, *Theology and the Church*, New York, St Vladimir's Seminary Press, 1980, p.83.
5. *Catech. XVIII*, 26; *P.G.* 33, 1048.
6. St Augustine, *In Psalm* VII, 7; *P.L.* 36, 101.
7. Hymn of Easter Saturday.
8. Hymn of the Feast of Epiphany.
9. Tertullian, *Adv. Marc.*, i, 14; see also H. B. Swete, "Eucharistic Belief in the Second and Third Centuries", in *Journal of Theological Studies*, 3, 1902, p.175.
10. Tertullian, *Adv. Marc.*, iii, 19.
11. *Ep*, 63,14, and 63,2.
12. Optatus, vi, 1: "quid enim altare nisi sedes et corporis et sanguinis Christi? [. . .] cuius illic per certa nomenta corpus es sanguis habitat"; and *ibid.*, vi, 2: "[. . .] calices, Christi sanguinis."
13. *De Sacramentis*, iv, 5.21: "[. . .] quod figura est corporis et sanguinis domini nostri Jesu Christi"; cf. the Liturgy of St Basil: "[. . .] Offering the antitypes (ἀντίτυπα) of the Holy Body and Blood of Thy Christ."
14. *Augustine the Bishop*, London, 1961, p.312 (though the French translation: *Saint Augustin, pasteur d'âmes*, Paris, 1959, 2 vols., is to be preferred).
15. Cf. also G. Bonner, "The Church and the Eucharist in the Theology of St Augustine", in *Sobornost*, 6, 1978, p.453.
16. *Rom* 2,2; *Smyrn* 2,2.
17. *Eccl. Hist.* III, 37.
18. N. Nissiotis, "The Witness and the Service of Eastern Orthodoxy to the One Undivided Church", in *The Orthodox Church in the Ecumenical Movement*, ed. C. Patelos, Geneva, WCC, 1978, pp.239–240.
19. St Ignatius, *Epist. ad Rom*, IV, 1.
20. *Hom.* IX, I in *Ezech.*
21. *Questiones ad Thalassium* 2 and 64; *P.G.* 90, 272, 256; see also L. Thunberg, *Man and the Cosmos: the Vision of St Maximus the Confessor*, New York, St Vladimir's Seminary Press, 1985, pp.58–59.
22. *In Psalm* I, viii, 10; *P.L.* 36, 698.
23. *Sermon* 45, 29; *P.G.* 36, 662.
24. G. Khodre, "Christianity in a Pluralistic World — The Economy of the Holy Spirit", in *The Ecumenical Review*, Vol. XXIII, No. 2, April 1971, p.120: "The Fathers of the Church continued to respect the wisdom of antiquity, although with a clearly apparent reserve. Gregory Nazianzenus declared that a number of philosophers, like Plato and Aristotle, 'caught a glimpse of the Holy Spirit' " (*Orat.* 31, 5; *P.G.* 26, 1373 C).
25. K. Rahner affirms that "the Church's first Pentecost was not presumably an accidental local gathering of a number of individualistic groups, but an experience of the Spirit on the part of a community as such. Such a 'collective experience' cannot and, of course, is not meant to take away from the individual Christian his radical decision for faith coming from his solitary experience of God . . ." *The Practice of Faith: a Handbook of Contemporary Spirituality*, London, SCM Press, 1983, p.23.
26. *Sermo ad Caesarensis Ecclesiae plebem* 2; *P.L.* 43, 691; and *ibid.*, III *Sent.* d.6a, II, ad I.
27. *On Prayer*, *P.L.* 79, 1193.
28. J. Karmiris, *op. cit.*, p.8; the term "mystery of the Church" exists from the early centuries, e.g. in Origen *Homely in Job* 20 in: *P.G.* 12, 1036.
29. *Ad Smyrn.*, VIII, 2.
30. Ch. Androutsos, *Dogmatic Theology*, Athens, 1907, pp.262–265 (in Greek).
31. Reprinted by Three Hierarchs Seminary Press, Maitland, Florida, w.d., pp.9–10 (first published in 1935).

32. St Cyprian of Carthage, *Letters* 55 and 73; and *On the Unity of the Catholic Church*; G. Florovsky, *Sobornost: the Catholicity of the Church*, "*The Church of God*", ed. Mascall, London, 1934, pp.54–74. This article is also found in G. Florovsky, *Bible, Church, Tradition: an Eastern Orthodox View* (collected works of G. Florovsky, Vol. 1, Nordland Publishing Company, Belmont, Mass., 1973). On this issue see also V. Lossky, *In the Image and Likeness of God*, especially the chapter called "Tradition and Traditions", New York, St Vladimir's Seminary Press, 1974; Th. Hopko, *The Spirit of God*, Danbury, Conn., Morehouse Barlow Co., 1976.

33. "History's Lessons for Tomorrow's Mission — What is the Value of Church History?", in *The Student World*, Vol. VIII, Nos. 1–2, 1960, p.16.

34. *Adv. Haer.* III, XXIV, 1.

35. G. Florovsky, *Bible, Church, Tradition, op. cit.*, p.62.

36. A. Khomiakov, "The Church is One", in W. J. Birkbeck, *Russia and the English Church*, w.d., section 9 (short but most valuable); and *ibid., section* 1.

37. *The Catholicity of the Church, "The Church of God", op. cit.*, p.63.

38. This idea of "becoming what you are" is the key to the whole ecclesiological teaching of the New Testament, in G. Dix, *The Shape of the Liturgy*, London, 1945, p.247.

39. See the *Declaration on Faith and Order* made by the Orthodox delegates at Evanston in 1954 where this point is put very clearly.

40. T. Ware, *The Orthodox Church*, London, Penguin Books, 1975, pp.243ff.

41. J. Meyendorff, "What Holds the Church Together", in *The Ecumenical Review*, Vol. XII, No. 3, 1960, p.298.

42. Cf. Florovsky, *Bible, Church, Tradition, op. cit.*, p.38.

43. *In Ephes. Hom,* 3,2 in: *P.G.* 12,26.

44. Explan. of *Epistle to Ephesians*, Vol. 2, Moscow, 1893, pp.93–94 (in Russian).

45. Kadloubousky and G. E. H. Palmer, *Writings from the Philokalia*, London, Faber & Faber Ltd., 1973, p.243.

46. See also J. Zizioulas, *Being as Communion*, New York, St Vladimir's Seminary Press, 1985: *Eucharist and Catholicity*, pp.143–169.

47. *The Justification of the Good*, transl. by N. A. Duddinton, London, Constable & Co. Ltd, 1918, pp. 199–298.

48. H. U. von Balthazar, *Liturgie Cosmique*, Paris, Aubier, 1947, pp.167–192.

49. St Maximus the Confessor, *Mystagogia* I, in *P.G.* 91, 665 CD.

50. Anglican-Orthodox Dialogue (The Dublin Agreed Statement 1984), London, SPCK, 1984, p.9.

51. *Ibid.*, pp.9–10.

52. T. Hopko, *All the Fulness of God*, New York, St Vladimir's Seminary Press, 1982, p.32; see also V. Lossky, *The Mystical Theology of the Eastern Church*, transl. by J. Clarke and Co., London, 1957, pp.46–64.

53. For the Orthodox theology empirically it is *hardly* possible to call the church "sign". We must pay attention to the institutional side of the church's life, to its character as sacramental institution and for the clear recognition that in the church there is always a co-existence of the Old Adam and the New.

54. Cf. V. Borovoy, *Life in Unity*, paper presented at the Sixth Assembly of the WCC, Vancouver, 1983, p.1.

55. *Oratio Contra Arianus* II, 43; and *ibid.*, 33.

56. Cf. T. Hopko, *op. cit.*, p.36.

57. *Church, Mission, World*, New York, St Vladimir's Seminary Press, 1979, pp.75–76.

58. B. Krivocheine (Mgr), ed., "Syméon le nouveau théologien, Catechèse I," in *Sources chrétiennes*, no. 96, Paris, 1964, introduction, pp.39–40.

59. St Irenaeus, *Adv. Haer.*, X, 10,2; and *ibid.*, 26,2.

60. "What Kind of Unity?", *Faith and Order Paper No. 69*, Geneva, WCC, pp.120–121.

THE MYSTERY OF THE CHURCH

Dumitru Staniloae

1. *Created by God the supreme mystery, the world is marked by mystery in its structure and its existence.*

The whole of existence is a mystery. The cosmos is a mystery; the world around us is a mystery; my own person is a mystery and my fellow human beings are a mystery. Although I understand much of these realities, none of them is capable of an exhaustive understanding on my part. None of these realities was produced by me, nor can I dispose of any of them completely as I choose. In spite of the fact that they satisfy my needs to a considerable extent, they do not, on the other hand, satisfy me completely. I note so many inadequacies and imperfections in these realities. Human beings are wonderful, but besides much joy they also create countless problems for one another. The same can be said of things and the cosmos. Moreover, linked with human existence are disease and death, which mark it as tragic.

The existence of individual human beings and of everything that surrounds us is a mystery, but it does not confront us as an absolute existence. It is not, thus, self-derivatory, not self-subsistent, and cannot be the ultimate reality.

The insufficiency of the world and of human beings is explained, according to Christian faith and doctrine, by the creation of the world

---

• Rev. Prof. Dumitru Staniloae, Romanian Orthodox priest and Emeritus Professor of Dogmatics at the Theological Orthodox Institute of Bucarest. Because of his advanced age and his state of health it was unfortunately not possible for Prof. Staniloae to attend the meeting, but his voice and witness were present through his contribution. For almost half a century Fr Dumitru has fought in Romania against a routine scholasticism which replaces substance and imagination with empty academic self-sufficiency. He has done this in the name of a truly "catholic" and dynamic Orthodoxy. Today he is one of the best known Orthodox voices in the world. All his life and theological work were an expression of a perpetual spiritual witness, "martyria", for the church. He is, indeed, a man of the church and deserves to be heard everywhere. (Editor's note) from nothing and its maintenance in being by a Creator who, by contrast, is self-subsistent, perfect and absolute.

This relationship of the world to its absolute Creator and Sustainer defines and augments its character as a mystery. In its existence the power of its Creator and Sustainer is manifested even though, on the other hand, he transcends it. The mystery of the world and the mystery of humanity are seen as an active presence of the absolutely Transcendent in their existence. But the world's own relationship with the Transcendent is itself a mystery. The Transcendent which is present and active in the world, on the one hand, imprints on the world a profundity and an ordered complexity and, on the other hand, shows it to be, in itself, lacking an absolute character; or, in other words, to have its profundity, complexity and duration not in itself but from the Transcendent who created and sustains it. This twofold aspect of the world has been described by the psalmist in unsurpassable words:

> O Lord, how manifold are thy works!
> In wisdom hast thou made them all. . .
> They all look to thee, to give them their food in due season. . .
> When thou openest thy hand they are filled with good things.
> When thou hidest thy face, they are dismayed;
> When thou takest away their breath, they die and return to their dust.
> When thou sendest forth thy Spirit, they are created;
> and thou renewest the face of the ground (Ps. 104:24, 27–30).

This bond between the world and its Creator is "participation", according to St Athanasius of Alexandria in his *Three Discourses against the Arians*. But who is able to understand what this "participation" means? In any case it does not mean that the divine powers become powers inherent in the world, even though the world, in a certain sense, also no longer remains separated from these powers. On the one hand, the powers of God act upon the world; on the other hand, it is by their operation that the world's own powers — which resemble the divine powers and attributes — come into being and are maintained in the world. In the created world's own distinctive energies and works, the energies and works of God are present and active.

Each of the world's component parts which exists in this relationship with the Transcendent, exists in the general mystery of the world or forms part of the world's mystery as a whole. But only the human person is conscious of this mystery of the world and of itself as constituting part of it, being itself a greater mystery than that of the world. It would be said that the mystery of the world's relationship with the Transcendent is powerfully realized in the human person. For in the understanding and experience of the mystery, the human person has an especial capacity for relationship with the Transcendent.

2. *Although by their nature limited, creatures have received the capacity to participate in the infinite life of God their Creator by the positive use of their freedom.*

The inadequacies of the world are not necessarily visible in its character as created reality. For the transcendent and absolute Creator could make these inadequacies good by his perfections. These inadequacies arise from the freedom of human beings as conscious creatures. God, the Creator and Sustainer of the world, has so ordered things that the world's full participation in his perfections depends on the freedom of the conscious beings for whom the world was created. He did not simply give the world inferior status of creature, but also compensated for its ontological inferiority, which is inescapable for it, by giving it the possibility of surmounting it by using the freedom of the conscious beings who form part of it. Thus the world can enjoy all the perfections of God as gifts bestowed on these conscious beings, provided that they respond to him by appreciating these gifts by the exercise of the capacity of understanding with which he has endowed them.

Since, however, these conscious beings have not used in a positive way the dignity of their freedom, either in themselves or in the world, many inadequacies arise in connection with their ontological status as creatures. And this is explained by the fact that the active presence of God in the created world has been diminished because of the free choice of the created beings. As a consequence of this, the character of the creation itself as a mystery has been weakened at the same time as the capacity of humanity to discern it.

3. *Jesus Christ: the climactic mystery of the unity of humanity with God and the centre of the enlarged mystery of the church.*

God brought the created world into being as a form of existence (other than his own) only in order to permit it to be filled with his perfections. He has not abandoned his initial goal, despite the sin of humanity, but employed another means in order to achieve it. He thus made the supreme mystery of his active presence a reality in the created world by uniting created humanity with his Son in an inseparable manner, by the fact that his Son personally assumed this humanity, becoming one human being among others, without ceasing, however, to be the Son of God, to enable him the more easily to keep human beings in the most intimate relationship with himself. By his human nature, which he united with his person, the Son of God ceaselessly remains among us human beings as an active presence, and is thus able all the more easily to communicate his divine perfections to us. He thereby became the centre of the mystery of the most perfect active presence of the divine Transcendence within the creation, the centre of the creation raised to the highest and fullest union with God, raised to the status of supreme mystery *qua* church. All who enter into communication (communion) with Christ as divine-human Person become in an enlarged sense his body, or his members, drawing even the world of things into this relationship with him. "Now you are the body of Christ and individually members of it" (1 Cor. 12:27).

Christ is the climactic central mystery from which a power of attraction operates permanently to draw human beings into union with him, making this union of which He is the centre the enlarged mystery of the church. Christ is the source from which the power which continually maintains the divine life in the church unceasingly springs. Thus, those who receive his power become increasingly united not only with him but also with one another. Because it is a life of love, the life which springs from Christ is communicated to them by another divine Person, the Holy Spirit. The Holy Spirit inspires human beings with love for Christ, makes them responsive to his love as their chief Brother, and breathes into them his filial love for the Father. For it is because human beings know themselves to be brothers and sisters of the one Christ, and therefore sons and daughters of the one Father, that they know themselves to be brothers and sisters one of another. In this way they enter into a life of fuller communion, inspired more and more by Christ, and are spiritually united with one another as members of his body. "For just as the body is one and has many members, and all the members of the body, though many, are one body, so it is with Christ. For by one Spirit we were all baptized into one body . . . and all were made to drink of one Spirit" (1 Cor. 12:12-13).

The Christ who communicates to us the life of his perfectly deified humanity is, however, the Risen One. He communicates to us the life of his risen humanity in order to prepare us, too, for the resurrection. The church is thus the spiritual locale where, gradually by his Holy Spirit, the Giver of Life, Christ communicates the imperishable life of his risen humanity to our humanity. The church is the laboratory in which God prepares us for and makes us advance towards the resurrection and the life everlasting. It is the place in which we are brought back to the forward movement which is proper to our nature.

4. *The church: the mystery of the perfectioning of human persons in their relationships of life and eternal love with God.*

Humanity was created for eternal life as a life in an eternal relationship of filial love with God the Father and of brotherly and sisterly love with God the Son, in the Holy Spirit who fills us with his life and unites us in love with the Father and with the Son. Every human being was created for eternal life, for we are all unique in our way of grasping the meaning of life, of living it and of giving ourselves to the eternal God and to our fellow human beings, as well as receiving from them the life they communicate. No human being can be replaced by another. None is ever duplicated. God did not create this richness of personal modes of existence, of understanding and loving communion, only to allow them eventually to be lost; on the contrary, his purpose was that each should be enriched in relationship with all the distinctive modes of understanding and loving communication between them. And each individual person is called to grow to infinity through the knowledge and reception of the infinite spiritual richness of God which is communicated to us in Christ. On this communication depends the inexhaustible capacity of the human person to communicate himself or herself in ever different ways to other persons and to receive from them what they have to communicate.

Each human being, moreover, is unique in the capacity to be enriched spiritually, to give himself or herself in ways that are inexhaustible and ever new, as a whole being composed of both body and soul. The uniqueness of every human being is reflected in his or her face; and this no matter how many myriads of human beings have already lived or will live in the future! In the face of every human being, there is reflected another way of spiritualizing the matter of the body, another way of communicating spiritually through material things, another way of imprinting on material things a spiritual significance and beauty.

But this communication is all the richer, all the more inventive and attentive towards other human beings, the less anxious a human being is to satisfy the blind passions of the flesh in an egotistical way. When this happens, their spiritual communication and the luminous sense shining in their faces are hindered by self-love, by the avid desire to acquire fresh means of satisfying desires by deceiving or dominating others, incurring thereby the distrust of many. Communicating thus becomes poor, monotonous, lacking love, and relationships between human beings are weakened.

Once the power of the spirit over the body is weakened, the latter becomes the prey to a process whereby its component elements disintegrate and which leads to death. This is how corruption and death were introduced at the beginning of humanity's sinful way. Since this process, however, affected the whole material universe, the only way in which death could be vanquished was in a body worn by the Son of God himself. But it was not by avoiding death that he conquered it, for such a victory could not have been appropriated by the ordinary human being who dies before attaining the resurrection. And if death had been vanquished without having first been accepted, this would have deprived us human beings of the possibility of growing spiritually into the condition in which, while knowing death is inevitable, we no longer fear it, believing very firmly in the God who will raise us again from this death which we shall undergo. More particularly, if death had been vanquished without having first been accepted, the Son of God would have been deprived of the opportunity of demonstrating the measure of his love for us, a love which even shares our condition as creatures subject to death, and we human beings of the opportunity of showing our complete detachment from the present order of the world, since faith in God and love for the neighbour call us to sacrifice our own lives.

5. *The life of the church is participation in the mystery of the cross and resurrection in the power of the Holy Spirit.*

From what has already been said, we can understand why the Epistle to the Hebrews so emphatically stresses the significance of the sacrifice of Christ for our salvation. This Epistle shows that our salvation was accomplished not only by the work of the Son of God in relation to human beings but also by the sacrifice he offered to God for us, a sacrifice which implies for us too the need to offer ourselves in sacrifice to God in order to be delivered from egotism and to show our love to God and our neighbour, and in this way to open ourselves to the love of God made known to us by the Son of God and to its effects on us. It is in order to communicate to us this spirit of sacrifice that Christ continues in a state of sacrifice before the Father. This is why he "holds his priesthood permanently" (Heb. 7:24). He is "the High Priest who is seated at the right hand of the throne of the Majesty in heaven, a minister in the sanctuary and the true tent" through the sacrifice "without blemish" in his blood (Heb. 8:1-2, 9:14).

Christ communicates himself to us as "priest for ever", in order that by his power to offer himself in sacrifice, we too should offer ourselves in sacrifice "to serve the living God" (Heb. 9:14). If, as St Cyril of Alexandria said, it is only in this spirit of unblemished spiritual sacrifice after having abandoned our egotism, that we can enter into full communion with the Father, and we can only attain this spirit of unblemished sacrifice through union with Christ, then it is obvious that Christ is constantly engaged in exercising his priesthood, since he not only offers himself in sacrifice to the Father but also draws us into this sacrificial action as well and, by the power of his sacrifice, makes us priests who offer up ourselves in sacrifice.

Our voluntary sacrifice of ourselves does not consist simply in the acceptance of death with a sense of committing ourselves to the heavenly Father but also in an increasingly complete purification and deliverance from the works of our sinful egotism. In this sense Christ, who communicates himself to us as the One who continually makes an offering of himself to the Father, "purifies our conscience from dead works" (Heb. 9:14). We ourselves also become, with Christ, more and more the sons and daughters of the Father and each others' brothers and sisters; in other words, ever more transparently sons and daughters of the Father and brothers and sisters of the Son, and in relation to one another.

It is in this way that we are prepared for the resurrection, namely, by participation in the power of the sacrifice of Christ who offered himself for us and was raised from death for us, by dying to the old humanity, spiritually dead, opaque to communion, arid and confined within the narrow walls of its egotism. It is in this way that we are made ready to enter into the broad and complete communion of the kingdom of God, which is simply the imperishable life obtained by the resurrection.

Without the struggle for the victory over our egotism by our union with the crucified and risen Christ in the power of the Holy Spirit, we cannot attain that full communion with Christ and one another in the future life, nor the kingdom of God, in which we shall each other be able to receive in him the whole life of God and of us all. Only in this way do we all become completely transparent and intimate, with no reticence due to distrust, no distance due to fear, and no opacity isolating us.

6. The church as anticipation of the eschatological mystery of kingdom of God.

As the anticipation of the kingdom of God, the church prepares us for the condition just described. This preparation for the perfect mystery in which "God will be everything to everyone" (1 Cor. 15:28), when by Christ's sacrifice all will be brought for ever to perfect communion (Heb. 10:14), is achieved by the permanent communion of all in Christ, the fruit of which is not only an increasingly greater participation in the perfect divine gifts stored up in his humanity but also the increasingly more complete union of all in him. This communion is achieved in a multiplicity of forms: by the common faith in Christ, by the prayers we offer for one another, above all in common worship, by a life cleansed of egotism and offered in love to God and to our fellow human beings, by various practical forms of mutual assistance, and pre-eminently by the sacraments or mysteries.

In all these ways, Christ maintains the character of the church as a global mystery; in these forms, the quality of the unitary mystery of the church is manifested. Through these forms, Christ communicates his Holy Spirit, which introduces into us his sacrificially offered and risen life so that our life, which has been destroyed by sin, may be renewed, in fulfilment of the psalmist's words: "When thou sendest forth thy Spirit, they are created; and thou renewest the face of the ground" (Ps. 104:30). By all these means our spirit is strengthened and prepares us for our resurrection, in a suitable body in which our spirit can freely manifest itself in a renewed, transfigured universe. This transfigured universe, moreover, will permit us all to communicate with all, without being hindered by distance, and to grasp fully the loving presence and work of God. This universe will become nothing other than the climactic mystery or global church, the supreme communion and transparence of all in Christ, God incarnate.

Even our physical death plays an important positive role in our forward march towards perfect communion with Christ and with those who believe in him, towards the kingdom of God. For the shock of death diminishes the motives which in our earthly life prevented us from giving ourselves to one another in complete communication and communion. Death relativizes these motives by showing us our total dependence on God and leaving us for a while deprived of the body with its earthly needs which in large measure feed our egotism. Our inability to communicate with one another any longer through the intermediary of our bodies is counterbalanced by the desire to communicate, for once in a perfect manner, also through the intermediary of our bodies.

7. *Fullness of participation in the life of the kingdom implies the fullness of faith.*

To this eternal and complete communion, however, only those are led who believe that Christ is the Son of God who assumed our humanity, that He gave himself in sacrifice for us on the cross and in his humanity was raised to life again in order to communicate himself to us as sacrificed and risen through the sacraments or mysteries, in which the general mystery of the church is actualized and by which the hope of the resurrection is nourished. Only those who are being prepared by this faith in Christ and this communion with him, within the setting of the mystery of the church on earth, for full communion with him and with their fellow human beings in the life to come, will be led towards the heavenly church — the mystery of the perfect presence of Christ and of the Holy Spirit and of the perfect union of all in the kingdom of heaven.

Nevertheless those who have only an impaired faith in the true Christ and practise only a reduced communion with him via diminished sacraments, or who are deprived of the full presence of Christ because they have weakened the experience of united life in the mystery of the church, which is a maximal mystery in the conditions of earthly life — they are not completely outside this mystery. Because, however, they are not partakers here on earth of the fullness of the mystery of the union of the logos of God with the creation, they are not preparing themselves for perfect communion with him and with those who are united with him, in the life to come. These will find themselves in the less illuminated, less transparent of the "many mansions" of the heavenly Father (John 14:2), and in a less complete communion with Christ and with those who are perfectly united with him. They will not have part, there either, in the fullness of the life of Christ, or in the spiritual richness of their fellow human beings who are in perfect communion with Christ because Christ is totally transparent to them and they are completely transparent to one another.

CHURCH AND WORLD IN THE LIGHT OF THE KINGDOM OF GOD

Jan Milic Lochman

I

We are otherworldly, or we are secular — but in either case this means we no longer believe in God's kingdom. We are hostile to the earth because we want to be better than the earth, or we are hostile to God because he deprives us of the earth, our mother; we seek refuge from the power of the earth, or we plant ourselves stubbornly and firmly upon it — but in either case we are not the wanderers who love the earth that bears them. Wanderers who love the earth aright do so only because it is on this earth that they make their approach to that alien land which they love above all else, except for which they would not be wandering at all. Only wanderers of this kind, who love both earth and God at the same time, can believe in the kingdom of God.[1]

Taken from an address given in 1932, these words of Dietrich Bonhoeffer are a memorable description of one of the fields of tension within which the central theme of the kingdom of God is set for the Christian community (and for Christian theology). This dialectic, which is quite fundamental for the biblical theme of the kingdom of God, can be threatened or even neutralized from two sides. Bonhoeffer describes both temptations. In the first place the kingdom of God can be taken to mean a reality which is utterly other, a transcendent other world beyond this one. In the pious radiance of this otherworldly reality, the earth pales into insignificance and ultimately becomes meaningless, hardly worth the religious person's wasting breath or energy on. The kingdom of God has nothing at all to do with the "labyrinth of the world" but everything to do with the "paradise of the heart". In that kingdom we can take refuge from earthly disappointments and tribulations.

●Prof. Jan M. Lochman (Swiss Protestant Church Federation), professor of dogmatics, University of Basle, Switzerland. Member of the Standing Commission on Faith and Order.

This piety of otherworldliness and inwardness is not difficult to comprehend from our human standpoint: situations arise in our earthly life — personal and social — when the pressure of circumstance and the burden of anxiety become so intense that people feel that only in that way can they attain some transcendent comfort in a comfortless world. Such comfort can be had fairly easily and is always to hand. "Whenever life begins to become oppressive and troublesome a person just leaps into the air with a bold kick and soars relieved and unencumbered into so-called eternal fields."[2] This "trampoline effect" is not to be mistaken for biblical faith in the kingdom of God. On the contrary, it comes within the scope of Karl Marx's well-known words: "Religion is the sigh of the oppressed creature, the sentiment of a heartless world and the soul of soulless conditions. It is the opium of the people."[3]

Tendencies to interpret the kingdom of God in otherworldly terms are matched at the opposite extreme by tendencies to interpret it in *secular* terms. There is no betrayal of the earth here. Earthly conditions and the responsibility of Christians for shaping them are here taken seriously. Efforts are made to "work for the kingdom of God" and much may even be achieved in that direction. That is not to be despised; quite the contrary. But this approach becomes the "secularist *temptation*" when the kingdom of God is consciously or unconsciously identified with some earthly goal or other, and the goal of the kingdom of God entrusted to the care of the church. We build God's kingdom: we are the architects not only of our own future but also of God's. On this basis, our plans and achievements are sanctified. It is not that the kingdom of God comes but that we come into the kingdom.

Both these dead-ends in the interpretation of the kingdom of God — that of privatization and that of precipitate secularization — are to be avoided. But how are we to find another, a "third way" to interpret the kingdom of God? A responsible description of the relationship between the reality of God and our earthly reality in church and world?

In the initial Bonhoeffer citation, the theme of "wandering" or *pilgrimage* appears twice. It is also specified that such pilgrimage accords with the kingdom of God only when the wanderer "loves both earth and God at the same time". The theme of "pilgrimage" with the kingdom of God as goal and standpoint reminds me of the historical church heritage which has particular importance for me: that of the Czech Reformation. In that tradition the guiding vision of the kingdom of God together with the personal and social commitment that vision entails plays a particular role, more prominent than in the sixteenth century Reformation, and indeed retains that role from start to finish. Let me give just one example, that of Jan Amos Comenius, the last great thinker of the Czech Reformation. He was, in a literal and very painful sense, a wanderer, one who for the larger part of his life was a refugee. "I have been a wanderer for my life long. I have no home. It has been a restless, continuous enforced moving on from place to place with never a fixed abode anywhere. But now already I see my heavenly home."[4] This pilgrimage to the heavenly goal, however, this journey from "the labyrinth of the world into the paradise of the heart" (to use the title of one of the best known of Comenius's works), was in no way an escape into privacy but rather an almost inconceivably multiform effort to achieve the reformation and a humane renewal of secular and ecclesiastical conditions in education, church and society. In the midst of this labyrinth of the world, hope in the kingdom of God is to be demonstrated in persistent humane initiatives and projects. Here, too, the truth is that one who is a pilgrim with the kingdom of God as the goal will love both earth and God at the same time.

II

We must next try to clarify the theme of the kingdom of God as to its *contents*. To see how necessary such a clarification is we have only to consider how often in the history of the church and the world this central thought of Jesus has been understood as a general concept. Certainly it is not just in the history of theology and the church that this theme of the kingdom of God plays an important role. It is a theme which has been emphatically present also in the history of Western philosophy and culture. We have only to consult Ernst Staehelin's seven volumes on *The Proclamation of the Kingdom of God in the Church of Jesus Christ*[5] to see how many variations there have been in the interpretation of this theme. I need only recall here the names of Hobbes and Locke, Lessing and Kant, Herder and Hegel — and there are countless others. When set alongside its biblical origin, the treatment of the theme here can be seen to be often extremely free and even arbitrary. We frequently get the impression that the "concept" of the kingdom of God is being used here as an "empty vessel" which we are at liberty to fill with contents of our own choosing in accordance with our own priorities.

There is no need for theologians to indulge immediately in vehement protests at such use or misuse of the message of the kingdom of God. This very diversity is itself a reminder that the kingdom of God is not something to be monopolized by the church but rather a reality which transcénds the bounds of the church. This, moreover, as we shall see, is entirely in accord with the original thrust of the theme itself. Many a truly humane initiative has been launched with the kingdom of God as its inspiration, even along unaccustomed ways. But the task of theology is and will always be persistently to draw attention to the New Testament contents of this theme. In the Bible, the kingdom of God is not a chameleon-like, protean concept. It has a distinctive shape which is embodied and delineated in the history of Jesus of Nazareth. Origen was right when he defined the kingdom of God as the *autobasileia* of Jesus Christ. And even Marcion, the great heretic of the ancient church, was right when he summed up the same insight in his dictum: *In evangelio est Dei regnum Christus ipse* (In the gospel, Christ himself is the kingdom of God), as quoted by Tertullian. [6] If we are to understand the second petition of the Lord's Prayer biblically, this is the direction in which we must look. When we do so, the message, the deeds and the fate of Jesus assume decisive importance.

Jesus' *message* is basically the good news of the coming kingdom of God, of the liberating promise and claim of that kingdom. "If the whole of the New Testament is gospel, this is the gospel of the kingdom of God." [7] We need only think of the parables, almost all of which are centred on the mystery of the kingdom, or, and above all, of the Sermon on the Mount, which is surely no other than the covenantal constitution and directives of the kingdom. Still more important, not only the words of Jesus but also his *deeds* make the kingdom of God a present reality. I am thinking of his healing miracles: these were understood as signs of the kingdom of God, not only by outsiders but also by Jesus himself: "If I by the finger of God cast out demons, then the kingdom of God has indeed come upon you" (Luke 11:20 ff.). Further and deeper still, the rule of God is realized not only in the action of Jesus but also in his *Easter destiny*, in his cross and resurrection. The unmistakable view of the New Testament is that on the way of the man of Nazareth from the manger to the cross and to the empty tomb, the kingdom of God has drawn nigh to us. "Jesus comes in and with his Kingdom." [8] Calvin rightly comments: "But when Christ could be pointed out with the finger, the Kingdom of God was opened." [9]

It is not easy to describe more vividly the idea and the reality of the kingdom of God as intended by Jesus. No "definition" is possible. The words (and the person) of Jesus militate against doing so. It is surely significant that Jesus spoke of the kingdom of God mainly in parables, i.e. in a form of discourse which is conscious from the very outset of its provisional character, indeed, which deliberately veils the mystery of the kingdom of God (in the sense of Mark 4:11), at the same time as it discloses that mystery. This surely means that we never have this mystery within our grasp. In attempting a sketch of this mystery we confine ourselves to one or two pointers.

In the New Testament witness to the kingdom of God two apparently quite heterogeneous strands are combined. In the one strand, the *basileia tou theou* is understood, so to speak, in spatial terms, analogously (if also in emphatic contrast) to territorial kingdoms. The characteristic terms point in this direction: one can enter the kingdom (Matt. 5:20; 7:21; 18:3, etc.)

and one can be thrown out of it (Matt. 8:12). Keys to this kingdom exist (Matt. 16:19), and it can be shut against human beings by other human beings (Matt. 23:14). The images of a house or a city are evoked. This has a very concrete application — in the parables, for example: they speak of the house of the Father, the house of the King, to which people are invited, and in which they are regarded and treated as members of the household.

This understanding of the kingdom of God, this "strand" of the message of Jesus, is largely new. Only peripherally in the Old Testament does the expression appear in a similar sense. But there is the "other strand". The *basileia tou theou* can be understood as God's "sovereignty" or "kingly rule". This preunderstanding is anchored deeply and centrally in the Old Testament. The Old Testament witnesses know that Yahweh is the true King of Israel and praise him as such. "Yahweh will reign for ever and ever!" (Ex. 15:18) is a credal affirmation which remains valid even if Israel chooses earthly kings in the manner of heathen nations. When this happened, it was not without hesitations and evident embarrassment, since it was feared, with good grounds, that the monarchy would mean rejection of the true kingship of God (1 Sam. 8). Yet the prophets kept alive the memory of Israel's true King in times of national decline in particular. And not just the memory; they also kept alive the hope of God's kingly rule, and did so indeed with an ever clearer eschatological vision. God indeed already sits on the throne today as yesterday, but the complete revelation of his rule is still to come. He has the final word. The future belongs to him.

The prophetic message of the liberating sovereignty of God is fully taken up in the words and deeds of Jesus. Without the eschatological note bound up with it, the way of Jesus cannot be understood at all. The presupposition of his teaching and healing is that the final decisive hour has already arrived: "The kingdom of God is at hand" (Mark 1:15). And the New Testament witnesses with their diverse voices unanimously confirm in their refracted experience of Easter that this presupposition holds good and that in the person and history of Jesus of Nazareth the sovereignty of God has once and for all "become flesh" definitively. In him God's kingdom was — and is — "in our midst" (Luke 17:21).

These two sets of ideas connected with the idea of the kingdom of God in the New Testament — i.e. the vividly concrete spatial and everyday one, on the one hand, and the confession of Christ's royal sovereignty, on the other — delineate the field of tension of the biblical theme of the kingdom of God. The tension between the two strands is quite fundamental for the New Testament understanding of the world, distinguishing it moreover from other eschatological and apocalyptic concepts of time. It "has stripped the idea of the coming world of the characteristics of apocalyptic fantasy and mystical indeterminacy, and has

given it the imminent reality of an historical event . . . God's apocalypti-
cally unique and eternal reality and his historically unique activity are
regarded as an event which happens here and now and in the future."[10]

III

What consequences does the kingdom of God as event have for the
biblical view of the church and the world, and for the ordering of our life?
The key statement of the message of Jesus indicates the way: "The
kingdom of God is at hand, repent and believe the gospel" (Mark 1:15).
The indicative of the first sentence here is matched by the imperative of
the second. The decisive concepts are "repentance", or better still,
"conversion" *(metanoia)* and "faith".

It is instructive that the first word of the "appropriate" response to the
coming kingdom of God should be the word *conversion*. This is anything
but obvious. As has already been pointed out, in the history of the
interpretation of the kingdom of God the idea has all too easily been
understood as a prolongation of human ideals, the ultimate climax of
human aspiration. The New Testament takes a quite different view. Far
from being the climax of our ideals or good-hearted intentions, the
kingdom of God passes a sovereign judgment on them, i.e. it calls for
conversion. The kingdom of God is certainly much more than a
polemical concept. It does nevertheless have its dissociative polemical
dimension. Augustine was not mistaken in contrasting his *civitas dei* with
his *civitas diaboli*. . . This contrast exists even if we find it impossible to
accept the philosophy of history underlying Augustine's statement. It is a
sobering thought — yet one essential to a biblically responsible view —
that the kingdom of God theme goes against the grain of our history to
the extent that the latter is the history of our interests or, to use Marx's
terms, to the extent that it is the history of the class struggle — which to a
large extent it is.

This problem rightly receives a good deal of attention from Karl Barth
in the final chapter of his interpretation of the Lord's Prayer in the
unfinished ethical section of the fourth volume of his *Church Dogmatics*.[11]
In this final chapter he is in fact dealing with the petition "Thy Kingdom
come!" He speaks here of "The Lordless Powers" and here mainly in a
critical perspective. What does Barth mean by "the lordless powers"?

The root of all evil is the destruction of cosmic order by our human
rebellion against the Creator. There is a paradoxical aspect to the tragic
consequences of this rebellion: "Parallel to the history of humanity's
emancipation from God there now runs that of the emancipation of
humanity's own possibilities of life from humanity itself: the history of

the overpowering of humanity's own desires, aspirations and will by the far superior power of humanity's ability. As with the spirits in Goethe's *The Sorcerer's Apprentice*, we become the prey of the 'lordless powers', which we have unleashed: we are no longer their masters, but they have become ours. So it is that human beings, the autonomous 'movers', are always at the same time becoming the 'moved'." We can only speak of this state of things, this entanglement in the world of evil, in mythological terms and the Bible does so by means of the vocabulary which the apostle uses — extremely impressively — in Ephesians 6:10 ff.

The stark connection between such mythologizing discourse and the realities of our world can still be made clear and concrete even today (and perhaps especially today). Barth offers a number of examples. He refers to the myth of the state, to the exaggeration and even absolutizing of its power which turns the instrument of cooperative human order into an apparatus of blind domination and oppression. He recalls the destructive power of mammon, the free play of vast interests concerned with profit, to which countless human beings — especially those at the bottom of society, but, in the last analysis, also those in leading positions — fall victim. But Barth also mentions the perverting sovereignty of the ideologies which so often try to force the human beings who create them into the Procrustean bed of their dictates and in this way to deform them. Barth also views critically the "chthonic forces" beginning with the power of technology, which, while initially liberating humanity, then also at the same time threatens and dominates humanity (today Barth would also be able to demonstrate this even more persuasively by reference to the increasing destruction of the human environment), but also including the more harmless "powers" such as sport and even fashion.

What is operative everywhere here is the related strategy, the same pattern of alienation: the potentialities and powers invested in the creation and in humanity as part of this creation are turned by our human rebellion against the Creator into false absolutes and are even absolutized in opposition to humanity. This strategy of alienation has brought us today to the very brink of the ultimate historical danger — in the shape of the accumulation and supremely dangerous "autonomizing" of the unimaginable arms potential, a development which we must today add to Barth's analysis as its ultimate critical culmination.

It is to this sombre background that the prayer for the coming of God's kingdom is related; it is into this dark abyss that it reaches. In this respect it is the first step of conversion and, in this sense, really the one thing needful. If rebellion against our Creator marks the beginning of the disease, the turning to God in prayer and intercession marks the beginning of the cure. "To put our hands together in prayer is the beginning of an uprising against the disorder of the world" — this frequent remark made by Barth in his old age is true. "The beginning of uprising" — not the end. A beginning which must be followed by sober factual analyses of the alienation mechanisms (of the kind Karl Marx furnished for dealing with an economy dominated by the profit motive) and by unstinting practical political efforts to find alternatives. The fact remains that, for the Christian, the prayer for the coming of the kingdom of God is the beginning, in the sense of setting out in a new direction; this is the first step in conversion.

But the message of the kingdom of God is not only the summons to conversion; it is at the same time the summons to *faith:* " . . . *and believe the Gospel!"* The kingdom of God is much more than an everlastingly critical authority; it is not just a warning light at the entrances to our individual and social dead ends. The gospel of the kingdom is certainly soberly aware of the reality of judgment and entertains no illusions on this score; it makes no secret of the seriousness of our human decisions; yet it does not do this wavering between "yes" and "no", light and darkness, but as *gospel,* as good news, bringing hope with it. By its very nature, the kingdom of God is the light, the light of Advent — *adveniat regnum tuum!* It is the word of promise and the reality of the promise, the invitation to faith and to life in the light of the promise.

How does this affect our understanding of the world and the way we order our lives? In my attempt to answer this question I want to refer to a central New Testament passage which has also remarkably often accompanied the ecumenical movement on its way, namely, to "Jesus' first sermon" according to Luke 4:14–21. The fact that this passage provides the Lukan parallel to the Markan summary of the beginning of Jesus' ministry enhances its relevance for our theme. The core of this Lukan passage is as follows:

> The Spirit of the Lord is upon me, because he has anointed me to preach good news to the poor. He has sent me to proclaim release to the captives and recovering of sight to the blind, to set at liberty those who are oppressed, to proclaim the acceptable year of the Lord.

This is a quotation from the prophet Isaiah; it is the basic affirmation of Israel's hope, the promise of God's liberating and reconciling future. On this text Jesus preaches his sermon, which is reproduced in succinct form in the statement:

> Today this scripture has been fulfilled in your hearing.

It is a short sermon yet one in which the entire programme of the kingdom of God is indicated. Jesus declares that what Isaiah had promised as God's final messianic future is now operative. Hope of reconciliation and deliverance is not a distant song of the far future, utopian and remote from reality. The promises invade our relationships and circumstances.

The way opens up to a new relation to reality. Not some fanatical way. Our actual circumstances are treated seriously. We are struck here by the sharp delineation of the various constraints and dangers in the world of humankind. Neither Isaiah nor Jesus soars off into the heavenly heights; both of them point down into the depths of the altogether real circumstances oppressing us all. The human beings who suffer, groups and individuals, are named; *the poor*, those who have come off badly in life, economically for example, the starving and the unemployed, but also in a moral or religious sense, the despised, the ignored, those cut off by the official church and society and considered suspect; then *the captives*, the prisoners, the people who have gone under or gone astray and are now at the mercy, or mercilessness, of rulers and the privileged; the servants and slaves, robbed of their freedom and rights as human beings. Then *the blind*, the physically and mentally disabled, the sick whose capacities for living are impaired, and *the oppressed*, the bruised: people whom life has broken because it has dealt them a bitter blow, or else because of personal failures and inner disintegration. . . . All these people are there in this text; the whole human race, every single one of us in his or her particular need. Evidently, Jesus did not ignore the circumstances and pressures of the time; on the contrary, he names them by name: poverty, injustice, sickness, oppression and brokenness.

In the light of the kingdom of God, however, this unvarnished view of our world is not the whole of reality: the whole human race, each of us in his or her need — but *not* in fact on our own, *not* left to our own devices, *not* abandoned to the naked superior force of circumstances — but indeed placed within the light of the promise. What Jesus, like the prophet, promises is: to the poor — good news; to the captives — release; to the blind — recovery of sight; to the oppressed — liberty and salvation. In short, if human distress takes many forms, the promise of God does likewise.

This, then, is the relation of the kingdom of God to earthly realities. It approaches these realities in as earthly a way as could possibly be imagined: biologically, economically, historically and materially. But never as isolated realities, never on their own, never elevated to the status of some immutable inviolate fundamental law of reality: no biologism, therefore; no economism, therefore; no historical materialism, therefore. For the world in which we live is not just its circumstances but always also the promises related to them. While the reality of the kingdom of God cannot be detected by any radar or understood by any computer, it is nevertheless present in the risen Christ and claims us and — above all — liberates us and sets us moving in the direction indicated by the promises.

Discipleship of the kingdom of God consists in attempts patiently and persistently to match human circumstances with promises and promises with human circumstances. This continues to be an urgent and relevant task down to our present time. The horizons of our world are darkening today. If we were to take only circumstances into account, only "the world as it is", the only honest reckoning would be an alarming and depressing one. The poet is right:

> To want the world
> to stay as it is, is to want it
> not to stay at all.[12]

It is precisely here, however, that we should and can pray: "Thy kingdom come!" This is a "word of defiance". Certainly not one which wipes out as if by magic the oppressive circumstances we have referred to but one which does bring them within the force field of the kingdom of God and thereby relativizes them and robs them of their seeming ultimate validity. *Kyrios Christos* — the Risen One is Lord of the "powers and authorities". This news liberates. We are no longer prisoners of an omnipotent fate. As in the apostolic age so today the faith in the kingdom of God takes the form of a resistance movement against fatalism. Our world does not have to "stay as it is". Resistance is possible. Our hearts and our circumstances can be changed. The "powers and authorities" no longer have us completely in their grip; we are no longer completely at the mercy of sinful entanglements and destructive structures. Our task is patiently to dismantle them and to direct our steps towards the coming kingdom of God.

It makes all the difference to any civilization and society if there are within it groups of human beings who, in face of the tribulations of their time, keep their eyes steadily on the kingdom of God by praying for its coming, by being its disciples, especially in the direction indicated by Christ's promises: advocating the cause of the poor, serving prisoners and the disabled, raising up the oppressed and broken, and, above all, proclaiming the "acceptable year of the Lord", God's liberating future.

IV

These groups of witnesses of the kingdom of God who try to "love both earth and God at the same time" are Christians (although not exclusively so), the pilgrim people of God, the church. But in the perspective of the kingdom of God they never appear alone, never in isolation, but always in company with countless human beings who take quite different ways, with their fellow human beings in their particular concrete world. This raises the question of how the kingdom of God relates to these two groups, the question of *church and world* in the light of the kingdom of God. I now turn in my concluding reflections to look at this question. I shall do so by focusing primarily — within the assigned

framework of our study "The Unity of the Church and the Renewal of
Human Community" — on the two key themes of unity and renewal.

I. UNITY

So far, in trying to outline the relationship of the kingdom of God to
the reality of our world, I have spoken in a unitary way, without
distinguishing between church and world. This was justified since, in the
horizon of the kingdom of God, church and world appear in their
fundamental, or rather, eschatological togetherness. It should be noted
that this is no undifferentiated, ontologically stabilized and monolithic
unity. It is no premature amalgamation and confusion between church
and world. There is a legitimate concern for the inalienable identity of the
church. We must take to heart what was said in Vancouver: "It is only a
church which goes out from its eucharistic centre, strengthened by word
and sacrament and thus strengthened in its own identity, resolved to
become what it is, that can take the world on to its agenda."[13] In the
course of history we must still go on making the distinction: the church is
not the world and the world does not become the church. The unity
between them can only be recognized and practised dialectically in hope,
i.e. in the light of the kingdom of God. In this light, however, this unity is
in fact promised and acquires a binding reality. "The church can go out to
the edges of society, not fearful of being distorted or confused by the
world's agenda, but confident and capable of recognizing that God is
already there."[14] For the kingdom of God is not only the church's future
but also the world's as well. In God's protological and eschatological plan
of salvation, it is impossible to separate church and world.

This dialectic of the unity of church and world has been stated in
exemplary fashion by Yves Congar:

> In God's unitary design the church and the world are both ordered to this
> kingdom in the end, but by different ways and on different accounts. Church
> and world have the same end, but only the same *ultimate* end. That they should
> have the same end is due to God's unitary plan and to the fact that the whole
> cosmos is united with man in a shared destiny. That they should have only the
> same *ultimate* end prevents a confusion that would be bad for the church, as
> raising a risk of dissolving her own proper mission in that of history, and bad
> for the world, as raising a risk of misunderstanding and hindering its own
> proper development.[15]

This view accords with the specific dynamic of the biblical theme of the
kingdom of God. Jesus' message of the coming kingdom is addressed
primarily and unmistakably to the disciples. They are called "the sons of
the kingdom" (Matt. 8:12); they are spoken of as "those invited" or as
"guests" at the marriage feast (Matt. 22:3, 8f.). Special communion with
the kingdom's King is promised them; they are permitted to "sit at table"

in the kingdom (Matt. 8:11), to "eat and drink" with the kingdom's King (Luke 22:30), to celebrate the marriage feast (Matt. 22:1 – 14; 25:1 – 15). Yet this special proximity of the group of disciples to the kingdom of God does not turn them into a closed society. The church has no monopoly on the kingdom of God. In contrast to certain tendencies within Judaism (or in the Qumran movement), the emphasis of Jesus is on the breaking of the firmly established barriers between, for example, the people of Israel and other nations — often indeed with a cutting polemic against "those born into the inheritance", "the sons of the kingdom". "I tell you, many will come from east and west and sit at table with Abraham, Isaac, and Jacob in the kingdom of heaven, while the sons of the Kingdom will be thrown into the outer darkness" (Matt. 8:11f.). The kingdom of God is clearly not under the management of hereditary administrators. What characterizes the "basic constitution of the kingdom" is Jesus' unmistakable practical concern for those who are excluded and discriminated against, his invitation to the "weary and heavy laden" (Matt. 11:28) and his table fellowship with notorious sinners (Matt. 9:10; Luke 5:29). Citizenship in the kingdom never means an arbitrary privilege but always a summons to discipleship and therefore to solidarity with people near and far.

Certainly it is possible to get this all wrong. Misunderstandings were already present in the company of Jesus' first disciples. The special intimacy of their commission was very soon transformed into a special claim: they coveted places of honour in the kingdom of God (cf. Matt. 20:21). This confusion, moreover, continues in the history of the church, despite Jesus' clear warning. There is one powerful, perhaps even the chief, temptation of church history: the temptation for the church to claim the kingdom for itself, to take over the management of the kingdom and even, at the limit, to present itself as the realized kingdom of God over against the world. Post-Constantinian Christendom, in particular, has been full of attempts and temptations of this kind.

In the light of the New Testament, all such attempts and temptations are to be firmly resisted. The kingdom of God is not the kingdom of Christians. Christians may and should, to be sure, already live, act and suffer with this kingdom of God as their goal and celebrate its presence eucharistically. That is the "special feature", the "distinctively Christian" dimension of the church's existence. But in this special light specifically, Christians cannot ignore the fact that what appears on the horizons of the kingdom of God is not a church without the world but the new heavens and the new earth, the new creation (and here it must give us pause when we notice that from the standpoint of the 21st chapter of the Book of Revelation just alluded to, there is not even a temple in the new city of God, the New Jerusalem). In the vision of the kingdom of God, the unity of the Church is never an end in itself but always basically oriented towards the renewal of the human community.

2. RENEWAL

For Christians, the renewal of the human community begins in the church. Asked in what sense the church is the people of the kingdom of God, Jürgen Moltmann answers:

> The church in the power of the Spirit is not yet the kingdom of God, but it is its anticipation in history. Christianity is not yet the new creation, but it is the working of the Spirit of the new creation. Christianity is not yet the new mankind but it is its vanguard, in resistance to deadly introversion and in self-giving and representation for man's future.[16]

We should note the strong *pneumatological* emphasis here. It is entirely justified. For it is certainly no accident that, in the Nicene Creed, the theme of the (one) church and of the (coming) world is dealt with in the pneumatological-eschatological Third Article. It is in the same direction that Paul points when he says: "*The Kingdom of God is. . .* righteousness and peace and joy *in the Holy Spirit*" (Rom. 14:17).

The pneumatological emphasis in the vision of the kingdom of God helps us to avoid all immobility in defining the relationship between kingdom of God, church, and world (an immobility easily encouraged by the "spatial" view of the theme of the kingdom). As the power of renewal, the Holy Spirit is a dynamic reality. And, determined by the Spirit, unity will also not be understood as a state but confirmed as a dynamic process, one related in fact to renewal. Just as in the vision of the kingdom of God, church and world are inseparable, so too unity and renewal are inseparable from one another in the perspective of the Holy Spirit.

Unless I am much mistaken, this is the view taken by the New Testament. "For by one Spirit we were all baptized into one body — Jews or Greeks, slaves or free — and all were made to drink of one Spirit" (1 Cor. 12:13). I find these words particularly helpful in the light they throw on the field of tension denoted by Spirit, church, world, especially so indeed in their two dialectical emphases. *Firstly*: the Holy Spirit places us in this concrete community, the church. The Spirit of Jesus is not a free-floating world soul, not a shapeless "cosmopolitan". He is the Spirit of his community. We cannot simply ignore this community, indeed are forbidden to do so. One can, one will perhaps in some cases be deeply pained by it; this was frequently the experience even of the apostle Paul. This community is no élite of the human race, not a "brilliant people" in the sense that it is culturally or morally superior.

"Not many of you were wise according to worldly standards, not many were powerful, not many were of noble birth . . . " (1 Cor. 1:26). Yet this human — only too human — community of faith is obviously the "object" of the Holy Spirit's working. The church becomes for us "the place assigned to us by the Spirit".

Secondly, however, another emphasis is to be noted: the fact that the church is the place assigned to us by the Spirit does not mean that we simply accept the concrete community of faith positivistically and resign ourselves to its actual mode of life. The Spirit of Christ is not a prisoner of Christ's body, as if his sole task were to maintain it in its existing form, but rather he seeks to mould it in the direction of renewal. The direction of this renewal is marked out by Paul as binding: the one Spirit of which we have all been made to drink binds us with our fellow human beings across all given frontiers and gulfs. It is surely not accidental that some of the most serious obstacles and rifts between human beings which are barriers to the achievement of unity — cultural, social and religious — are referred to in the apostolic passage just quoted. The Spirit combats these barriers and gulfs, in particular. While it is true that the Spirit blows where he wills, it is clearly in this direction that he is determined to blow — to overcome obstacles and to tear down barriers which keep human beings apart and sooner or later lead them to oppose one another, so as to renew human community. Every form of "apartheid" is sin — indeed, in this concrete sense, the sin against the Holy Spirit.

It is in the church that the renewal of human community begins for Christians. At the same time, in the power of the Spirit, the Church leads them (along with itself) beyond itself. Another classical New Testament passage on the Spirit, Romans 8, claims our close attention here. In a most impressive way, this passage combines the personal and ecumenical dimensions of the biblical witness to the Spirit. The Spirit comes to aid us in our weakness, "pleads for us" in the midst of our most intimate spiritual need, when we "do not even know what it is right for us to pray for" (v.26). Rooted in the vicarious action of the Spirit, however, this inner freedom sets us free for our fellow human beings, indeed, for our fellow-creatures generally. It is not just a question of the new human existence of Christians but of the new creation. The Holy Spirit does not reach his final goal in the church — not even in a truly ecumenical catholic church. Paul describes this "open-endedness" of the Spirit poured out on Christians by using a remarkable image and speaking of the "first fruits of the Spirit" which we Christians already have (v.23). In other words, as Christians we have not got a corner on the Holy Spirit; the Spirit is not a predicate of Christian existence, still less a monopoly of Christians. It is counter to its very nature for this "first fruits of the Spirit" to be commandeered and misused for selfish needs of our own. On the contrary, it is characteristic of it to open our eyes and hands to the "eager expectation of the creation", to the threat of annihilation which affects the whole created world as well, including that part of it outside the church (v.19ff.).

The new creation of man by the Spirit is not a flight of faith into heaven or an abandonment of this imperfect world. . . On the contrary, the new creation means beginning to see the world as it is, suffering with it and taking its suffering to heart. . . The work of the Spirit is to make us aware of our solidarity with the world.[17]

The Holy Spirit leads — in the light of the kingdom of God — into a fellowship with "the whole creation" in its destiny and its hope. The only consistent response to the movement of the Spirit, therefore, is an all-inclusive ecumenical view of the world and practical solidarity on the part of ecumenical Christendom which strives for unity and renewal.

The hour when the church today prays for the coming of God's kingdom drives it for better or for worse into the company of the earthlings and worldlings, into a compact to be faithful to the earth, to its distress, its hunger, and its dying.[18]

NOTES

1. Dietrich Bonhoeffer, "Thy Kingdom Come", in *Preface to Bonhoeffer*, D. Godsey, Philadelphia, Fortress Press, 1965, p.28.
2. *Ibid.*
3. *Early Writings*, New York, McGraw Hill, 1964, p.43.
4. *Unum necessarium*, X, 10.
5. *Die Verkündigung des Reiches Gottes in der Kirche Jesu Christi*, Basel, Reinhardt, 1951–64.
6. *Adv. Marc.* iv, 33.
7. K.L. Schmidt, in *Theological Dictionary of the New Testament*, Gerhard Kittel ed., Vol. 1, p.583. Grand Rapids, MI, Wm. B. Eerdmans, 1964.
8. *Ibid.*, Vol. 2, p.670.
9. *Institutio*, II, 11, 5.
10. E. Lohmeyer, *The Lord's Prayer*, London, Collins, 1965, pp.99–100.
11. Edinburgh, T. & T. Clarke, 1949–.
12. Erich Fried, *Status quo zur Zeit des Wettrüstens*.
13. *Gathered for Life*, report of the Sixth Assembly of the WCC, Vancouver 1983, ed. David Gill, Geneva, WCC, and Grand Rapids, Wm. B. Eerdmans, 1983, p.50.
14. *Ibid.*
15. *Lay People in the Church*, London, Bloomsbury Publishing Co. Ltd., 1957, p.88.
16. *The Church in the Power of the Spirit*, New York, Harper & Row, 1977, p.196.
17. Eduard Schweizer, *The Holy Spirit*, Philadelphia, Fortress Press, 1980, pp.109–10.
18. D. Bonhoeffer, *Gesammelte Schriften*, Munich, Kaiser, 1958, Vol. 3, p.274.

A RESPONSE TO "CHURCH AND WORLD IN THE LIGHT OF THE KINGDOM OF GOD"

Jorge Pantelis

Since I basically agree with the treatment of the topic, I do not have particular criticisms of its content. However, let me express a few comments on the implications of Prof. Lochman's essay.

If we define church and world in light of the kingdom of God more or less *abstractly*, we will not face the painful and divisive issues which appear when we deal with the themes concretely and historically. In this case, however, our theological discourse faces risks and ambiguities of all kinds. Prof. Lochman's paper — in spite of making significant allusions to the concrete world and church — avoids consideration of today's concrete world and church. Furthermore, our understanding of the kingdom of God in the light of the New Testament will appear in a fresh way if we develop it in the light of today's concrete world, sharply divided as it is between rich and poor nations and social classes, between East and West as they struggle ideologically and militarily. In the midst of this our churches have become accommodated and "domesticated" to such divisions.

Prof. Lochman refers to the statement (from Luke 4 and Mark 1:15) that the kingdom of God is present in Jesus' deeds and words, as a calling to *metanoia* and faith in favour of the *poor*. This is, certainly, the very heart of the understanding of church and world in the light of the kingdom of God. Prof. Lochman is quite correct in calling our attention to the fact that the *poor* for Jesus were not just the economically poor. The New Testament understands it in a broader sense. But that does not excuse us — also according to the New Testament, where it is prophetic of the final plenitude of the kingdom — from recognizing that human sin has separated us from

---

●Dr Jorge Pantelis, Methodist pastor from La Paz, Bolivia. Member of the Faith and Order Commission.

God precisely in the brutalizing effects of an unjust world situation, which keeps so many people economically and socially poor.

In spite of the fact that the kingdom of God is always beyond our definitions of it — as Prof. Lochman adequately stresses, since in the New Testament it appears as a sign — it is always both a *judgment* on and a *direction* for our world and church. In this sense it is not enough to say that the relation between the church and the world from the eschatological perspective of the kingdom is *dialectical*. It is also an analectical relationship. It is a matter of choices, of *options* between types of historical projects, and types of churches, which are possible today (recognizing all of their precarious historical relativity). It is a question of how we can best point to the plenitude (*pleroma*) of the final promised kingdom of God. In light of the demands of this kingdom — as they are presented powerfully and concretely in Jesus Christ — we are forced as Christians to take sides critically and obediently. *Cui bono? In favour of whom* do we discern the kingdom?

The *preferential option for the poor* is the only obedient way to answer that question, because — according to Jesus — the kingdom is promised to them. But, as Prof. Lochman has noticed correctly, that does not mean a sacralization of the poor as often appears today. They are preferred in the kingdom because they are the *victims* of a sinful world and because their condition is the consequence of a reality which denies the kind of kingdom that God is offering in Christ.

According to the New Testament there is another element that is not always adequately noticed. Those *poor* to whom Jesus has promised his kingdom are not the proletariat in general, but his disciples. In Luke 6:20 (those who are economically poor) and in Matthew 5:3 (the poor in spirit, like the *anawim*, those who share a total disposition to follow the Lord) Jesus is addressing his followers. The *church of the poor* here appears as the ecclesiological correlation of the kingdom of God. The poor here are not the objects of Christian charity or mission, but they are the church. For today's churches — which are captive of bourgeois values and ideologies — that ecclesiological perspective will always be a disturbing and challenging demand. The poor inside the church are a presence which expresses God's judgment upon his church and a directive as to where we should go: the hope of a new world of the kingdom. It is in the unity of being *poor* and *poor in spirit* that the true church is located, in light of the kingdom of God.

There is another element with which Prof. Lochman has not dealt explicitly. The preaching of the kingdom in Jesus' words and deeds includes a clear prophetic denunciation of the false religious elements within the various Jewish sects of his time, particularly the Pharisees and Scribes. Jesus totally rejected a religion which seemed to be a substitute for love and justice. To participate in God's kingdom is possible only by doing his will as it appears clearly in Christ (Matt. 6:11 – 12; 7:21ff.). The New Testament understanding of the kingdom of God will always emphasize such a criticism of "religion".

THE CHURCH AS EUCHARISTIC COMMUNITY AND THE RENEWAL OF HUMAN COMMUNITY

Edouard Boné

Permit me, if you will, to approach the subject given me from the standpoint of scientific anthropology, which was the principal object of my intellectual activity over many years in interpreting the phenomenon of hominization. By extrapolation I should like first to attempt to reach an understanding of the future course of humankind in its concern for renewal. Then I should like to go deeper and discuss the organic place of the eucharistic community of the church within that concern. With those two starting points of anthropology and theology we can then arrive at an almost stereoscopic vision of the human community which is being built in the course of history.

1. First of all, to extrapolate the evolutionary curve beginning with the parameters set by hominization, which is acknowledged today as taking place over some ten million years in the history of life. With our knowledge of the equation of that curve, can we predict the course it will take in future? That would be the aim of a sort of "paleontology of the future". For the generalized evolution which is now accepted as a paradigm by contemporary science is not random turmoil — it has both direction and meaning. The process of hominization and the resultant emergence of humankind are not accidental. We are not dealing with a chaotic whirlpool, in which the only coherence to emerge is that of a levelling entropy. Certainly in former days people could speak of humankind as being descended from a leech or as a bacterium gone wrong! And speak of life as coming unhappily into being as a result of some aseptic failure! But contemporary science knows otherwise. It

•Rev. Prof. Edouard Boné (Roman Catholic Church), former professor of practical theology, University of Lovanium Neuf, Belgium; currently director of Centre d'études bioéthiques, Brussels, Belgium.

acknowledges evolutionary series and the path they follow. It perceives the creativity of evolution, the "probability of the improbable", "the openness of a world whose activity produces novelty, whose drift is innovative". I am quoting there from *Order out of Chaos* by Prigogine and Stengers. Matter is weighted with life, it has been said, and life rises towards spirit (Teilhard de Chardin). Humankind is at the axial point where the stuff of the cosmos is being transformed, the spearhead of evolution.

2. How can we extrapolate from this? In an inevitably rather simplified way let me remind you that the process of hominization, which began some eight to ten million years ago, is marked by two major acquisitions: first, the primate's standing up on its hind legs, thereby attaining an upright position, walking on two legs and having the free use of its foreparts, its hands and face; and, secondly, exponential growth in the size of the cranium. With the appearance of the hominids this latter phenomenon speeds up spectacularly, takes off and prepares for the emergence of a new form of life, a life marked by consciousness and reflection.

Two major acquisitions with immense implications for the future of humankind: the upright position and walking on two legs. That is much more than a mere alteration in the body's axis or a simple change in habits of locomotion. "Proud *Homo sapiens* began with the feet," Leroi-Gourhan delights in repeating. What can be said here? The upright position and walking on two feet gave a greater mastery of the environment and opened up the possibility of exploring a world of ever-increasing variety. The result was that the human race spread rapidly over the whole surface of the earth, and the same specific form appeared in places as far apart as Tanzania and China and Europe and Indonesia. The species thus became, in the strictest sense, planetary. But individuals themselves were no longer restricted to a limited territory or tied to their sources of supply: with their arms free, they could carry things; families could move to new areas. The hand appeared with all its instrumental capabilities, and beginning with the rudimentary shaping of a simple pebble, through the progressive refinement of skills, the computer and the laser beam are naturally predictable. The use of hands and tools freed the whole facial area from its instrumental role. Lips and cheeks, tongue and larynx now became available for mimicry, expression and language. The face lit up and became the face of a person.

And parallel to that, of course, and producing an impressive feed-back, the size of the cranium — the second decisive factor in hominization — underwent exponential growth. During the eight to ten million years known to paleontology the brain certainly increased three, four and even five times in volume. But above all it was the cortex of the brain which used the increase in volume to its advantage. Now, it is known that the cortex is responsible for the brain's most important functions of discrimination, and, in due time, consciousness and reflection. Its role is to stimulate, restrain, channel and control instincts and the activity of the nuclei.

It is the cortical function of conscious control and heightened mastery which was specific and characteristic of the emergence of humankind in the course of evolution and gave it its true direction.

Let me try briefly to outline the inevitable and thus predictable direction which these new abilities will take on the planetary scale in the future, abilities which will inevitably be used and exploited by every effort at renewal which we see being made by the community of humankind at the end of the twentieth century. Beginning with the fact that evolution has produced consciousness, reflection, personality, mastery, and the ability to think symbolically — and all that above all converging in a single biological species, we may reasonably outline the challenges ahead:

a) First of all, the inescapable need for the four and a half thousand million human beings alive today, and for the ten thousand million we shall certainly be tomorrow, to create one large human family, which will doubtlessly respect our distinctive features, but also be capable of overcoming our divisions. The European Community, the Council of Europe, the United Nations, UNESCO, the universal longing for peace — through all these we are seeking a "common soul", and a sense of being human is coming to birth, and they both are laboriously forging the instruments indispensable for achieving tomorrow the global village which earth is becoming. Cultural exchanges, international trade, the world economy, the community of interests, sharing of resources, the rule of international law — all these are the only way forward for our species, and, if we fail to make the breakthrough, we shall die . . . .

b) Parallel to that, our consciousness and knowledge, multiplied and exchanged exponentially, provide humankind at the end of the twentieth century with an ever-increasing capacity for prediction. Planning will thus become more urgent. Our mutual responsibility one for another will be greater. Sharing of resources throughout the whole human family, particularly between north and south, is becoming, and will continue to become, more and more a reality. The plunder of the earth and the protection of the environment are becoming ethical issues and we shall need to take the generations to come into account in our planning. We are gradually discovering that we have new duties towards those yet to be born, with whom we are bound in a solidarity projected forward in history.

c) Humankind is increasingly controlling the motive force of the world, determining its laws and taming its energies. We are even controlling our own species and the most intimate details of our own biology. I am thinking of the cracking of the code of the DNA molecule, of our control of reproduction, of our transplants and synthesis techniques. It would be impossible to stop the human spirit from probing, testing, using its ability to change our environment and our very nature. There is nothing as biblical as technology, Jean Danielou once wrote. It is, and will increasingly be, the nature of human beings to use their skill to make things: we can even now speak of a certain human *autopoiesis*. However, all our powers are not destined by fate towards true advancement of humankind. They are ambiguous. Science and technology are superb tools for gaining knowledge and accomplishing tasks, but they do not possess in themselves their operating rules or their instructions for use. I do not think that we can reasonably hope to put a brake on research; I do not think we could ethically attempt to do so. I do not think that we can morally advocate — except very temporarily and locally — a moratorium or a freeze in experimentation, for that would be unworthy of humankind. We must even prudently allow people the right to make mistakes. But that does not relieve us of our duty to discern and criticize, nor of the corresponding obligation to change direction when we recognize that we have taken a wrong turning, i.e. impaired human values in our society. There is no doubt that we have now entered a technological age, which is at once attractive and disturbing, and that there is a concomitant urgent need for research into ethics and for a sense of values, so that we can use aright the structures and new powers which we achieve or happen upon to create a world which is a warmer, more humane community of persons.[1]

d) The voice of the individual person, with his or her legitimate autonomy, will continue to make itself more clearly heard in this world of the growth of the human and of future becoming.

Recent decades have certainly made us more aware of the need for the advancement of women, respect for children, freedom from the colonial yoke, and the expression of distinctive cultures and regional identity. All this immense ferment produces its excesses and confusions — but they are ripples on the surface which time will doubtless enable us to see in their true light and history will quickly efface. On the geological time-scale of the millions of years taken by the process of hominization, many events, even painful events, take on positive meaning. But the impetus is there, and no institution will be able in future to remain exempt from this longing for personality and respect. The churches themselves, especially mine, and in particular inspired by the Second Vatican Council, have deliberately become involved in this movement of participation, the laity's coming of age, the affirmation of religious freedom, the reinstatement of personal moral awareness, and also greater tolerance towards theological research.

3. Human becoming, renewal of human community — they are some firm markers for the way forward which we are all but compelled to follow in view of the processes already set in motion by the progressive hominization of our species. What is happening now is an essentially psychosocial evolution, no longer a rigorously biological evolution. This is a new revolutionary mutation in evolutionary conditions.

At this point I should like, however, to anticipate an objection and reject a possible naive interpretation of my extrapolation of the evolutionary curve. I wish to point out that nothing in all this can be viewed as inevitable, foreordained and therefore certain. With the transition to civilization, i.e. to what is human, biological evolution in fact ceases precisely to obey natural selection and the strict determinism of physical chemistry. Blind mutations, competition for life in the narrow Darwinian sense, physiological or socio-biological necessity as presented by Wilson are definitely no longer adequate categories to deal with evolution at its human level. Human beings are free — at least basically — and they never cease to show it. Consciousness, autonomy, personal life, a sense of values certainly exert attraction on them, but not as a matter of fate, and we cannot rule out the danger or the possibility of a wrong choice, with negative results for human advancement, for what Legros Clark has aptly called *the Humanity of Man* . . . .

There are risks and dangers in freedom and its lack of coherence, standstills, missed opportunities, dead-ends in which the human race could lose itself, sin in all its various individual and collective forms, which could destroy what evolution has attained in humankind and worked towards over many millions of years. Those are the risks which freedom in all its richness and fragility entails. It can never be infringed without the risk of its being destroyed — and of being able to destroy itself freely, not as a matter of fate — and sink forever into non-existence. Faced with such risks, we exhibit greater or lesser degrees of optimism, which, I suppose, is only a matter of temperament. Certainly we can point to crises successfully overcome or, on the contrary, put the emphasis on the unfortunate choices made in recent years. I, for my part, am more impressed by the generally positive movement of the whole produced by the evolution of humankind during the some two million years it has been governed by consciousness and freedom. Beyond the chances and setbacks of history, it is difficult not to admit that in the final definition there is more freedom, more respect, more tolerance, love and poetry, more comfort and true quality of life in humankind today than there was in the paleolithic age, the iron age, or even the age of colonialism, the Third Reich, or the Third Republic . . . .

4. The main reason for my optimism, however, and the profound conviction I have that human freedom will succeed and will make the

right choices for its future in the medium and long term is to be found in the security of my Christian hope. And that leads me to move on from what humankind will *become* to the subject of our *hope* and the role of the *church as eucharistic community*. To become is to obey a law of nature, to help forward a process of inner growth, of which we are at once the inspiration, origin and driving force. But to hope is to wait for what occurs without our causing it, what we receive without its being in any way our due. To speak of the hope of humankind is inevitably to view humankind from the standpoint of faith — for us, from the standpoint of faith in Christ. It is to see humankind in the light not of science, but in the complementary light of theology. It is to attempt to understand humankind no longer as the product of the history of evolution, but as the child of God's dreams. The two standpoints are not contradictory. They are obviously different but, in the strictest sense, complementary. If need be, they are adequate when taken alone, but our thirst for unity, understanding and universal meaning makes the one imply the other and vice-versa. It is thus natural for me in this lecture to use both.

To begin our thinking in this direction, let me refer briefly to trinitarian theology. I do not intend to plunge into the intellectual deeps of the divine procession, but simply to examine the basic teaching of the enduring revelation. In his innermost being, God is Father and Son, the seat of an everlasting eternal generation: the Father who from all eternity generates the Son, and the Spirit as the substantial relationship of love between them making them one. This supreme activity of generation within Godhead in the depths of being of his eternal nature can also be seen as the pattern and example of God's contingent activity *ad extra*. If God creates, if he takes the initiative to reveal himself beyond himself, then it is reasonable and consistent to think that he will necessarily reveal himself (out of ontological necessity) in conformity with what he is typically in his deepest nature, i.e. in conformity with the pattern of generation. In creating, God could do no other but create sons and daughters, gathered around and in his Son. He could do no other but create sons and daughters in order to transmit to them his own life, through and beyond biological life, by linking them, by incorporating them into the mystical body of his Son. Emile Mersch, one of our great theologians of the 30s, wrote somewhere that "the sole mighty act pursued by God in his creation is to give his only-begotten Son the ultimate mystical extensions of his being".

To make that statement from the standpoint of theology is certainly to make humankind the centre of the created world and the *raison d'être* of the whole of cosmic history, humankind as the sole purpose of God within his creation. Everything else, from the big bang to the succession of galaxies, to the chaotic swirling of the stars, everything else (the kaleidoscopic evolution of living forms, from bacteria to anemones, to the insect population, to the world of the phoronidea, to the fish kingdom, to the amazing variety of reptiles, to the extraordinary adventure of the mammals) — everything else being nothing but the precondition, preparation, material and matrix, support and background for the birth of humankind. That is certainly explicit intentional anthropocentrism, adduced here for theological reasons, but which connects in its way with a certain scientific apprehension of the phenomenon of humankind. (I am thinking of all those, like Huxley, Piveteau or Teilhard, who speak of a new kingdom, a new species of life being manifested in humankind; or of the Soviet authors, who, in speaking of the pleistocene age, even invent new words like "anthropozoic", "psychozoic" or "anthropogenous", as if humankind were for them the veritable criterion and key of interpretation for the geological and zoological sciences.)

Theological statements about humankind, however, go further than its biological or natural reality. To repeat Emile Mersch: "The sole mighty act pursued by God in his creation is to give his only-begotten Son the ultimate mystical extensions of his being." He is speaking here, to be sure, of humankind, but of it as much more than its cultural and biological reality as a being of flesh and blood: rather, of humankind in its capacity to become God's children. As St John says in the prologue to his gospel, " . . . to all who received him, who believed in his name, he gave power to become children of God; who were born, not of blood nor of the will of the flesh nor of the will of man, but of God" (1:12 – 13). A result of the will of God, a child of his dreams, as the word and Christ into whose body they are incorporated by the divine hope, humankind is thus born into the divine life, and their own hope, conscious or unconscious, drives them into that deep intimate relationship with their creator. St Peter does not hesitate to use powerful figurative language: " . . . . born anew to a living hope . . . like living stones be yourselves built into a spiritual house" (1 Pet. 1:3; 2:4 – 5). And we must not forget the organic nature and vigour of St Paul's thought in his letters to the Colossians, the Ephesians and the Corinthians. "God chose us in Christ before the foundation of the world, that we should be holy and blameless before him. He destined us in love to be his sons through Jesus Christ . . . according to his purpose which he set forth in Christ as a plan for the fullness of time, to unite all things in him, things in heaven and things on earth" (Eph. 1:1 – 10). Or again: "Christ is . . . the first-born of all creation; for in him all things were created . . . through him and for him . . . in him all things hold together . . . He is the head of the body, the church" (Col. 1:15 – 18).

The word "church" is in itself deeply significant and rich in meaning, which we run the risk of sometimes not appreciating today. The church is first of all the *ekklesia*, from the Greek kaleô = I call, the assembly of all those are called, invited and raised up to be organically incorporated into the body of Christ, to enter God's family, to share the divine life, and to be the heirs of the kingdom. But, as I have just suggested, that is the very purpose and sole *raison d'être* of creation. The dream of the creator God, the implicit expectation of all earth's matter, the muted hope at work throughout evolution, the silent longing in the hearts of all humans, whether they are aware or not of the gift given them, is that they should be thus gathered, built, ingrafted, incorporated, included, adopted, welcomed into the body of Christ, and live with that fullness of life, beyond the level of the biological and the cultural, but imbued with them, enduring beyond time and space, although those latter are tools and material which must be used proleptically to build the city which is to come.

Teilhard de Chardin locates that statement of faith organically within the intellectual coherence which he puts forward of the world, his "vision", and, as I share it — in its essential elements, at least — I shall present it here as a help to us in our thinking on the eucharistic community of the church and the renewal of human community. " . . . the Universe, conceived in experimental or phenomenal terms, is a vast temporo-spatial system, corpuscular in nature, from which we cannot sensorially escape (even in thought) in any direction. Viewed in this light everything in the world appears and exists as a function of the whole. This is the broadest, deepest and most unassailable meaning of the idea of Evolution." Such a system, which by its nature is both organic and atomic, shows signs of containing within itself a favoured axis of evolution, which may be defined in terms of the following four successive theorems, each of which clarifies and substantiates the one preceding it on a single line of experience and thought:

a) *Life* is not an accident in the material universe, but the essence of the phenomenon.
b) *Reflection* (that is to say, man) is not an incident in the biological world, but a higher form of life.
c) In the human world the *social phenomenon* is not a superficial arrangement, but denotes an essential advance of reflection.
d) The *Christian phylum* is not an accessory or divergent shoot in the human social organism, but constitutes the axis itself of socialization. [2]

The first two theorems are today widely acknowledged and accepted, and are almost commonplace. "It is beyond this point — beyond Man in his anatomical and spiritual individuality — that the path vanishes in the undergrowth and the dispute begins." [3] For Teilhard the phenomenon of human society and the forces of socialization are underestimated in that they are not in their turn perceived as an expression of the law of cosmic complexity and arrangement, and are thus merely "reduced to the level of a regulated epi-phenomenon, having no value or substance of its own, and therefore no future in its own right". He considers that "through the prolonged effect of 'cosmic coiling', the human layer is weaving and folding-in upon itself. On this basis the fundamental evolutionary process of the Universe does not stop at the elemental level of the human brain and human reflection. On the contrary, at this stage the 'complexity-consciousness' mechanism gains an added impulse, acquiring a new dimension through new procedures. It is no longer simply a matter of cells organized by the hazards of natural selection, but of completed zoological units inventively building themselves into organisms on a planetary scale. Adopting this organic view of the social phenomenon, we find that not only does the structure of our terrestrial society become meaningful" — technological and social pressure, progressive accultur-ation, the gradual interdependence of peoples and nations — "but the whole process takes on a convergent aspect: the human phenomenon, seen in its entirety, appears to flow towards a critical point of maturation . . . corresponding to the concentration of collective Reflection at a single centre embracing all the individual · units of reflection upon earth", indeed on other inhabited planets . . .

That is, very sketchily, the deep significance of the forces of socialization at work. But, Teilhard admits: "Further than this we cannot see and our argument must cease — except . . . in the case of the Christian, who, drawing upon an added source of knowledge, may advance yet another step" — theorem number four above.

"The belief that the human individual cannot perfect himself or fully exist except through the organic unification of all men in God" (by slow "evaporation" through the death of individuals; and also by subsequent incorporation into the mystical body, whose maturation will be completed at the parousia) "is essential and fundamental to Christian doctrine. To this mystical super-organism, joined in Grace and charity (and known only by faith), we have now added a mysterious equivalent organism born of biology and sociology: the 'Noospheric' human unity gradually achieved by the totalizing and centrating effect of consciousness and Reflection. How can these two super-entities, the one 'supernatural', the other natural, fail to come together and harmonize in Christian thought; the critical point of maturation envisaged by science being simply the physical condition and experimental aspect of the critical point of the Parousia postulated and awaited in the name of Revelation?"

5. If this vision has some internal coherence, I can now bring together some conclusions to the train of thought I have been developing in the course of this talk. From the standpoint of traditional theology, we can affirm that the sole purpose of God in creation is to complete the mystical body of Christ, i.e. the fullness of the church. And from the standpoint of

the natural philosophy of evolution, we can acknowledge that human-kind is converging by socialization into a community, of which the Christian phylum forms the historical axis, at once highly explicit and charged with hope. The fruitful bringing together of these two axioms is the basic justification for the place and role of the eucharistic community of the church in face of the urgent needs of the world in its search for renewal and completion. But again this requires a further excursus . . .

On the basis of the revelation of scripture and of tradition, we have reached an understanding of the ground and object of human hope, but now the dual question arises which we cannot evade, and it will lead us directly to the eucharist.

The first question, which is perfectly legitimate: we may ponder the reality of this invitation to all to be incorporated into the body of Christ; we may further be amazed at the modest way in which it is formulated, or be scandalized at the apparent thwarting of the divine purpose. If all men and women are truly created ultimately for the sole purpose of building and completing the body of Christ, how do we understand why so few are aware of it and live in hope of it? For, after all, humankind existed for one to two million years before the coming of Christ. At least some 40,000 generations of men and women preceded the birth of Christ. The question is not unanswerable: we find it answered in the very words of Jesus himself in Matthew 25, in that description of the last judgment, the parable of the sheep and the goats. "Come, O blessed of my Father, . . . I was naked. . . I was hungry. . . and you came to me." "Lord, when have we seen you naked or hungry. . . ?" "Inasmuch as you did it to the least of these, you did it to me." They are the men and women who are solemnly declared to be "the blessed of my Father, the heirs of the kingdom" for having acted, not with conscious reference to Christ, but in accord with the demands of the kingdom. They have acted without reference to Christ, but they are saved, these millions on millions of men and women who have never heard his name, never acknowledged his godhead or lordship, who have been deceived or disappointed by the counter-witness of a sinful church and inconsistent Christians. In other words — as Jesus states it for us — what counts on the "great day of judgment" is not so much having known Christ explicitly, as being acknowledged by him, i.e. having in fact lived in the spirit of the Beatitudes. Orthopraxis, right action, becomes the true sign of our orthodoxy.

This final assembly, the *ekklesia*, is being structured and built to the extent that our behaviour accords in fact with the demands of the kingdom. Christians certainly have here a considerable privilege and their responsibility is on the same scale as God's dream and plan in creation which it is their task to advance. But the gift is for all and the Lord comes to all, because he has raised us all up to share his life. The church, "outside which there is no salvation", is beyond the institutional church. It is the body of Christ and the great assembly at the end of history. The "salvation" proclaimed is the richness of life, the untrammelled freedom, the unfailing love and the unalloyed bliss which every human being has always longed for. These things are beyond our reach, and *by our own efforts we can attain* only pale passing reflections of them, but they *come to us* in their fullness and reality and can in fact fulfill our hopes, when we open ourselves concretely so that he in whom all things consist may invade our being. . . .

I have just contrasted what we attain by our own efforts and what comes to us. The fundamental identity of the world is not only that which man gives to it when, by *culture*, he makes the world into his own body, in the sense that Marx means and explains; the fundamental identity of the world is the identity which Christ gives it when he acquires in his *resurrection* the "power which enables him even to subject all things to himself" (Phil. 3:21). "As it is", says scripture, "we do not yet see everything in subjection to him" (Heb.2:8) and in this, moreover, we are fortunate, for it is this obscurity surrounding the glorified identity of Christ that makes history possible. If the world were already seen here and now in conformity with its potential truth as very body of Christ, this would mean the conflagration of the world in the glory of God, and so the parousia too. But history must endure, and man must "become" in a world which he makes his own, by culture, as he does his body. We would, therefore, seek in vain for the least real incompatibility between the two phases of one single genesis: the *cultural phase* which makes the world man's *historical body*; and the *parousiac* fulfilment, founded upon the resurrection, which makes from the world Christ's *glorified* body and humanity rising again in Christ. Christ, as second and last Adam, in no way annihilates the first Adam. We may say more, that he is really himself only by "seconding" the historical genesis of our humanity. He supplants our humanity, it is true, but only at the final term, when man proves that he suffers from an incurable cultural weakness, and the risen Christ, without ever having dispensed us from the duties implicit in history, reveals to us and gives us an absolute fulfilment which is drawn from the power and glory of the Spirit.[4]

However, on this side of the mystery of the church which will reach its completion at end of history, we have our churches, which are part of this advancing world of time and develop within it, and which are working towards that church in the hope of its coming into being. I quote again from Gustave Martelet:

> Built up from the very foundations by the energies of the resurrection, which unite the countless multitudes of men in the body of the Spirit, the church continues to exist also only because she is continually given strength by the risen Christ. Under the temptation that we all experience of shutting

ourselves up in the prison of man's resources alone, the people of God gathered into a church is destined to be the permanent centre of a defiance as much as of a rejection; and both of those bring freedom. The church differs from the "world", not because she is concerned to stand out against the world, but because she is aware of her origin and of her responsibility to bear witness; and, as a community of the resurrection, she sees that she is withdrawn, in her source, in her duties, and in her end, from everything in the world which tends blindly to throw men back upon themselves. She bears witness to, and must bear witness to, an origin, a road, and a goal, of which Christ himself, sharing this with nothing and nobody, is "the Alpha and the Omega, the first and the last". But if the church is really to hold firm in the confession of a "mystery" which governs the fulfilment of the world in salvation, forbidding it to find its own self-sufficiency in itself and yet fulfilling its deepest hopes, then she must not only be *born* initially, once and for all, of the Spirit — that happened at Pentecost — but she must also be *fed* every day from the body of Christ and given to drink from his Spirit: and that food and drink are the eucharist.[5]

6. The eucharist is the symbol of unity — unity in the church and unity of humanity as a whole, symbolizing the dimension of hope and the full stature of the body of Christ. In St Paul, the early Didache, St Cyprian of Carthage, the whole of the church's tradition, the chorus rises through the centuries from the early churches of Corinth to the liturgies of the present day. "Because there is one bread, we who are many are one body, for we all partake of the one bread" (1 Cor. 10:17). "As this broken bread was scattered upon the mountain tops and after being harvested was made one, so let thy church be gathered together from the ends of the earth into thy Kingdom."[6] " . . . in like manner as the many grains, collected and ground and mixed together into one mass, make one bread; so in Christ who is the heavenly bread, we may know that there is one body, with which our number is joined and united".[7]

The symbols of the eucharist speak predominantly of food and drink, of meeting, sharing and fellowship at table. For the Christian community first of all but, beyond it, for the wider human community of which it is the foretaste and precursor, these symbols thus emphasize the call to gather together in celebration of the kingdom which the Lord's Supper proclaims and anticipates. As we have said, orthopraxis is the true sign of orthodoxy. The bread and the wine, far from placing the eucharist beyond the control and the economy of the community, actually place it under that control, for they are the most eloquent signs of the human. From the very beginning the church and the apostles have reminded us that the Lord's Table is the first support-base for the work of justice required of society. Paul reminded the Christians in Corinth of this: "When you meet together, it is not the Lord's Supper that you eat. For in eating, each one goes ahead with his own meal, and one is hungry and the other is drunk! What! Do you not have houses to eat and drink in? Or do you despise the church of God and humiliate those who have nothing?

What shall I say to you? Shall I commend you in this? No, I will not." "In fact, the Lord's Table, being bread and wine offered and shared without distinction between rich and poor, is incompatible with *any* table which would be an insult to the poverty of a part of the world. What is needed, as the Apostle says, is 'equality', that is to say justice, and that the abundance of some may supply the want of others, (1 Cor. 11:20–23; 2 Cor. 8:15 and 14) thus securing a balance which was encouraged by the 'distribution' and 'collection' in the Apostolic Church".[8]

Guy Goureaux has asked: What actually is this community which claims to be formed in the church out of people who are engaged (without finesse) in the struggle of political, social and economic life? What is this community which says it is in the service of the poor, the deprived, but is itself essentially composed of people who are well-off and is a place where the poor do not feel at home?[9] St James himself refers to it: "For if a man with gold rings and in fine clothing comes into your assembly, and a poor man in shabby clothing also comes in . . . " (2:2–5). We certainly have to ask ourselves about the social, political and economic limits of Christian realism. There have been hundreds of reminders: "If faith is not expressed in charity that transforms the world, it means nothing."[10] Our churches know full well the urgency of the questions raised here: while it is reasonable to recognize the possible ambiguities inherent in them and to guard against the dangers of dubious commitments, this does not absolve us from tackling the challenges they represent, in Christian faithfulness and obedience. Indeed, the realism of the eucharist within the community of the church should help us to resolve them truthfully.

7. I can well imagine a second question: "Created in the hope of God for the completion of the body of Christ which must be given its ultimate mysterious extensions . . . . " How, concretely, can we live out this hope in the circumstances of our earthly life, our human physical condition and the regime of time and space in which we live? How are we to bring "becoming" and hope together in the human heart? This is a fundamental problem: if we fail to provide a satisfactory answer the people of today will remain insensible to the attraction of Christ's gospel, while Christians themselves will remain divided and hesitant. Basically what we must do is to show the organic links between the Christian hope and human hopes. Once again the eucharist which is at the very heart of the church points the way and gives the grace. They are very simple humble things, the bread and the wine offered on the table of the eucharist to be transfigured into the food and cup of the resurrection, the body and blood of Christ. Wordlessly, and again by symbols, the substance of the sacrament recalls the essential goal of hominization. For these basic products of human activity say very forcefully that effort,

labour, science and culture all together only acquire their true value when they become for human beings the food of existence and the cup of love — radical *service*. We might feel the temptations of a proud, promethean spirit, and the ever-present seductive power of technology is there as an eloquent illustration of the dangers ahead. Throughout his life Teilhard de Chardin was deeply aware and lucidly critical of the dual attractions of the two stars which beguile our contemporaries. Science, art, civilization, progress, the development of our planet, technology: the immense *faith in the world* releases their energies, makes them inventive and creative, demands their devotion and sacrifice for a religion that *drives forward* and the human "becoming" it promotes. At the same time another faith, the *faith in God*, the religion that *aspires upwards*, has always disturbed and tempted the human heart, striking its deepest chords. Through all their many faltering traditions, myths, symbols and rites human beings have always sought to reach their God and be one with him. They have studied the stars and observed the most insignificant signs; they have listened to the prophets, deciphered the scriptures, sounded the Spirit in themselves, burning with impatience to place their lives and hearts in the hands of God and ready, in order to do so, to make the most heroic sacrifices, in the hope of meeting him face to face. Two stars, two religions, two faiths which we feel to be in competition with one another, whereas in fact our human hopes are the very stuff out of which our Christian hope is woven. There is no other road that leads to heaven apart from earth — the earth is the workshop of paradise. And as we seek to develop fully all the forces of creation, to be in close communion with God's dream which is manifested in creation through the evolution towards life, consciousness and convergence in human community, we prepare the way for its final consummation. The successful completion — truly successful — of our planet and the world (of which we are the stewards, continuing the creation in God's name) must be the guarantee of a new heaven and a new earth, the body of the city of God. In the change, both scientific and technological, which our world is undergoing at present and which may lead to the renewal of a human community at the crossroads, the symbolism of the eucharist — the symbols of the bread and the wine, the simple produce of the earth, the objects of sharing and the instruments of fellowship — reminds us in its own way that none of our knowledge and our powers, nothing in our culture can serve and satisfy humankind unless it remains faithful to the unfathomable depths of love and is organically directed towards the building of the kingdom. By joining loyally, in faith and in charity, in the work of this earth, the community of the church which springs from and is upheld by the eucharist brings the transfiguration of the sacrament into the whole wide variety of human activity: it participates in the renewal of human community and ensures its constant redemption.

NOTES

1. This was the whole concern of the conference organized by the World Council of Churches in Boston in 1979 on "Faith, Science and the Future", cf. *Science sans conscience?*, texts selected by J.L.Blondel, Geneva, Labor et Fides, 1980

2. Cf. P. Teilhard de Chardin, "Turmoil or Genesis", in *The Future of Man*, New York, Harper & Row, 1964, pp.214–26. I have myself developed these thoughts further in "La vision dynamique de Teilhard de Chardin sur l'univers", *Rév. théol. Louvain*, 13, 2, pp.163–85, 1982.

3. *Ibid.*, p.221.

4. G.Martelet, *The Risen Christ and the Eucharistic World*, London, Collins, 1976, pp.163–64.

5. *Ibid.*, pp.161–62.

6. *Didache*, IX, 4.

7. Cyprian of Carthage, Letter LXIII, 4.

8. Martelet, *op. cit.*, p.38.

9. Le Marxisme dans l'Eglise de France, IDOC Intern., 39, 1971.

10. *COSMAO*, Le monde, 3 June 1971.

A RESPONSE TO "THE CHURCH AS EUCHARISTIC COMMUNITY AND THE RENEWAL OF HUMAN COMMUNITY"

Keith Watkins

Introduction

a) To borrow from musical terminology, this paper can be described as having:

— A unifying motif that weaves together its main themes: the body of Christ which is a transhistorical, transbiological unification of all things into a mystical super-organism that is the culmination of God's intention for creation.

— A tonal quality that gives the paper its emotional, or spiritual coherence and force: rational tranquillity or intellectual optimism.

b) There is a grand dimension to this paper that takes its readers beyond their immediate experience into a timeless and transfigured world for which the world of daily experience is the preliminary and partial symbol.

c) The eucharist is the connection between the heavenly reality and its earthly counterpart. (I think of Thomas Merton's description of attending mass in New York during his pilgrimage to faith and finding the streets of that city transformed into the Elysian Fields.)

d) The question to be discussed in response to this lucid and hope-filled paper is this: How do we move from the current condition of humankind, the current level of hominization, to the condition of the "evolutionary curve" that reaches its conclusion in the parousia? Three scenarios can be presented.

1. The first scenario is the gradual evolution of the transformed world of God's dreams.

a) This is one way of exegeting some passages from Deutero-Isaiah, for example, 44:2—8, which affirms that God will pour water

---

• Dr Keith Watkins, pastor of the Disciples of Christ, professor of worship at Christian Theological Seminary, Indianapolis, USA.

on thirsty ground; people will then call themselves by the name of the Lord.

— The people live in captivity but will be released to return to their own land which will blossom again. While there are hints of warfare, struggle, and disaster, the major theme is peaceful transformation and completion of creation and the human community.

— There are intimations of distress, as in 50:1 – 3, but they are expressed as rebukes by which God brings people to repentance.

— Then come the servant passages in which the suffering servant is lifted up. The servant is in great distress, bearing not only his own sins but those of his people. Even he is an exile from the good land and whole life, and will be released to return to that fullness.

— The climax comes in 55:1 – 13 with its eucharistic overtones. The beautiful and fruitful earth is the means of human fullness and of relations with God.

b) There are echoes of this passage in the New Testament — John 6 and Revelation 21, for example — but the sustained discussion, the full cosmic vision is not clearly expressed. The tendency is to move either to individualized spirituality (as in John) or to a post-historical epoch, a time beyond time (as in Revelation).

c) One strand of Christian tradition continues this idea that the course of world history, natural and cultural, is moving towards fulfilment and perfection in historical time, and that this time of completion will bring about the heavenly realm described in Revelation. In traditional Protestant thought, this view has been called post-millennialism; it is the idea that we will move to a thousand years of peace and justice, probably ruled by a theocratic government, after which Christ will come in glory.

d) Liberal Christianity, especially the Protestantism of late nineteenth and early twentieth centuries, represented this point of view. Jesus is the exemplar of the new humanity and by following his example the golden age of God's dreams (and of ours) will come into being. Even people like Walter Rauschenbusch, who were keenly aware of the terrible conditions in the new urban centres brought about by industrialization, seem to have believed that the kingdom would come in this world and relatively soon.

e) In America this progressive scenario has had a secular version which at one time was clearly expressed in an idea often called "manifest destiny". It not only believed that everything was moving towards its perfect state, but it also was convinced that the United States of America was destined to be the leader and fulfilment of this movement—and that because its moral qualities and language were so much superior to that of everyone else and because the developing life of America was in fact a foretaste of the golden age to come.

f) In this scenario the church is the foretaste and precursor of the fulfilled human community. The church embodies God's dream, although in a not yet perfected form; but by studying the church we can discover the character of humanity in its perfected form.

g) And the eucharist? It is the food and drink that the church requires as it continues in its journey. By feeding upon the resurrection body of Christ, we move towards the realization of our destiny which is to become united with that body. And the eucharist "recalls the essential goal of hominization" which is that the earth is the road that leads to heaven.

2. *A second scenario also appears in scripture and the witness of the church through time.*
   a) In Isaiah 65ff. the imagery is stronger than earlier in the book. There will be great disaster and those whom God favours will be saved (see Isa. 66:15–16; 22–23).
   (b) And this prepares us for New Testament passages like Luke 22:5–36 and Revelation 18. The destruction of the earthly city is the prerequisite for bringing the new Jerusalem.
   c) This scenario has also become deeply entrenched in Protestant Christianity, and is called pre-millennialism. It emphasizes the violent overthrowing of the current structures in order for the rule of Christ to begin. In Christian tradition this view is ambivalent about human activity. What we do is instrumental but not causative. The real actors are in heaven, God and Satan, but they wage their battle on earth.
   d) Pre-millennialism is especially troubling when it is converted into political forms. Its chilling implications include:
   — Nuclear disaster should not be feared but welcomed because that is God's way of bringing the millennium.
   — The destruction of the environment is not a reason for alarm since it will all be destroyed as God remakes the earth.
   — Political violence, especially in the Middle East, is preparation for the biblical battle of Armageddon.
   e) The church is the community of people who can read the signs of the times. It is a community of people who can wait until God brings it all to pass. Members of the church are given the task of preaching the message of repentance; and they have the task of caring for each other until the time comes when Christ returns in triumph and remakes everything.
   f) In such a view of history and the church, the eucharist is a strong connection to the atemporality and ahistorical character of redemption. It contains a clue to the meaning of nature and history. It connects people now to the ultimate source of their salvation.

3. A third scenario is becoming a strong contender for the church's support, composed of the following elements.

a) The earth is intended to be a cosmic sacrament, with humankind the priests using creation as the mode of communion with God. This use of the natural world is vividly portrayed in the first creation account in Genesis and is implied in the sermon on the mount where Jesus talks about birds of the air and lilies of the field. This idea supports the natural theology of Romans 1 and 2.

b) The fact of human history is that we have failed to use creation as God intends. Sin has cursed the earth. The process of hominization increases our capacity to wreak destruction as well as our ability to move towards the parousia. The prognosis for a worldwide system of justice and joy is not very good. (An eloquent description of this result of hominization is Robert Heilbroner's *The Human Prospect.*[1])

c) Jesus and the early band of Christians developed a course of action that contained both the vision of God's intention and a clear recognition of the sinfulness of history. Their scenario is expressed in Jesus' commission to the twelve in Matthew 10. The message is brief: "The kingdom of heaven is at hand," which in its expanded form includes the command to repent (Matt. 4:17).

— The assignment Jesus gave the disciples illustrates the meaning of the message: they were to heal the sick, raise the dead, cleanse lepers, and cast out demons. Although these duties were non-political, the results of these actions turned out to be intensely political. The disciples were dragged before governors and kings. Jesus says that he did not come to bring peace but a sword. In this context Jesus says that those who do not take up their cross and follow him are not worthy of him. And he seals this commission by giving up his own life as the result of non-political activity that was perceived to have revolutionary implications for the social order.

— In its early period, the church found that this kind of revolutionary impact could be expected when the message of Christ was preached. An example is the uproar in Ephesus (Acts 19) that came about because Paul's preaching threatened the economic structure of the city and thus the political structure was also put into turmoil.

d) In the church of our time, this scenario has become persuasive to people who no longer can accept the presuppositions of liberal progressivism or the quietism of apocalyptic Christianity. For much of this century it was possible to believe that liberal culture was fundamentally good despite the occasional aberrations such as Stalinism and Naziism. Increasingly, our generation is persuaded that the problem is deeper, that liberal culture necessarily brings about racism,

poverty, militarism, and systemic injustice. Thus, the very structures
of the modern world need to be transformed. Yet, the inactivity of
apocalypticism seems to be a sign of unfaithfulness to God and disloyalty to Jesus, the suffering servant. Active work, after the model
of Jesus and the early disciples, seems to be the only way open to
faithful people.

e) In this scenario, the church is the community of people who
dream God's dream, recognize the pervasiveness of sin, experience
forgiveness through the cross of Christ, and commit themselves to
the never-ending struggle to overcome sin and bring about a society
that is more just and joyful than any we have known. Yet this
church is tempered by the realization that in the world of time and
space the perfected order will never be realized. That can come only
in the time still to come that only God controls.

— This kind of church may be recognized in at least three historical
modes: The small communities of people who are linked by geo-
graphy and common cause, such as the base communities of Latin
America; alternative communities, such as the Amish in the
United States who live in contra-distinction to the main culture
and make their decisions about accommodation corporately rather
than individually; and black churches in the United States. Martin
Luther King, Jr, and Jesse Jackson, with his Rainbow Coalition,
illustrate how this third form of the church can concentrate upon
fundamentally religious goals and in the process radically challenge
the existing political structures.

f) In this kind of church the eucharist is the sacrament of suffering
and of overcoming. It portrays the suffering servant, the man of
sorrows, acquainted with grief, the crucified saviour. But it also is the
sacrament of overcoming, the assertion that all of God's faithful will
someday wear white robes and shoes and walk all over God's heaven.

— Thus, the eucharist is a counter-cultural force. An interesting illustration is its contrasting status in two branches of American
Methodism. In white Methodism, as strongly acculturated as any
form of the church could be, the eucharist is avoided. On Sundays
when the eucharist is celebrated, attendance usually drops, often as
much as 40 per cent. In black Methodism, however, the response
is quite different. In these churches, whose people have suffered at
the hands of the dominant culture, the eucharist places that suffering in cosmic and redemptive perspective.

— The eucharist is a sign of both aspects of human and natural history. This feast is a clear sign of the use of nature as a means of
communion with God, thus continuing the meal symbolism of the
Hebrew scriptures (e.g. Ex. 24:9—11 and the tradition of communion sacrifices). The eucharist is also a sign of the depth and per-

vasiveness of sin. It is built upon an ancient foundation of death as the necessary means of restoring relationships between God and the people.

4. *These three scenarios about how "the kingdom of this world will become the kingdom of our Lord and of his Christ" (Rev. 11:15) are not easily reconciled; and faithfulness to the gospel calls upon us to choose between them.*

a) Is the choice a function of temperament? If so, facts from the natural and historical world and faith in God have diminished bearing. As an American living under a president who seems to have this optimistic temperament but still pursues warlike policies, I am very uneasy when the entropy of the natural order and the continued violence of the political order are swept away by the assertion that one's stance towards such matters is a function of temperament.

b) Or is one's view a function of biblical faith and the unbroken tradition of the church? This conclusion also seems to be unsatisfactory because all three scenarios are attested in scripture and tradition and can be empowered by the conviction that God is in control and will accomplish the divine purpose when the time is right.

c) Is our response a function of our station in life? If so, those who are comfortable would prefer continuity and be inclined towards the hopeful, evolutionary view, while those who are dispossessed would look towards cataclysm and the radical overturning of history. Yet even this view does not hold up under scrutiny because some very comfortable people are apocalyptic in their views and some very poor people seem able to live in relative equanimity despite the unjust structures of life.

d) Yet some movement towards consensus among Christians is necessary. As Paul states so eloquently (Rom. 8), the whole creation groans, waiting for its redemption; and the church is to be engaged in that redemptive work.

5. *A major restating of the topic of the paper would result if we were to give greater prominence to its secondary theme (the kingdom of God) and give greater attention to our current historical and cultural setting.*

a) All evidence points to the fact that the natural world is running down and the form of Euro-American culture is broken. We face the prospect of nuclear disaster, over population, and the failure of the biosphere. Neither dominant economic system seems able to respond to the threat facing humankind and nature because both of them are based on similar presuppositions of exploitation, consumption, and industrialization. Some argue that the socialist system has a slight short-term advantage, but even this way of life seems to have little to commend it in the longer perspective.

b) The conclusion to human life is likely to be one of the following: nuclear destruction with a long nuclear winter; gradual dissipation of energy and culture, with the tragedy of northern Africa as a foretaste of what will come to pass everywhere; or the emergence of a secular monasticism as the dominant form of social organization, a communal way of life that is both ascetic and disciplined.

c) The church, in such a vision of time to come, could be a paradigm of what life should become, an example of people who voluntarily limit consumption, yield their demands for power, and give themselves in the kind of service that Jesus models. Such churches would likely find themselves strongly opposed by the principalities and powers, as was Jesus, and as churches in Latin America and South Africa now find themselves. They would find themselves to be the accusers of the powers, as the American bishops of the Roman Catholic Church have become in their two recent pastoral letters.

d) The metaphor of kingdom seems more faithful to this vision of the church than the metaphor body of Christ. Indeed, Prof. Boné's paper becomes more eloquent and more persuasive when he speaks more as a citizen of this world and less as the scientist, when he subsumes the metaphor *body* under the metaphor *kingdom*. In the synoptic accounts of the institution of the eucharist Jesus says that he will not drink again of this fruit of the vine until "I drink it new with you in my Father's kingdom" (Matt. 26:29). In Matthew's account, the institution follows parables of the kingdom that point towards its revolutionary character. The greatest of them is the narrative of the final judgment, when Jesus declares the importance of caring for the hungry, the alienated, and the oppressed. Does it not seem reasonable to believe that Jesus' reference to the kingdom in the narrative of the institution is closely tied to the ideas of the kingdom in the preceding parables?

e) Eucharistic celebrations need to include both joy and penitence. A standard interpretation of the New Testament teaching on the eucharist is that in the early period the church's celebrations were marked by ecstasy and joy. There was such an emphasis upon the experience of Christ in majesty that the crucifixion was overlooked. It was Paul's task to recover the historical dimensions of our Lord's passion, the reality of human sin that led to crucifixion, and the need for repentance in order to come to God. A modern version of this same corrective is given by Frederick Herzog who states that the purpose of worship is to help the people "grasp the crude shape of what God has done in Christ". Herzog accuses some writers on worship, such as Evelyn Underhill, of emphasizing the glory of worship and thereby losing the foundation in human experience which is necessary to make any celebration credible.

f) Eucharistic life needs to be rooted in historical experience (and here I must acknowledge my debt to Rafael Avila's book *Worship and Politics*).[2] This means at least the following:

— The eucharist needs to be celebrated in the context of a community that is engaged in ethical discussion and social action.
— The eucharist should use language and ceremony drawn from real life, including the struggles for freedom and justice.
— The eucharist should be celebrated in association with the dramatic turning points of social history and at the cracks of contemporary life. For example, American Christians should celebrate eucharist on the anniversary of the death of Martin Luther King, Jr, whose Christian witness led to his assassination — just as the church was preparing for the celebration of Palm Sunday.

g) The eucharist, drawing upon the anthropology of Victor Turner, is the sacrament of the body and blood of Christ. It summons to consciousness the fundamental life experiences in which blood is shed, experiences which are the source of our most powerful emotions, and it connects these emotions with the values of the primary community in which we find our life. Such a sacrament makes us want to do what has to be done if we are to live. The sacrament of Christ's blood depicts the tragic dimension of creation in which sin has become so prominent and in which the death of God's incarnate presence became necessary. This sacrament generates within us, too, the willingness to live this same kind of life, a life that is marked by tragedy as well as grandeur. The social functions of the eucharist are intensified by the more personal functions of nourishment and medication that are so prominent in traditional eucharistic theology and piety. The emotionally charged character of the sacrament is impressed upon worshippers who eat and drink "body and blood". Furthermore, we become what we eat. The medicinal metaphor addresses our needs for healing and protection. Thus the eucharist cures our maladies, innoculates against the threat of disease, and fortifies us for the hard work of struggling for justice and joy in human life.

NOTES

1. New York, W. W. Norton & Co., 1974, p. 5.
2. Maryknoll, NY, Orbis Books, 1981.

THE CHURCH AS A SACRAMENTAL VISION AND THE CHALLENGE OF CHRISTIAN WITNESS

Nikos A. Nissiotis

Ecclesiology remains the crucial issue for Christian theology in ecumenical perspective. Because of the growing interchurch dialogues resulting from the ecumenical movement, this special item in systematic theology becomes more and more the focus of interest in modern theological research. At the same time, it becomes evident that in ecclesiology the vast spectrum of theological study assumes a concrete shape and a specialized expression. As a response to the challenges for intensifying interchurch relations, or for making theology more explicitly relevant and concrete in the modern world, ecclesiology today becomes the meeting point for church-centred ecumenism and church-centred theology.

It is not astonishing, therefore, that such a rich theological production has been manifest in this area of theology during these last seven decades. One cannot fail to appreciate the intense ecclesiological research work based on sound biblical premises and historical-patristic studies. Ecclesiology has therefore contributed not only to better understanding between separate Christian confessions, but also towards a more complete self-understanding on the part of each confession; indeed, it has given a new impetus for the renewal of Christian theology itself.

The question now is how to evaluate this extremely rich production, and use it in an appropriate comprehensive and synthetic way, not so much for producing additional statements of confessional ecclesiological positions — this only risks repeating positions which are well known already — but rather in the service of *renewal* both in ecumenism and in theological work. It seems to me that our tasks at this moment are to use this enormous ecclesiological literature and attempt a new type of

• Prof. Nikos Nissiotis (Church of Greece), professor at the Theological Faculty of the University of Athens, former moderator of the Faith and Order Commission. He died on 17 August 1986.

ecclesiological approach, with the intention of promoting an ecclesiology of *convergence* and mutual enrichment between our one-sided ecclesiological positions. It is precisely this kind of ecclesiological approach, which is behind, or better, at the basis of such preconsensus documents as "Baptism, Eucharist and Ministry" of Faith and Order.

There is clear and sufficient evidence that all ecclesiological approaches can be distinguished into two main streams of thought. Without risking a dangerous generalization — because there are a lot of variations within each one of them — we can detect in all ecclesiologies in contemporary systematic theology on the one hand a pro-catholicizing tendency, and on the other a pro-congregational tendency. There are many attempts at mutual appreciation and at a gratifying exchange between these tendencies, but we are still in the process of constructing a genuine, all-embracing ecclesiology incorporating both elements.

When one regards ecclesiology in ecumenical perspective, we become fully aware, after half a century of work, that there is still a strong dualism prevailing in contemporary ecclesiological thinking. There is a certain "distance" resulting from the opposition between two different ec-clesiologies. The first is an ecclesiology conceived on the basis of incorporation of all in Christ, and sharing in the same experience in an inseparable single communion as common members of one "sacra-mental" body. The second is an ecclesiology deriving itself from the fact of the regathering of the people of God by his word, and sharing in the prophetic actualization of the evangelical message in the world.

The one tendency, in other words, emphasizes the element of belongingness to the body of Christ through definite sacramental events as the *sine qua non* of the church's existence. This is accompanied by a mystical experience of an inner, spiritual communion with all the saints of the church as immaculate and holy. The other tendency emphasizes belongingness to the body of Christ as a result of a Christ-centred appeal and vocation within the gathered community, which "hears" or acknowledges the absolute supremacy of the word of God addressed to, and exercised in, the world in a prophetic way.

Experience within the mystical body of Christ on the one hand, and kerygmatic-prophetic adherence and consistent devotion and action on the other, are the fundamental elements — amongst many other ones resulting from them — which distinguish these two tendencies in ecclesiology.

Certainly, this schematic (and perhaps, in some respects, too easy and arbitrary) separation does not do justice to the reality of church life in either case. This is because, in ecclesial *praxis*, i.e. in the actual *praxis* of the churches and their devotional, liturgical and evangelical-missionary action, there is an inevitable interpenetration of the two tendencies as described above. But I would still maintain that there is clear evidence, especially in ecclesiology as well as in the positions taken over current issues of the life of the church in relation to its own renewal and to the renewal of the world, which make this distinction clearly manifest. Of course we can defend the idea that the "mystical body" tendency includes the kerygmatic-prophetic tendency, and vice-versa, but in reality our ecclesiological thinking, and the corresponding presence and action of our church in the world, betrays our commitment to one view over the other and this one-sidedness is at the basis of all later disagreements over specific ecclesiological issues.

There is, on the Eastern Orthodox-catholicizing side, a permanent reference to a kind of ecclesial "ontology", i.e. a special ontological affirmation by faith and praxis — expressed especially in the liturgy — of the being of the church in itself, beyond the adherence, the loyalty or disloyalty, and the holiness or sinfulness of its human members. This affirmation is due to the direct and unshakable connection between the head, Christ, and the body, the members as maintained by the operation of the Holy Spirit cleansing the church and preserving it *as holy* (though composed of sinful members). Without denying that a similar trend exists in the life of the churches of the other type, and perhaps that a kind of church ontology can be found in some of the leading reformers also, the truth is that there is no similar insistence there on the permanent, transcending element in the existence of the church itself. This is seen clearly in the different appreciation each side has for the value of church tradition, for the *priestly* nature of ministry, and for the permanent validity of church structures in their continuity throughout history.

It is because of this ecclesiological "ontology", for instance, that the Eastern Orthodox "never treats the earthy aspect of the church in isolation but thinks always of the church in Christ and the Holy Spirit. . . and starts with the special relationship which exists between the church and God". It is because of this reference that the priorities given in ecclesiology are expressed by subjects like the body of Christ, or the bride of Christ, the insistence on the Trinitarian basis for the communion of the church, the interpretation of the church as a continuous Pentecost, or as the celestial Jerusalem established in history, reflecting in it the permanent divino-human intercourse as the image of the incarnate word.

We may speak here of a verticalism of ontological affirmation and mystical experience in the liturgy and the sacraments, with an attendant strong pneumatological-charismatic, eucharistic-sacramental, and eschatological elements. But historical facticity and reality are equally important for a wholistic ecclesiology which wants to be based, as it should be, on authentic Christological premises. The question remains, however, how far this kind of ecclesiology could include such historical elements without losing its own "ontological" and sacramental self-affirmation. Certainly this attitude or, better, this necessary extension, would be expected from the evangelical-congregational tendency and from the notion of the people of God in order that both tendencies might converge into one common, more complete ecclesiology capable of contributing to the study of the relationship between the unity of the church and the renewal of the world.

1. The catholicity of the church in relation to the universality of the world

The first and paramount task of the Eastern ecclesiology would be the more inclusive concept of church *catholicity*. This seems to me to be the key-notion and reality for the study of our theme of church unity and the world's renewal. This is because catholicity is very important amongst the marks of the church directly related to the unity of the church. In fact, all of the four marks of the church are attributed strictly to the church as such. But it would be a great error if we use them as statements of identity only, and not also as points of reference. As there cannot be a self-sufficient oneness of the church for itself alone, without reference to and for the world's realities of a broken human community, in the same way there cannot exist a self-limited and self-perfected catholicity without a reference to the already existing self-consciousness of humankind as experiencing life in a universal, worldwide history. It is especially an Eastern Orthodox ecclesiology which has the task of expounding such an idea of church catholicity based on its traditional, all-embracing and all-inclusive cosmic Christology and pneumatology.

a) Qualitative with geographical catholicity

Orthodox ecclesiologists usually give priority to the qualitative notion of catholicity over the commonly accepted geographical, quantitative understanding of the term. They use the etymology of the Greek word "katholikos" as composed of καmore a and όλον, thus pointing to wholeness rather than to universal meaning, because in the latter case one should use a term deriving from κατά παντός or ματά πάντας. In this case the Orthodox intend to underline the fullness of grace and truth given to all ecclesial gatherings sharing in the sacramental life with the bishop at their centre. On the other hand, they want to reduce the simplistic, massive and centralized quantitative-universalistic catholicity. Their intention is to prove the priority of "what" and "how" of God's full revelation of his truth over an objectivized and universally institutionalized reality.

This fundamental approach in Orthodox ecclesiology centres around the fullness of God's act and presence amongst his faithful, gathered into one visible communion through the Christ event and in the operation of the Holy Spirit. Accordingly there is a priority of the sacramental-eucharistic communion over the universal extension of it which is its result. When we say "catholic", we mean first "comprising all truth" and not expansion of the institution established on a worldwide scale. We emphasize the depth-dimension of catholicity as representing the totality, wholeness and perfection of the triune God's act of creating, restoring and fulfilling his cosmos as a whole through a personal, concrete re-establishment of his communion with specific persons in a given place at a given time.

Catholicity is, therefore, a notion which can be applied in its qualitative sense for describing the wholeness of God's act of creating, saving, and restoring humankind and the whole world. God, because he is love and therefore personal communion in himself, gives his whole and full grace when he acts in divine economy in and through three distinctive persons. Wholeness of personal communion pre-exists, precedes and essentially postulates the basic creative act of God as well as all of his saving acts in history. Personal-ecclesial communion has priority over all other forms which make it manifest in history.

It would have been, however, a one-sided conclusion of this qualitative priority if one had interpreted it as an individual-mystical experience excluding, or even minimizing, the importance of the historical worldwide facticity of the same notion of qualitative catholicity. The emphasis of the Orthodox, here, intends to ground on a more solid basis the "spiritual" value of the visibility and universality of the church communion in the whole world. Catholicity, expressed and experienced as a total act of sacramental communion, here and now in history and the small local eucharistic communion, validates, exalts and enacts more deeply and fully the universal dimension of catholicity. The quantitative-geographic notion of catholicity is not a secondary one, but it is inherent in the qualitative one as inseparably linked with it. Priority here does not mean exclusiveness or absolutization. On the contrary, this kind of qualitative catholicity "makes" the geographical its immediate outcome, the proof and the absolutely necessary reality of God's total act in and for the whole world.

The concepts of "wholeness" and "everywhere" relate now "ontolo-gically", i.e. they are both grounded in the one total act of God as equally God-given by his immediate personal contact with humankind through distinctive persons in communion, and in a whole redeemed and restored Creation. "Wholeness" and "everywhere" relates as do "personal" and "cosmic" in the salvation story of the Christian faith. One revitalizes the "whole world" as a restored wholeness of the truth made in it through a concrete person, Jesus of Nazareth, who is proved in the Spirit to be the Christ of God. The cosmic dimension in Christian faith passes through personal communion and universalism for becoming catholicity in both the qualitative and quantitative-geographical senses, but always out of a "small" concrete event, the communion of the *ekklesia* in each place through which and only through which one becomes a member of the catholic church "everywhere". It is in this way that one should better understand the patristic phrase "the catholic church which is to be found in the whole oikoumene". Universality, which in the ecclesiological sense is a fundamentally ontological term and therefore more deeply grounded in the creative and saving act of God, is of absolutely greater importance since it corresponds more fully to the qualitative "catholic" sense of creation. This is also "not in place but in essence", as God made everything out of the wholeness of his being as love and "his full will and logos".

b) Ekklesia with ktisis

This understanding of qualitative catholicity, including the historical reality and the whole created cosmos, makes us conceive the church always in relationship with and together with the divine act of creation. It is only in the ecclesial sacramental communion that we can conceive a full doctrine of creation. The origin, means and purpose of creation can be grasped only in the church and in connection with the "wholeness" and "everywhere" dimensions of the ecclesial reality, i.e. with the total revelation of God as creator of "all things" restored by him in Christ. The self-evident consequence of "wholeness" and "everywhere" is "all things" (τά πάντα), as implied by the inseparable connection of God's full action revealing the "wholeness" of his truth through the *ekklesia* to the whole world as the creator of "all things" by and in his logos and renewed and fulfilled in his Spirit.

The ecclesial understanding and experience of the creation is deeply grounded, ontologically and existentially, in the biblical affirmation that God "created" everything, "recapitulated" all things, and "restored" them in his logos, who has been given by him to be the head of the body which is the church (Col. 1:18), and further that the Holy Spirit fulfills the destiny of the whole creation, which is expecting together with the children of God, and in travail and groaning, its final liberation (Rom. 8:21–22). The ecclesial communion represents, incarnates and enacts this biblical basis by incorporating the whole of creation within its sacramental being and existence in and together with the world in an inseparable unity.

This approach to the ecclesial understanding of creation has immediate and important repercussions for the themes of church unity, sacramental vision, and witness in the world and further for their relation with its renewal.

First, there is a deeper and broader unity of "all things" rooted in the creative act of the Trinity of God caused by his essence, which is love, leading to communion, communal operation in creation, and communal experience of it in and through the church. The logos's creative "principle" is life and the creative energy transcending, permeating and uniting all things. The logos, as hypostasis, endows the whole creation with love and meaning by communicating life which is in him (John 1:4) and his life is identical with meaning, sense and reason, i.e. intelligibility, value and beauty, will, goodness and feeling. His life is in this sense relating material, biological and spiritual elements in an absolute unity within human beings and through them in the whole cosmos. That is why "his life is the light of men" (John 1:4) and in him everything is recapitulated "becoming thus the head of the body" (Col. 1:15−18). The creative "arche" (principle) therefore is fully identical with the unity realized within time in the ecclesial communion by the Spirit in virtue of the logos incarnate, crucified and risen, and of the event of Pentecost. The unity principle is deeper and broader than the confessional church unity which is a nucleus, a sign, a manifestation and also the real presence, as microcosm, of the unity of the whole creation. The cosmic dimension of the logos' creativity implies that unity is the authentic proof of the logos being, as creator, the life-light of all men. The unity of the whole cosmos, then, is the fundamental life-principle and power, as a continuous process of life from the origin of the creation by God, "who has made of one blood all nations (and everything) to dwell on all the face of the earth" (Acts 17:26). The purpose of the creation is the unity of all things under the authority of God so that "God may be all in all" (1 Cor. 15:27). Unity of all things is given in creation and in the process of life towards its fulfilment. Alongside the given unity in "One Faith, One Baptism by the One Spirit" we have to struggle "till we all come to the unity into the measure of the stature of the fullness of Christ" (Eph. 4:13). Cosmic unity is the fulfilment of the creation as its *telos* in logos, as he is given to be "the head over all things to the church, which is his body, the fullness of him that filleth all in all" (Eph. 1:22−23).

Second, this understanding of creation leads to a comprehensive image of the whole historical reality realized and experienced in the ecclesial communion. Creation, as nature (*physis*) with all of its realities, appears to be like a living organism with a deep, unshaken, inner coherence. Alongside the *ekklesia* but always together with it, and through it, there is the biblical term *ktisis* for creation. *Ktisis* includes God's creative act out of his love, the meaning of creation in his logos and the continuous perfection and renewal of all things in Christ by the Spirit: "If any man be in Christ (he) is a new creature; old things are passed away; behold all things are become new" (2 Cor. 5:17). In this way God, man, nature and "all things" are expressed by the term *ktisis* and are inseparably linked, and share together, in the creative, sustaining and all-renewing and uniting one grace of God. *Ktisis*, as the biblical term for creation, speaks of the meaningful act of God in his logos creating "all things" with a definite purpose. *Ktisis* denotes the solidarity of man with nature which is given by the creator, within the one and same creative and renewing act in the logos, struggling to fulfill their purpose together in this history. *Ekklesia* is always therefore with *ktisis*, in solidarity with it, being its hidden focus, a restored image and a prefiguration of its fulfilment and *telos*, in the kingdom of God which is already among us and is still coming and shall be finally realized at the end of time.

Third, it becomes evident that this approach to the full sense of catholicity (qualitative *and* geographical-quantitative) endows history and material things with a paramount value in the logos of creation. History becomes a meaning-bearing event with inner cohesion and continuity as a process of life towards a definite telos. In the logos which takes flesh is revealed also the supreme value of *material* things for a meaningful creation. History and material things are not simply the place in which the sacred history of the divine economy is taking place, but they are organically inter-related with revelation as its form, i.e. as its qualitative presence here and now. This goes beyond any kind of historical dialectical materialism which professes the autonomy of man, man who deals by his own spirit with the infinite possibilities of nature, thus reducing history to a closed system which realizes only its own purposes. This qualitative-quantitative understanding of ecclesial catholicity incorporates history and matter organically within the creative act of God in logos. Nature is no longer merely instrumental or exploited material. It belongs, as *ktisis*, to the existence and positive reality and givenness of creation out of God's love and purpose for it. The "logos-ktisis" as creation becomes *ekklesia* and renewed human existence. Therefore, nature shares (as the self-evident event) in the revelation as a living organism, having the same origin in God's love and the same purpose: the liberation of the children of God. History is becoming *ktisis*, also, and nature becomes a historical meaningful event. Matter is neither itself the creator, nor does it have autonomous life from itself, nor is it a simple instrument of inferior value in God's creative plan and act. Matter is the open possibility for new life by the creative logos with men. Matter is *sine qua non* in the one catholic-cosmic act of creation. Without matter there is no historical being, and no reality is possible. To be a human person means to be a bodily existence. New life in the resurrection cannot be but bodily, while history is a receptacle of divine economy and revelation by, in and through matter. Over against the term "historical dialectical materialism" we should use the term *theo-materialism*, pointing to the pivot-event of history as being God-in-nature creating, restoring, renewing and fulfilling his cosmos, as it is experienced in the ecclesial communion in full solidarity with the world as *ktisis*. Therefore, any anthroponistic vision and use of the matter and nature as ktisis is a sin in the most authentic sense of the word. Our whole technical civilization which has also biblical-Christian roots and makes us all as Christians co-responsible for the abuse of nature today, distorts nature as *ktisis* as we have to conceive it through the sacramental vision uniting church and all things in the world.

Fourth, the catholicity of the *ekklesia* conceived in this sense of creation manifested and experienced in the ecclesial communion can preserve Christian theology from all kinds of monisms or dualisms, which try to conceive the doctrine of creation unilaterally and thus destroy the appropriate and dynamic relationship between church and world. Christian theologies of creation without strong ecclesiological bases are easily tempted to fall into the approaches of theistic idealisms or pantheistic monisms, and, in some cases (for the sake of a "pro-worldly" attitude), into mechanistic autodeterministic naturalisms. The cause of all of these deviations is the dualism between spirit and matter and the discontinuity between creation and cosmos, or the confusion caused by an unreflective fusion between creative act and creation. The creation conceived through the catholicity of the *ekklesia* safeguards the distinction of creator from the creation in which he acts. Nature as *ktisis* includes the whole of created reality as an organism composed of distinctive elements of being and existence. They are in full relationship and interdependence as they are created out of the love of a personal God as creator. He is in distinctive full communion with all of them, renewing "all things" by his creative logos. The clear distinction between creator and creation as well as between the different beings and their modes of existence, becomes thus the dynamic power of inner coherence without either dualistic separations or monistic tendencies, or fusion and confusion between them. The ecclesial communion is the *locus* for experiencing the catholicity, i.e. the fullness and distinctiveness of the creative act of the Trinitarian God, securing both the distinction between creator and creation and also continuity and personal relationship between them.

c) The broken catholicity or the catholicity of the Fall

This understanding of qualitative catholicity and geographical catholicity as an inseparable whole should not be regarded as an abstract vision and contemplation. It is, simply, the first reality and mystical experience within the sacramental life of the ecclesial communion, as a foretaste of the final fulfilment of the continuously renewed creation as *ktisis*. It is not an irenic-static, introverted and esoteric attitude of the sacramental gathering enjoying the beatitude of grace in isolation from the realities of this world. This would have been an illusory vision or meta-historical fantasy and chiliastic interpretation of history, and against the premises of the authentic understanding of catholicity within the ecclesial communion according to which "all things" are brought into a new relation for the sake of their continuous process of renewal.

Within this reality of catholicity there is, as a reality which permanently resists it, the "catholicity of the Fall", i.e. of the broken relationship between Creator and creature (which is also experienced as redeemed in the sacramental life of the ecclesial communion). The distinctive act of brokenness by one person binds together all human beings and all things. Everybody and everything everywhere and at every time in history is in solidarity with this one person Adam, whose act is causing brokenness of communion — ἐφ'ᾧ πάντες ἥμαρτον ("in whom", or better, "with whom and his act *all* have sinned", Rom. 5:12). But it is, precisely, the love of God that preserves the plan of the whole creation as it is revealed and experienced within the sacramental life of the ecclesial communion by another "catholic act", i.e. "concluding all men in unbelief that he might have mercy upon all" (Rom. 11:32). This solidarity of Fall and sin is again the result of a concrete act by a concrete person at a definite time so that through another distinctive person at a concrete moment in history all men and "all things" might be restored into the communion with God (Rom. 5:17).

This negative aspect of "catholicity" makes church catholicity a permanent experience of a continuous tension between opposed realities. They are, of course, redeemed, and the fullness of God's grace has overwhelmed the brokenness of humankind by his new personal communion in the *ekklesia*, but the opposition is still there, both inside the church and in the whole universe. The catholicity is a process of God's grace creating, redeeming and saving all men and all things. Grace binds everything together into a strange Oneness. In the *ekklesia* and its sacramental reality the negative side is overcome, because the brokenness as a reality in the whole of creation happens outside the Being of God and concerns man's relationship with him. The sin is in the mode of existence and not in the essence of God's being, or in some imperfection in his divine ikon in mankind. Therefore, the sacramental communion is possible as redeeming and restoring the communion of "all things" with God.

This approach to the mystery of "including all men" into the sin of Adam through the concept of sacramental communion within the church prevents any minimizing of the reality of the brokenness in creation or, at the other extreme, making it a *fata morgana* devaluing human life and history. It preserves the absolute, overwhelming power of the grace of God over sin and acknowledges at the same time the historical reality of sin and its destructive presence mainly in the world, but also within the ecclesial communion. The brokenness has been once for all defeated by God, as received in the sacramental life of the church, but the historical reality of all human relations are still subjected to the rule of "concluding" all men into the oneness of sin so that they might be all together saved. The negative "catholicity", as universal Fall, is the main element in human relationships and "deeds", reflected also in all created things; but sacramental communion within the *ekklesia* is happening within these broken relationships as a sharing in the restored communion of God.

It is very important that an ecclesiology should keep this curious and unique dialectic between unshaken communion in *essence* and brokenness in *existence* in the whole creation. This is because the *ekklesia* as sacramental communion is absolutely holy, and a sure guarantee for sharing in the full communion with God by his grace, but all men yet remain sinful and in broken relationship both in the ecclesial communion and in the world. There is an immense difference, however, between redeemed sinfulness in repentance and non-repenting human sinfulness outside the ecclesial communion. There is a great difference between a broken unity within the sacramental communion and a broken humanity outside of it, but on the other hand there is also an inevitable reciprocity and mutual interdependence between the two as being subjected to the one and the same historical predicament of sin and brokenness. The church is one communion, but it is also reflecting the brokenness of the world within its communion. The world, on the other hand, is broken but strives for unity on the basis of qualities and aspirations which God has given to all human beings. The ecclesial sacramental communion is thus the focus and image of the redeemed brokenness of the world and the world is brought back into the personal communion with God. The unity of the church and the renewal of human community are thus inseparably linked not as two separate entities but as two concentric circles around the one, unique and the same pivotal event in history: God redeeming brokenness and bringing back into his communion "all things" in order to renew them. There is one and the same redeeming, uniting and saving grace of God, which is connecting the ecclesial communion with the whole creation, as cosmos and *ktisis*, restored to his communion. The final stage of communion, in its as yet unfulfilled eschatological sense, unites, in hope, the ecclesial sacramental communion and the broken human community into a single worldwide community which is in process of growing towards unity around the unique, pivotal historical event of the divine economy.

In other words, the "sacramental vision" is an anticipation of the coming kingdom of God in which we participate in hope and which exercises an immediate pressure on history. The not-yet fulfilled ecclesial sacramental communion looks forward to its final fulfilment. But it already participates by anticipation in the coming kingdom of God by sharing in the gradual restoration of the whole creation-*ktisis* as it also expects the same fulfilment at the end of time. Eschatology, thus, becomes in the sacrament a real presence in history.

2. The sacramental vision as a witnessing process

This broad understanding of church catholicity is due to the sacramental nature of the *ekklesia*. It simply means that the church as a distinctive concrete event and institution has its origin in God and its members are called out of the world but, on the other hand, its existence is with and for the world, of which the *ekklesia* is one inseparable part. The church's origin in God prejudges and postulates its being in and for the whole world, because its Founder is the Creator of "all things" and has endowed them with meaning and purpose. The church is an event manifesting the permanence of the personal relationship of God *with* the whole creation in a specific way and through a chosen human community.

"Sacramental" means the self-communication of God through human realities at a specific moment. The "sacral" event consists in the fact that God has singled out a channel of communication, specific and visible, by using worldly elements in order to penetrate history and restore the broken communion with man, giving his grace anew in a special way. The whole created cosmos is a gift of grace. There is nothing in the creation which is not a gift of the Holy Spirit. But the sacrament as a particular distinctive intervention in time comes out of the same grace and of the same essence: the love of God in order to overcome the brokenness of humankind and restore its broken community.

The ecclesial communion is, therefore, sacramental by its nature and function; it preconditions, by its visible, concrete existence here and now, all sacramental acts happening within it. The church is animated by the special grace in virtue of the incarnate logos, the cross and the resurrection. It is cleansed (as restored communion with God) by the Spirit. A sacramental act offers a channel for the grace of God to penetrate, in specific ways, the elect community of people in the world, so that through this community and these worldly elements grace flows into the whole world and to all of humankind.

The church as the one and unique sacramental event, containing all specific sacramental acts, makes manifest the co-existence between grace and the world, between the invisible gift of God and the visible elements from among material created things. The sacramental being of the church is grasped only through natural, worldly means, which are indispensable as receptacles of grace and as its channels for the whole world. The grace of God singling out the church as distinctive community conditions its being as an existence in-solidarity-with-the-world. Sacrament is the permanence of the presence of God through his elect community in solidarity with the world. The act of sanctification, setting apart distinct people by specific actions, becomes the new starting point of a restored communion of God with the human reality. Sacrament means (as we have seen in the understanding of catholicity) *distinction for re-establishing relation*, a separation or "setting apart" in order to ground the communion more deeply by singling out a special channel for restructuring the divine-human communion.

When, then, we speak of "sacramental vision", we mean the reality of the church as a link and a channel, specially visible and unique, between God and history in unity and communion, and as a regathering of humankind into a oneness which redeems the broken relationship with God. The "vision" therefore is not a simple individual mystical experience and contemplation. It represents and enacts the divine grace within human realities. "Sacramental vision" is synonymous with realized divine-human communion here and now, for the sake of transmitting the saving and uniting grace of God to "all things" for building the new community of love in history.

In other words, "sacramental vision" denotes that the church does not possess its own being as a self-perfected community but it exists *from* God and *for* the world, making manifest the restored communion between them. Its origin in God and its purpose for being is conceived only as being continuously *in via* from God to and for the world. Its ontological status can be grasped only as a perpetual movement towards the whole world as a specific "sign" or, better, as "instrument" of the recapitulation of the God-man movement and relationship. "Sacramental" is, in this sense, God-being-with-man in a new, renewed, specific way. The "vision" here points to the relation of the whole world with God. "Vision" — from the biblical word "horô", to see — signifies not simply visual action but existential relationship, and this is mainly emphasized when we speak of "seeing" God or Christ and the divine glory (John 1:14; 1 Cor. 13:12).

The church, then, as sacramental event, together with the "sacramental vision" of its members of the reality of the restored relationship of God and man for the sake of the whole world, is in itself a permanent, witnessing act. Witness is not simply a moral obligation but it is identical with the faith in the sacramental nature of the church. In the sacraments God is acting through human means in the world, and the sacrament is a presence of God in time. Consequently, the sacrament is a continuous witness of his presence amongst men. "Sacramental" points to a reality about witness: God is with us and for the whole of humankind.

In the eucharist, where the elements of the sacramental nature of the church directly express the grace of God communicated by the Spirit in virtue of the cross and resurrection of Christ, we offer our thanksgiving with worldly means, and on the part of the whole world, so that we all become, anew, sharers in the body and blood of Christ and at the same time "we do show" the death of Christ (1 Cor. 11:26). The eucharist, as a culminating action of the sacramental nature of the church and a recreating act of the body of Christ, points to the identity between "sacramental vision" and the witness to the renewed divine-human communion in the *ekklesia* of God.

It is because of this identity of "sacramental vision" and witness that the whole church as such, and all of the church members sharing in its sacramental reality are, inevitably, living witnesses of the faith and hope in Christ for the sake of the world. The evangelical commandment to witness is inherent in the sacramental being and vision. Our whole sacramental sharing is ontologically a permanent process of confessing, witnessing, and serving in the world. Presupposing catholicity as I have explained it in the previous paragraph, and the consistent interpretation of "sacramental vision" above, we can now approach the multiform expression of this witnessing process of the "sacramental vision" of the ecclesial communion within the world.

a) Witness in and for solidarity with the world

The first and most important aspect of witness is identical with the sacramental nature of the church. The point of departure is the thesis that "all things" have been created out of the love of God, thus excluding all dualisms between created order and ecclesial communion. Witness, therefore, is shaped, actualized and proclaimed out of sincere, frank and permanent love for all men and the honest will to serve in all human conditions in the world. Our solidarity with the world thus witnesses to the real presence of Christ amongst persons struggling for the improvement of human life in all of its areas, wherever this is needed.

Witness is the verification of our faith in action with respect to the image of Christ. If the "sacramental vision" is a manifestation of the restored relationship with Christ, then the question is what do "we see" when we look at him. By looking at Christ, we relate our lives to him (vision = communion) in the midst of the world, which is in process of liberation through the defeat of all negative elements existing in the broken human community. We bear the marks of this brokenness within the church also. Witness as solidarity with the world is of the essence of the sacramental communion within the *ekklesia*, which does not allow either a separation from the world or an absence from all sincere struggles to recover a fully human existence. The human struggles "outside" of the church for justice, peace and liberation are not foreign elements in the one creation of God, elements outside of his love. There is no opposition between the two concentric realities, church and world, but rather continuity. The constructive character of the church's action in the world makes our solidarity even more pressing and urgent.

Sexism, racism, classism, exploitation of the weak, poverty, famine, injustice and threats against peace are destructive symptoms within the human community in the world, as well as in the church. Here we have to remind ourselves of the "catholicity of the Fall" and our solidarity in sin, where God has "concluded us all in order to save all of us together". Our witnessing process, therefore, is a witnessing act for us and for the communion of the church which also inevitably bears the human brokenness. The church is not only a divine institution but also a human, "sociological" one in the full sense. Those who forget this are, in *praxis*, monophysists, and their "sacramental vision" is introverted, seriously defective and therefore fruitless.

b) Witness as a prophetic judgment of the world

Certainly we might have regarded the element of "solidarity" in witness as a one-way traffic, a sentimental understanding and application of God's love made manifest in creation and in the sacramental nature of the church. But this would have been a serious misinterpretation.

The catholicity of the Fall implies a resistance and an opposition from all human enterprises in the world and in the church. Witness cannot be full if it is not, therefore, also prophetic judgment, with priority given to the judgment within the ecclesial communion. "Judgment must begin at the house of God" (1 Pet. 4:17), but we must bear in mind also that "the saints shall judge the world" (1 Cor. 6:2). In neither case do we have people as members of the church judging, out of their own authority, the world. Rather it is a prophetic act of witnessing, i.e. of giving, in all humbleness, God's judgment: "But them that are without, God judges" (1 Cor. 5:13), because the "prince of this world is judged" (John 16:11).

Prophetic judgment must be effected as the consistent witness of God's presence in the midst of history. It has to take into consideration the resistance of sin in all human efforts which struggle between good and evil. The particularity of Christian witness as service, and in solidarity with the world, consists in making visible to the world the particularity of God's special intervention in the realm of human struggles. The peace of Christ is different from the one that the world gives (John 14:27), not forgetting that Christ came "not to send peace but a sword" (Matt. 10:34), and bearing in mind that the justice "that the world may achieve today can be proved to be injustice tomorrow".

Witness must always be an authentic application of God's saving act by judging all autonomous human enterprises. It means a total devotion to the gospel, which both judges and reconciles at the same time, as well as to the total cause of humanity in the process of its liberation from the bonds of human sin. Within the humanist's framework and in the vast array of political-economic struggles there are also some illusory, optimistic and self-satisfied anthropocentric programmes. Witness out of "sacramental vision" in solidarity with them means an open, direct and honest judgment on behalf of the gospel, otherwise the witness offered out of the "sacramental vision" of the church is not appropriate and full.

It is only by challenging the principalities and powers of this world that we can serve the world, and remain in dynamic solidarity with it on the basis of the love of God. Human self-confidence may be based only on ideological or idealistic, humanistic self-affirmation in all kinds of struggles for the sake of humanity and justice. A witness of the Christian church which neglects challenging this self-confidence does not fulfill its sacramental mandate to witness in all given situations, both in the church and in the world. We should seek the origin of all prophetic witnessing acts within the church and understand them within the church community, as particular gifts of grace for facing specific circumstances and concrete cases. Witness is expression of the dynamic evangelical message serving the church in its existence for the world. It shares with it in the common effort for the renewal of the world in concrete instances where the church's dynamic presence is needed to prepare the way towards the unity of all through the incorporation of "all things" in Christ.

The final perspective of the prophetic judgment is therefore the realization of a new human community uniting all people in Christ for the sake of the unity of the whole world. It is at this crucial moment that witness can be tested as authentic and evangelical. Though all of the struggles for justice and peace are absolutely necessary, the ecclesial community remains the final reality and, as such, both the origin and fulfilment of all kinds of the acts of witness which it performs in the world.

c) Witness as martyria to the glory of God

The prophetic enactment of witness in the world, with the church facing the brutal opposition of the principalities of this world, renders witness to a process of *martyria* to faith and requires it to face the possibility of martyrdom as the highest proof of its authenticity. Unless Christian witness is not a *martyria* which causes a certain kind of opposition, it has not yet reached its ultimate development. Martyrdom as *martyria* does not signify immediate bodily suffering or an open persecution. Oppression is the most polyform phenomenon in the world. It can take for Christians the shape of scorn, irony and hidden devaluation of one's personality and dignity. It can cause marginalization of the faithful in human society and demoralization of their personal life.

Persecution of all kinds as a counterpart of witness is a mystery which cannot be explained rationally. History reveals its non-sensical side. The victims would never dominate their persecutors by becoming martyrs, as they actually do, out of a naive innocence with respect to the image of Christ. "If the world hates you, you know that it hated me before it hated you" (John 15:18). This kind of opposition of the world against the gospel message is growing alongside an intensified witness on the part of the ecclesial communion. That is why the Spirit, who establishes this communion in history and renews it by the sacramental life, is promised by Christ to be the *Paracletos*, i.e. the Comforter or, better, the advocate defending all of the witnessing members of the church. They are, as it were, facing a perpetual accusation in the world's court.

Witness in the form of a martyria-martyrdom is the outcome of the sacramental communion with Christ in his unique and once-for-all sacrifice: "If they have persecuted me they will also persecute you" (John 15:20). Witness cannot be an accommodated, comfortable operation in the world. If it is linked with the love of Christ experienced in the sacramental relationship with him, the solidarity with the world includes and implies a strange combination of deep satisfaction and profound frustration. Without this dialectical or, better, contradictory, experience, witness cannot become efficient. This element of contradiction is not absent even in the most explicit acts of love and solidarity of the church with the world.

The paradox now is that this opposition to Christian witness results in an indirect praise to God and his glory. In the Eastern Orthodox iconography most of those who execute martyrs are presented as if they are performing a solemn duty or an act of praise, because the moment of martyrdom in this extreme form is a testimony of the authenticity of witness as a parasacramental act of sacrifice and praise to the glory of God. To a certain extent one can maintain that, unconsciously, a persecutor recognizes the truth of a witnessing act of Christ's love to the whole of humankind, and by his act of execution is transformed into a God-celebrating person who is on the way to his conversion, thus prefiguring the return of all humankind, through the most cruel experience, to the all-embracing love of God. "The time has come that whosoever kills you, will think that he does God service" (John 16:2). Behind all acts of witness there is the crucified and risen Christ.

Finally, witness as a result of a "sacramental vision" in the *ekklesia* is performed (in its right form and in connection with sacramental life of the church) not simply for increasing the number of proselytes but, primarily, because of the consistent desire to make known the gospel message as good news to the whole world. Witness, identical with "sacramental vision", enacts the love of God for humankind. This is the final and crucial issue and moment of Christian witness as living *martyria*, overcoming all the threats of martyrdom and suffering. Therefore one is offering his witness as a para-eucharistic act of thanksgiving together with the whole of the *ekklesia*. It is one more act, perhaps the most important act of offering, as a grateful response to the sacramental communion established by Christ through his sacrifice and victory. Witness, finally, is dominated by the image of Christ Victor and Pantocrator and is operated as a eucharistic hymn to the glory of God. Glory is of the essence of the triune God and a synonym of his love, and the main element of his revelation in history. Witness, then, as *martyria* has to be a thanksgiving response to the love of God and a rendering of honour to his glory.

Contemporary ecclesiology, in summary, has to relate the givenness of the church's existence and structure to the whole of the divine economy and the life of the Holy Trinity, but also, and equally, to the historical realities of the world. This is implied by the Christological premises, because Christ reveals the full communion between divinity and humanity. The concept of qualitative catholicity implies the inclusion of the world as created cosmos, as part of the one and undivided reality restored within the communion of the church.

We can discuss neither the subject of dynamic witness to the gospel in today's world, nor the relation between the unity of the church and the renewal of humankind, unless we start from the inner coherence of the whole created cosmos as it is represented and enacted within the sacramental ecclesial communion. Only then can we enter into the debate about witness as solidarity in love and judgment of the world. Only then can we proceed to necessary specific references to actual world problems in the realm of politico-economic or racial issues, in order to contribute in a special way to promoting all efforts to support justice, liberation and humanization.

The Eastern Orthodox tradition is offering a clear proof of the ecclesiological foundations of witness through its "sacramental vision" of the church. It is necessary, therefore, in the third part of my paper, to try very briefly to exemplify how this tradition has actualized these ecclesiological principles in history, and how the world's and humankind's renewal today can be positively affected by it. The contribution of the Orthodox can be of importance, because it will stand against all kinds of dualistic approaches regarding church and world, gospel and law, grace and nature, as well as all monistic tendencies in interpreting the doctrine of creation. Unity and communion of the church, witness, mission and renewal shall be kept in unison and interdependence, with priority given always to the specific saving act of the Triune God in the church as one, holy, catholic and apostolic, but always also to the church keeping its inseparable connection with the realities of the world.

3. Eastern Orthodox tradition as ecclesial martyria in the diakonia of the world's renewal

The inner connection and interdependence between sacramental vision and witness in the world as a contribution to its renewal through a continuous martyria-martyrdom seems to be one of the main characteristics of church life in the East throughout its long history. Due to the insistence of the Orthodox on the devotion of the total human person to Christ as the unique archetype of the renewed humanity on the way to its *theosis*, the life of a faithful Christian, as a member of the church sharing in its sacramental vision, has to be an imitation of Christ's prototype: a continuous martyria through suffering, service and diakonia within the world to the glory of God.

The intense sacramental-liturgical life of the Orthodox can give the impression of an introverted praying community, closed to the outside world. In reality, however, praying, sharing in the eucharist, and enjoying the ecclesial sacramental vision significant for the Orthodox, has been in their long history a *prefiguration* of their full conformity to Christ's diaconal witness to the world, and at the same time a *martyria* through martyrdom to him.

a) Philanthropia justice as a witnessing diakonia

Because of the historical circumstances in the Eastern European countries, it has always been necessary for church life to render witness and service to the world through a manifold martyrdom. Neither worldly wisdom nor social work have ever enjoyed, in the East, primacy over this simple, direct, and effective martyria. Faith has survived in the East because of this continuous dynamic witness: martyrdom as living example of existence in Christ. That is why martyrs, hermits, staretzes, monks and totally devoted lay persons were always the backbone of the ecclesial community witnessing through martyrdom. The phrase of St Basil: "Thus Christ has taught, the apostles have proclaimed, the Fathers have maintained, the martyrs have confirmed" summarizes the patristic thought on the value of martyria as the confirmation of Christian-ecclesial faith in and for the world.

It is within this tradition of witness that the whole evangelical-missionary work of the Eastern church has always been conceived and practised. While there were not organized "missions" in the modern sense of the term, Orthodoxy has never ceased to be a missionary ecclesial community. Patristic theology was fundamentally kerygmatic-evangelical in so far as it had underlined that faith is not primarily and only an individual possession but is ecclesial, and a faith for others who have not yet joined the Christian community. St John Chrysostom writes that if one keeps his faith to himself then he is unjust to those who do not have it, and to himself also; his faith he makes passive and inactive. Mission flows out of the essence of God who is love, and therefore witnessing to Christian faith for and to others is the first expression of being rooted in God's love. No personal problems should make us "neglect to save one who is in danger of drowning in the waves of the sea: precisely the same thing makes our witness become at every moment urgent".

Christ himself as the archetype "has not remained in Jerusalem but went out to find and save people". Therefore, "you also do all possible things to make those who are ignorant and deserted from faith return to it".

The most evident expression of living faith, or existence in Christ renewed by sharing in his deified humanity, is witness and evangelism — not for increasing membership but because this is the heart of the kerygma: love for the salvation of others. For the Christian life "the cornerstone is our neighbour", writes Abbe John, and Makarios of Egypt: "There is no other way to share in salvation than through the other."

On this basis the Eastern church witnessed to and transformed pagan cultures, and Christianized the heathen world. There is a magnificent simplicity, and at the same time a deep Christological foundation of ecclesial witness in the East, right from the beginning of the Christian era. There are no professional trained missionaries or systematized projects of evangelistic work, but only a deep devotion to Christ's witness for the salvation of all people within a total experience of the ecclesial life as continuous witness. Ecclesiology for patristic theology is a *praeludium* to the witnessing life of the community. If Christ is the Lord of history and of the whole world, then his lordship makes sense only if ecclesial witness makes it manifest in the world, abolishing the separation between sacred and profane. Ecclesial witnessing presupposes, for the Byzantine tradition, the recapitulation of all things in Christ, who is given as the head of the church. Therefore it springs out of a given unity and is offered for the sake of the coming unity of all things in him. Catholicity and apostleship are inseparably linked in the theology of the Greek Fathers. The wholeness of truth for the whole world is exercised in evangelism. Christ's truth, fulfilled, flows out into mission.

This is the source of power for the weak missionary who renders witness in a strange, foreign, or hostile environment. The simple monks of the Eastern Church incarnated this true connection, showing a catholicity in apostleship flowing from love for humankind: "The ministry of the monks is in its very nature very close to that of the apostles, both witness to the sovereignty of Christ over history and over the world."

b) Witness as diaconal service to the renewal of the world.

It is within this simplicity, as well as on the Christological foundation of ecclesial witness, that the Eastern churches understood witness also as a diaconal service to the world for the sake of its renewal. In the true affirmation of the gospel, the suffering neighbour is a loving presence of Christ. To be "philanthropos" for the church fathers is not a moral obligation but the consistent outcome of being "philotheos" in Christ. In church hymnology, "philanthropos" is a synonym for Christ as saviour. The term is not used in a sentimental-moralistic-compassionate sense, but as denoting the basic archetypal image of God who is love and who calls upon human beings for constant action in the world. We find the term used by St Athanasius to denote the leading motive of God in incarnating the logos, "who assumed humanity that his brothers might partake of divinity; this philanthropic attribute of God demands that many should imitate it and manifest it in his relation with his fellow men".

The Byzantine church first, and then the other autocephalous churches which shared this concept of *philanthropos* Christ, have developed a remarkable social programme for all persons in need as an inseparable part of their preaching and celebrating. In this realm, they were the first institution of their times, acting to erect the first organized hospitals, houses for the aged, for orphans, the blind, widows, outcasts, and crippled persons. "The bishops were bound by universal church law to do charitable works. . . and on many occasions led their flock in expressing the concern of the whole church for philanthropy."

Many of the church fathers who are most famous for their theological and missionary achievements are also those who gave first priority in their pastoral care to organizing charitable work in their diocese. This has been true from ancient times up to the present day. In countries where they are still allowed to act in the social welfare field, the Orthodox churches always and everywhere practise "philanthropia" based on the sound Christological principles, i.e. Christ who came to save all people, heal the sick and protect the poor and weak. This is done together with the kerygmatic, catechetical, and evangelical work which they do by their very nature. The Eastern churches in their best expressions can be especially proud because they have succeeded in remaining in solidarity with the simple, poor and martyrial people of their societies. In many instances they have offered them the only refuge and the only milieu for moral and material recovery, and for achieving human dignity. In this respect not only the parish churches and the church's charitable institutions but especially the monastery have permanently practised, as their first commitment to Christ's example, all kinds of humanitarian assistance to the weak — Christians and non-Christians alike. "The monasteries assumed (of course in a primitive way) all of the phil-anthropic responsibilities of modern welfare states."

Apart from this immediate involvement in acts of philanthropy, the church's contribution in this area of witnessing to God's word has been immense in yet another way. This is by continuous preaching from the pulpits the gospel of the poor and underprivileged. This unceasing pleading on their behalf has influenced the attitude of the civil authorities in their countries. Indeed, most of these countries have been created as independent states *by* the Orthodox mission, and preserved as such by the Orthodox churches through very hard historical times. Very early, from the fourth century on, in the Byzantine Empire and then in all the other states of Arabic, Slavic and Roman background in the East, state authorities have been urged to organize an extended and efficient welfare programme as a response to the church's appeal and example. Taking into consideration the historical circumstances, limited resources and spirit of these patriarchal societies, it is astonishing to read how many public philanthropic institutions, bearing Christian names of saints and church fathers distinguished by their social work, have been created in all of these "Orthodox countries". Thus Constantinople offered the first city with an organized system of philanthropy, so that "an eye-witness of its collapse lamented that when it fell under the Turks, the famous city could no longer maintain its many philanthropic institutions".

To be sure, this kind of language praising philanthropy and charitable work may sound strange to contemporary Christians who are involved in social work in the name of Christ. I know that supporting the poor in this way is sometimes worse than not helping them at all, i.e. if you are not creating new conditions for them by restructuring society. Giving alms may sound today scandalous to revolutionary Christians who are trying in the name of the gospel — and rightly so! — to abolish the unjust structures of contemporary society. But first one has to reckon with the spirit of these earlier times in the East, and their total lack of conscientization towards such social reform; second, the churches had to act, as the first institution to "sensitize" state authorities and public opinion in desperate situations, in an elementary, philanthropic way (which is also important and highly commended in the Bible); and third — and most importantly — the teaching of the church fathers and the pulpit did not in fact ignore the acute problem of justice and solidarity beyond simple philanthropy. St Neilos expresses authentically the patristic spirit of the East with his words "the religious person is not the person who distributes alms to many but one who treats no one unjustly". Plitho Gemitza, writing some centuries later and deploring the fall of Constantinople under the Crusaders' rule, "insisted that restoration of social justice was a pre-requisite for the revival of the Empire". His works remind us of the phraseology of contemporary theologians of liberation who demand that we "prevent the stronger from crushing the weaker. . . so that one person does not oppress another".

In the Eastern church tradition throughout its history, then, philanthropy is not practised as dissociated from the demand for justice. These churches have been in this respect the initiator of the dynamic process of restructuring unjust societies. This follows from their primary concern of protecting human persons who are called to become participants in the nature of God and aim at his theosis. On this solid theological basis and on the faith of the generating and liberating power of the Holy Spirit the church fathers defended, with the language of their times and in their own historical circumstances, human rights and the authentic equality of men and women. They pleaded the case of the weak against the strong and oppressors. Refusing to admit that there can be an identity with any kind of civil, secular authority, they did not hesitate to risk their own lives and privileges within a system which closely connected church and state. In this context, some of the phrases of Eastern church leaders should not sound very strange to us, because they resemble what contemporary radical revolutionaries are saying. Chrysostomos appears as one of the very early radical Christian socialists when he writes: "The rich withhold the goods of the poor even if this wealth is honestly acquired or legally inherited."

This social radicalism was practically expressed by the monastic ideal with its total rejection, for the first time, of private property, and the replacement of it by the communal possession of goods after the example of the first church in Jerusalem. Certainly this was a *monastic* rule and not an immediate church request addressed to the entire secular society. But it has played an enormous role as a teaching of the church, pointing out the purpose of human life beyond the material welfare offered by indi- vidualistic capitalist economy; opening the way for radical Christian social ethics in the light of the gospel; focusing patristic teaching and thought on the point that all material goods did not belong to the individual but are God's, that we are only stewards of them. Chrysostomos again, facing the allure of private property at the expense of spiritual life and social values, remarks: "We have distorted the order of things, requesting unceasingly material goods instead of the spiritual ones — and that is why we lack both."

c) Diaconal witness in culture

Liturgically the Eastern Orthodox use the term "diaconate" for the whole of the priesthood of the church. This is because the main qualification of the priest is, for them, their service liturgically and as a permanent witness in service to the world. This service of priesthood (in which women also, as ordained deaconesses, express directly and clearly this witnessing dimension) corresponds to the spirit of the sacramental community in permanent service to the church and to the world as two inseparable entities. To be a church member means to be in diaconal service. The existence of a Christian, as a renewed person everywhere where he lives and acts should be a living witness. Before and beyond all types of systematically organized witnessing and service programmes, which could resemble those produced by secular humanists in various ways, Christian life should be a witnessing act by itself.

"Diaconate" is an expression of the democratic, and at the same time family, church *ethos* that the Orthodox try to maintain in all realms of church life and self-discipline. It is the "system" where love and charity have absolute priority over any institutional, legalistic, systematic self-centred organization which seeks to apologize to, or polemize against, other secular institutions, or to copy the principles and methods of action of other ideologies.

This kind of "sophia" (wisdom) of the serving diaconate is the basis of one of the greatest contributions of the Eastern church tradition, as it serves by making a renewed witness to its environment. I refer to its witness through *serving* the people's culture, or in other cases renewing it or even creating a new one. Since culture is the human effort to transcend barbarism and to help human beings become distinctive persons in front of their Creator and in his image, promoting culture has always been for the Orthodox churches one of their sacramental duties in their witnessing service to the world. This did not come from an anthropocentric belief but, again, was an implication from *Christology* for a renewed anthropology.

In fact the churches in the East found themselves in a culture prominent and fascinating by virtue of its achievements in all their brilliance, i.e. philosophy, art, theatre, literature. This culture content was one of the greatest achievements of the Eastern Orthodox tradition and was also due to its diaconal-witnessing-renewing spirit. This was the way in which moving beyond a formal negation of the culture, or seeing it as its antithesis, they transformed this culture *from within*, giving to it a more human face and a new *entelecheia* in God. Sharing in this tremendous philosophical heritage, the church fathers made an exemplary effort to relate human reason to the personal revelation of God — without identifying them or confusing them. Their attitude towards the ancient classical wisdom and culture was openly appreciative; they viewed it as God-given, as part of God's sustaining and renewing all through grace. This helped them to teach how human cultures, as gifts of grace, can relate to the biblical revelation and serve mankind in a new age within a renewed world. Here is where church witness, as diaconal service in the renewal of the world, has to recognize its culminating point. And the West has rightly recognized the patristic contribution to its secular cultural environment, especially by Gregory of Nazianzus: "Through Gregory the church took its place at Acropolis of spiritual culture forever."

The logos theology of the Eastern churches, using this ancient wisdom carefully and selectively, moved culture towards creating new forms, new ways of theorizing, new applied scientific knowledge, and favoured new ways of artistic expression. The church mission of the Byzantine church tradition has been at the origin not only of our autocephalous churches, but also of new cultures which joined with pre-existing ones to create new genuine Christian expressions of philosophy, art and literature. Out of the admirable ancient wisdom the church witness within the realm of culture created a renewed, dynamic, cultural society. The logos Christocentric theology, with the all-renewing operation of the Holy Spirit, modified the ancient wisdom and made it one of the most important elements after the Bible for the renewal of the world. Our main preoccupation today with the church's witness in the social realm for establishing justice and liberation should not make us forget this continually important area of church witness, in which the Orthodox tradition maintains one of the most distinguished places.

d) Ecclesial sharing in the world's renewal

It is in this way that one has to think of the relationship between church witness as diaconal service and the ongoing renewal of the world. In other words, we should not think that churches are going to create renewal processes in the world. Renewal in the world is a permanent event. What is new in the world becomes self-evident in the renewing power that all things in nature possess once they come into positive and creative contact with the human intellect. Science does not need to create theories about renewal of all things, nor do sociologists. All things appear to have a permanent existence in space and time, but in reality their reason for being is to be found in a process of change, renewal and development. We can consider this process to be the primal reality in history; it is not a blind process, but one which can be scientifically explained, and to a certain extent mastered, without referring to metaphysical or supernatural causalities.

The church as a witnessing service to the world has to recognize this "autonomous" event as happening also within the grace of God — of course, with the restrictions imposed by the historical predicament of human sinfulness. We should not posit an opposition of sacred and profane renewal, but an irreparable co-belongingness within the one creation which is in permanent process of renewal. The church as sacramental reality and vision is in the midst of this renewing process of all things, and must always be the primary reality of a world which is changing and renewing itself. It does this by sharing in this renewal through the people of its day who move and structure it. Therefore the church's life and theology is also subject to renewal for itself, and its renewal is the only possibility of establishing a point of contact with the renewal of the world.

The first question, or problem, is therefore the one concerning the church's renewal in light of the renewal of all things. We cannot easily distinguish between church renewal, reformation, and transformation, because we cannot easily reconcile the challenge to share in this world's process of renewal with the desire to preserve and keep the past inheritance in unbroken continuity with the future. It is the problem of how to link the special renewing intervention of God in Christ, and through the Spirit, with the ongoing renewing process happening in the world by and within the same grace of the Trinitarian God. The renewal problem for the church, and especially for the Eastern churches today on the basis of their age-old tradition of diaconal, renewing service, is central for their authentic identity in a world which is also continually changing and renewing itself.

The biblical message that everything becomes renewed in Christ and is called upon to share in this newness as the purpose of human life is not an abstract contemplative and visionary notion. The sacramental vision of renewal is the primary central reality of world history from the Christian point of view. The apocalyptic phrase "behold I make all things new" (Rev. 21:3) summarizing the gospel message denotes the divine sovereign act of God acting in Christ by the operation of the Holy Spirit at the centre of history. The scriptures have as their last chapter the vision of "the river of the water of life, clear as crystal, proceeding out of the throne of God and of the lamb. In the midst of the street of it . . . was the tree of life, which bare twelve manner of fruits . . . and the leaves of the tree were for the healing of the nations" (Rev. 22:1–2).

In this image we can trace symbolically the grace of God flowing from his throne through the tree of life with "its twelve fruits", i.e. the apostolic church and its kerygma and sacramental life which is in "the midst of the street", at the centre of the world, "for the healing" of the world. The movement starts from God through the church as the centre of the world and in inseparable unity with it so that it might offer its diaconal witness for the improvement, correction and perfection of what is already happening in the nations.

We are not, therefore, introducing renewal to the world but sharing of God's grace in it and healing the nations. If we lose sight of this vision of renewal both in church and world as one inseparable event out of God's grace, then we risk all kinds of extremist one-sided positions, either isolating the church from the ongoing process of renewal of all things or identifying it with this renewal process entirely losing thus the "healing" aspect of renewal as a distinctive witnessing church contribution in the renewal of the world.

Christian faith, based on the Bible, is at the origin of the most dynamic modern concept of history laying emphasis on its continuous process of renewal and historical development towards the future. There should not be a discrepancy between keeping the past of the church life and doctrine unchanged and the need to share in the renewal of the world by and through the renewal of the church. Progress is the target of renewal in the service of humanity but progress means continuity with the past and continuity therefore means the right use of the past event in Christ and the wisdom to interpret in anew through the renewal of the church in contact with the renewal of all things.

The secular world thus becomes an appeal to the church reminding it of being at the origin of the whole renewal process beginning with itself, otherwise it risks not to be a witnessing church. But while renewing itself the church does not respond to the temptation to easily identify itself with the world's renewal, because it fulfills this ongoing renewal in the world by the specific intervention of the continuous pentecostal event that it represents, i.e. uniting everybody and all things by this process of renewal caused by the operation of the Spirit. The wholeness of this renewing act of the world by the Spirit implies the new specific event of regathering all people into God's oneness, which implies the defeat of all kinds of race and sex discrimination, the improvement of human conditions, the protection of human dignity and the abolition of injustice and poverty.

The unity of the church in this way has to be understood as the focus of renewal of the whole world in a new perspective i.e. as one human family struggling to recapture its high destiny in God. The unity of the church therefore does not fulfill a self-purpose but it is a renewing process of church life as a sacramental community and as a living diaconal witness in the midst of a self-renewing world, aspiring also for its unity by overcoming all obstacles caused by human sin and failure and which have broken its unity. Thus unity, witness and renewal in church and world constitute the means of the whole of history to fulfill its purpose in God. That is what is grasped from the perspective of the sacramental vision of the church.

The tradition of the Eastern Orthodox should always be maintained because of its insistence on church continuity, sacramental distinctiveness, special witnessing, service to the world, i.e. the special renewing church contribution to the world's renewal but at the same time the solidarity of the church with the ongoing renewal of the world in which the church is sharing in all human efforts in developing human values and world's unity. The example of the church patristic tradition in this respect, initiating and sharing out of the sacramental life of the church in all of the genuine efforts for improving the human race in personal, family, social and cultural life, is very instructive for the Orthodox church life at the present moment.

At the same time this central purpose of witness should become the cause today for an honest self-criticism of the Orthodox as they are finding it hard to reinterpret the patristic thought and action in contemporary terms and by witnessing acts of renewal for the sake of the unity of all. Liturgy is instructive of a continuously renewed dynamic style of life in the world, but when it absorbs the total sacramental vision then diaconal renewing witness in the world risks failing. Orthodoxy today is tempted to fall into an introverted ecclesial life. There, where hostile church authorities prevent the church from acting as a witnessing community in the world, the renewal issue is hindered by the survival problem, but unfortunately there where full freedom for this is allowed, a sclerotic conservatism negates the practising of the renewal process as a witnessing diaconal martyria in the secular realm. The dynamic process of uniting all things into the oneness of God by diakonia and witness can be then negated by an illusory self-sufficiency in God and a confidence in "our" unchanged church structures and scholastic dogmatism.

A RESPONSE TO "THE CHURCH AS A SACRAMENTAL VISION AND THE CHALLENGE OF CHRISTIAN WITNESS"

John Hind

Prof. Nissiotis's paper may be summarized as follows. Ecclesiology is the central theme of theological reflection today, and the chief ecumenical task is to achieve a reconciled ecclesiology in which the pro-catholicizing and pro-congregational tendencies are allowed to enrich each other. Starting from the Eastern Orthodox position with its emphasis on the ontology of the church seen always in its relationship with God, Prof. Nissiotis demonstrates the way in which this approach may include a systematic understanding of the relationship between the church's own unity and the renewal of the world. Catholicity is perceived as the vital concept in this task. The Orthodox opt for the priority of the qualitative over the quantitative understanding of catholicity, although seeing the latter entailed in the former. One reason for this is the desire to avoid dualism: catholicity is *deep* first, because it is rooted in the mystery of God himself, and *extensive* second, because God is the Creator, Redeemer and Restorer of all things. The church is already one and perfect, catholic in both senses, because it already shares in the communion of the Holy Trinity; but in the second sense the church is also catholic because it shares too in the universal sinfulness and brokenness of the world, in the full disclosure of whose restoration the church has an essential part to play. There should be no opposition between the joyful acknowledgment of the church's unity with God and its witness to the as yet unreconciled parts of his creation. Sacramental vision and Christian witness belong together, and our responsibility must be to avoid dualism on the one hand and monism on the other. The eucharist is the most characteristic act of the church which is both a

---

● Rev. Canon John Hind (Church of England), principal of the Theological College, Chichester, Sussex, England.

sacramental and a witnessing body. Like the church itself the eucharist proceeds by taking the things of this world — already redeemed in
Christ — and through thanksgiving restoring them to their full and
proper end. Through unity with Christ the church is both a sign of
this end and a channel of God's grace whereby it is being achieved.
Simply by being this, the church is already a prophetic, witnessing
body; its existence in the world points to the world's true nature. In
this being-and-witness the church is inevitably a judgment on the
present form of the world. Thus while the church should collaborate
with every venture that concerns the promotion of human dignity,
this can never be an uncritical collaboration. The criticism is not one
born of ideology, however, but of the church's own essential being.
Such witness including judgment is bound to lead to suffering, an
inescapable implication of the sacramental vision. Without on the one
hand solidarity with God and on the other hand solidarity with the
world in both its whole and broken aspects, there would be no possibility and indeed no need of sacraments.

In this section I shall attempt to show how some aspects of historic
Anglican experience and thought reflect the main themes of this
study.

Ecclesiology

Anglican experience certainly confirms the importance of ecclesiology. Our history has repeatedly raised questions concerning
relations with other churches and concerning Anglican self-
understanding. At an early stage of the development of the Church
of England there was a struggle between the Celtic and Roman
traditions, and throughout its history there has been a certain tension
between the desire to preserve an insular independence and the desire
to be an integral part of the wider world; ecclesiastical and secular
aspects of this ambivalence have not always been clearly
distinguishable.

When the Western church was divided at the Reformation the
course of the schism in England has to be seen not only within the
context of the religious ferment in continental Europe but also in the
light of this earlier history. With the gradual separation from Rome
new questions were posed: these concerned firstly relations with the
churches of the continental Reformers and such continuing contacts
with Rome as were possible, and eventually with the Orthodox
churches as well. During this period certain characteristics of a distinctive Anglican ecclesiology emerged: these included the supremacy
of scripture within and over tradition; the God-given nature of episcopacy; respect for Christian antiquity; a strong sense of nationhood
in its relation to the church; a distinction between the two "gospel"

sacraments and other sacramental acts of the church (the former being seen as uniquely constitutive of the church); a vernacular liturgical tradition with direct access for all the faithful to the scriptures; a balance in both liturgy and life between word and sacrament. Alongside these features was a willingness to recognize as churches within the catholic family other bodies which lacked some aspect or other of what the Church of England itself considered to belong to the fullness of the catholic tradition. The concept of the *via media* (which should not be misinterpreted in a negative or reductionist way) suggests the steering of a middle course between other paths in the light of which there must be a process of continual self-assessment. There thus emerged a kind of confessional position, unlike others in its lack of a fixed confessional statement and being contained above all in liturgical formularies and practise.

The civil disabilities and persecution suffered by dissenters (both Protestant and Roman Catholic) were consequences in part of the Church of England's self-understanding as the catholic church in England, the concrete form in which the one church of Christ appeared there. Passing years brought changes in the position of dissenters and these led the Church of England increasingly to be seen either as the *established* church (with a tendency to emphasize its role as the religious manifestation of the nation), or as merely one *denomination* among several (with a tendency to seek a clearer confessional identity — although the very comprehensiveness of the earlier settlement led to increasingly divergent understandings of what that identity involved).

A significant new factor in the past century has been the growth of the Anglican communion. A worldwide family of churches, united by communion with the Archbishop of Canterbury and sharing many common features but no single confessional statement other than the common patrimony of the "undivided" church and a shared reverence for the English Reformation, raises ecclesiological questions which have as yet found no wholly satisfactory answers. Thus within Anglicanism both universal and national elements are to be found, congregational and catholic tendencies both find a place. It is arguable how far we are successful in holding these tendencies together, and how far they simply "co-exist". More recently the ordination of women to the presbyterate in some Anglican churches has introduced new questions for the self-understanding of the communion, for relations with other churches and for the interpretation of tradition. The difficulty is not just that the protagonists fail to agree about whether the issue is primarily one of ecclesiology or primarily one of sexual equality, but also that what constitute ecclesiological questions is disputed.

At an earlier period when Ecclesia Anglicana meant the Church of England, understanding itself as the church of the English, there was an undoubted connection between the being of the church and its social responsibility, the two being seen as aspects of the one reality. The historical developments I have outlined have rendered this connection more problematic. Having become first a "denomination" and then a worldwide episcopal family has led Anglicans to face major ecclesiological questions. Developing conciliar practise (the Lambeth Conferences, synodical procedures of church government), a quest for clearer organs of authority (primates' meetings, the international theological commission) and a permanent instrument for communication (the Anglican Consultative Council), together with a developing role for the Archbishop of Canterbury are altering the ecclesial experience of Anglicans.

Catholicity

Anglican churches believe that they are parts of the "One, Holy, Catholic and Apostolic Church" (cf. Canon A.1 of the Canons of the Church of England). They deny that they are, whether severally or all together, *the* catholic church *tout court*. Both qualitative and quantitative understandings of catholicity have been held; in the seventeenth century John Pearson thought that the original sense of the term had been geographical, but that it had quickly led on to a consideration of the nature of the geographically universal church. William Sherlock on the other hand regarded it as "downright Popery to judge of the Catholic Church by its multitudes or large extent, or to judge of the Catholic faith by the vast number of its professors".[1] He argued that "the profession of the true Faith and worship of Christ (is what) makes a true Church, and all true Churches are the one Catholic Church, whether they be spread over all the world, or shut up in any one corner of it, as at the first preaching of it the Catholic Church was nowhere but in Judaea".[2] It could be argued, he went on, that "were there but one true Church in the world, that were the Catholic Church, because it would be the whole Church of Christ on earth, and were the true Christian faith professed in but one such Church, it would be the Catholic Faith still, for it is the faith of the whole true Church of Christ, the sincere belief and practise of which makes a Catholic Church".

In his consideration of the meaning of catholicity, Pearson identified four principal senses in which the church may be described as catholic:
1) the "diffusiveness" of the church (teaching all nations);
2) the universality of necessary and saving truths retained in it (teaching all things);

3) the universal applicability of its teaching;
4) because of "all the graces given in it, whereby all diseases of the soul are healed, and spiritual virtues are disseminated, all the works and thoughts of men are regulated, till we become perfect men in Jesus Christ".

Like Sherlock (quoted earlier), Pearson considered that "the Church which is truly Catholic containeth within it all which are truly Churches" so that "whosoever is not of the Catholic Church cannot be of the true Church. That Church alone which first began at Jerusalem on earth will bring us to the Jerusalem in heaven; and that alone began there which always embraceth the faith once delivered to the saints. Whatsoever Church pretendeth to a new beginning pretendeth at the same time to a new Churchdom, and whatsoever is so new is none, so necessary is it to believe the Holy Catholic Church."[3] The universal truthfulness of the church is the vindication of its catholicity rather than its universal extension, although it is necessary to notice that this saving truth is contained in an historical and identifiable visible society, continuous from the apostolic church of Jerusalem, and concretely realized in particular "churches". Furthermore this church contains all grace necessary for completing the building of the church — catholicity has an eschatological reference as well. Pearson sees the holiness of the church as residing in its "institutions and administrations of sanctity" and in those of its members who are genuinely holy. Thus the church with its ministry of word and sacrament and the actual sanctity of some of its members already demonstrates the holiness of God and is a sign of the completion of the activity of Christ.

Catholicity of church and world

An important aspect of this wholeness/holiness is the extent to which it led the Church of England, and through it the wider Anglican tradition, to stress the coterminousness of the church's concerns with those of the world. In England the parochial structure means that "every blade of grass is in somebody's parish", and that people everywhere consider that they have a claim on the church and the care of the clergy. It is also significant that the canon law of the Church of England is part of the civil law. There is admittedly a less attractive side to all this, and it has endangered the church with Erastianism and an all too frequent secularism (not to mention the problem of nominal church membership). Despite the dangers, however, this historic role of the church in English life has safeguarded a sense of responsibility for the whole of society, and has marked the pastoral approach of Anglican churches even in countries where the social, legal and constitutional position of the church is very different from that in England. There have moreover been serious attempts to understand this social position and responsibility theologically.

There is a predisposition in Anglicanism to see the church in relation to the entire creative, redemptive and restorative work of God. William Temple wrote characteristically: "By living amongst men the sinless life, the life of perfect obedience (Christ) became the Head of a new society, the pivot of a new moral system, of which perfect obedience to God is the animating principle. This is the Church; and so far as men consent to be raised to the fulfilment of their own destiny, it will at last include all mankind in the unity of obedience to God through their participation in the Spirit of Christ."[4]

The church, like the incarnation of which it is the outcome, is thus the disclosure of the real meaning of human life and nature, which can only be revealed through the indwelling of God. There must be no playing off of redemption against creation, for they are different aspects of the divine will. God's creative-redemptive activity is seen as being complete at the ascension; what now remains is the application of this completed action to the whole creation. Human history is now the outworking of causes which are now irrevocably transforming the world of man, nature and history.

The church is therefore a divinely instituted body, existing prior to the individual human beings who become members of it; they come into actual union as they respond to God's act. And so we find affirmed the primacy of God, but also the ambiguity of the church which is itself divine and human, eternal and historical. In an important passage Temple reflects on this ambiguity: "The ideal Church does not exist and never has existed; some day, here or elsewhere it will exist; meanwhile its 'members' are members also of 'the world'. The Church only exists perfectly when all its 'members' are utterly surrendered to Christ and united to Him. Some such there have been and are. Mostly the members of the Church are still in process of reaching that consummation and have by no means reached it yet. So the Church appears under the guise of a compromising institution; but the true Church is the Body of Christ, and consists of men so far as they are members of that Body. For this reason we ought not in strictness ever to speak of the failure of the Church; we should speak of the failure of Christians. The failure, which is conspicuous enough in history, is a failure of Christian people to be thoroughly Christian; insofar as they thus fail, the Church does not exist on the historic plane, where it exists it triumphs, though its triumph, like the triumph of its Head, often appears to the world as failure till the passing of ages brings a true perspective. The true Church does not fail, but the true Church is still coming into historic existence; that process is the meaning of History from the Incarnation onwards; it consists both in the drawing of men and nations into the fellowship of the Holy Spirit, and in the completion of His work upon them in perfecting their surrender to Christ and their union with Him."[5]

Similar emphases are apparent if we turn from Temple to one of the nineteenth century fathers of modern Anglican theology, F. D. Maurice. He writes of "a Church Universal, not built upon human inventions or human faith, but upon the very nature of God himself, and upon the union which he has formed with his creatures: a Church revealed to man as a fixed and eternal reality by means of which eternal wisdom had itself devised".[6] Maurice seeks to ground the existence of the church firmly in the nature of God as He is in himself and as he relates to his creation. It follows from this that the church's first responsibility is to acknowledge its origin and to assert the primacy of God and his universal creativity which sin has established, a unity deeper than sin but which sin has damaged and defaced. "My desire is to ground all theology upon the Name of God the Father, the Son and the Holy Ghost, not to begin with ourselves and our sins, not to measure the straight line by the crooked one."[7] "We see beneath all evil, beneath the universe itself, that eternal and original union of the Father and the Son . . . which was never fully manifested until the Only Begotten by the Holy Spirit offered himself to God. The revelation of that primal unity is the revelation of the ground on which all things stand, both things in heaven and things on earth. It is the revelation of an order which sustains all the intercourse and society of men. It is the revelation of that which sin has ever been seeking to destroy and which at last has overcome sin. It is the revelation of that perfect harmony to which we look forward when all things are gathered up in Christ."[8]

In Maurice's view therefore the unity of the church is ultimately identical with the unity of the whole creation, restored to its true nature. Ecclesiology must never be narrowly "ecclesiastical" but must take as its scope the purpose for which the church exists — the reconciliation of all things in Christ. "The world contains the elements of which the Church is composed. In the Church, these elements are penetrated by a uniting, reconciling power. The Church is, therefore, human society in its normal state; the World, that same society irregular and abnormal. The world is the Church without God; the Church is the world restored to its relation with God, taken back by Him into the state for which He created it. Deprive the Church of its Centre, and you make it into a world."[9]

This catholic vision is thoroughly traditional in Anglicanism, and reflects the synthesis attempted by Richard Hooker who in the sixteenth century sought to ground the Church of England and its share in the whole church of Christ within the universal purposes of God. He saw a fundamental unity between all things, because God himself has created them, and that they therefore need each other as well as depending absolutely upon him.[10] In Hooker's view all effects in some sense contain or at least resemble their cause. Hence "all things in the world are saide in some sort to seeke the highest, and to covet more or lesse the participation of God himselfe."[11]

The "influence of deitie" not only creates but unceasingly sustains everything that exists, while the incarnation creates new possibilities of participation (an important word for Hooker).[12] The church he sees as formed "out of the verie flesh, the verie wounded and bleeding side of the Son of Man. His bodie crucified, and his blood shed for the life of the world are the true elements of that heavenlie being which maketh us such as himselfe is of whom we come."[13] Within this church word and sacrament alike have "regenerative force and virtue".

Hooker was an important apologist for the role of religion as the bond of social cohesion; this followed as we have seen from his understanding of God and creation. Piety and justice although by no means the same thing need each other, and thus he laid foundations for an "ecclesiastical" polity which is as concerned for the world in which the church is set as it is for the church itself.

The catholicity of the eucharist

Against this background we can understand the assertion of the 1978 Lambeth Conference that "in true worship, the whole of life is offered to God".[14] It has been characteristic of the Anglican tradition to see the liturgy as the bearer of tradition, and the teacher of theology. Maurice regarded it as "a perpetual testimony that the Father, the Son and the Spirit, the one God blessed for ever, is the author of all life, freedom, unity to men; that our prayers are nothing but responses to His voice speaking to us and in us."[15]

William Temple considered that all human life is already caught up in the self-offering of Christ: "The sacrifice of Christ is potentially but most really the sacrifice of Humanity. Our task is, by His Spirit, to take our place in that sacrifice. In the strict sense there is only one sacrifice — the obedience of the Son to the Father and of Humanity to the Father in the Son. This was manifest in actual achievement on Calvary; it is represented in the breaking of the Bread; it is reproduced in our self-dedication and resultant service; it is consummated in the final coming of the Kingdom."[16] He saw it as the perpetual reassertion of the divine indwelling which in the incarnation disclosed the true nature and possibilities of humanity. Anglicans have been traditionally unwilling to speculate on the precise relationship be-

tween each eucharistic celebration and the one perfect sacrifice of
Calvary, and the ambiguity of the ascription of the term "body of
Christ" to both church and eucharistic elements has for the most part
been a cause of rejoicing rather than embarrassment. Hooker, who as
we saw described the church as formed from the crucified flesh of
Jesus, also said of the eucharist that "these mysteries doe as nails
fasten us to his verie crosse."[17] The universal scope of God's creative
activity and of the redemption of creation by Christ implies directly
the universality of the scope of the eucharist.

Moreover, it is Christ himself who is perceived as the actor in
Christian worship; in it "he offers himself and his whole Body to the
Father in the power of the Holy Spirit. The Eucharist is the heart of
Christian worship because it is the showing forth of his death and
resurrection until his coming again. Worship is never initiated by
human beings. Rather we are caught up into an ongoing action already taking place."[18] This means that the celebration of the eucharist is at once the place at which the nature of the church is most
plainly seen, and also the disclosure of the true part the things of this
world occupy in the sacrifice of Christ. To celebrate the eucharist is,
as Temple said, to proclaim the divine indwelling. It is therefore a
share in the effect of the incarnation which "binds all action, all
experience, all creation, to God, and supplies at once the motive and
the power of service."[19]

This close association of the eucharist with the incarnation means
that, for many Anglicans, to celebrate the eucharist at all involves
Christians in an act of public and frequently political proclamation.
Lionel Thornton expressed the underlying principle when he wrote:
"If the Son of God took the nature which is common to us all, and
by so doing declared the spiritual dignity of every human being, then
the present social order is an open denial of Christ, for it condemns
the majority of mankind to be economic slaves ministering to the
selfishness of the minority."[20]

This has become a fairly common view among Anglicans, linking
creation-incarnation-church-eucharist-social action; it has challenged
both the esoteric ecclesiasticism of "Anglo-Catholics" and frequently
socially unaware individualism of "Evangelicals". It found weighty
support in the Lambeth Conference of 1978, to which reference has
already been made. "As God in Jesus commits himself to our humanity, the worship of God through Jesus directs us towards every
human search for freedom, fulfilment and joy; and brings us up
against everything that distorts, imprisons, or ignores the lives, needs
and hopes of men, women and children. Because we worship God in
his glory we are called to seek the glory of man . . . . For us the
very continuing of the Church in worship, in fellowship, and in

hope, amidst the realities of sin and bewilderment, is itself a sign and sacrament that there is a God in whom all may realistically trust and to whom all may look for salvation."[21]

A personal postscript

I have tried in this paper to illustrate a few of Prof. Nissiotis's main points from Anglican experience and thought. There is much in this tradition that challenges contemporary Anglican practice and theology. In a final brief section I attempt a resume and reinterpretation.

God alone is good, the Source and Creator of all things. All that comes from God is good, and exists by union with him, and possessing a real although frequently concealed union with all other elements in creation. The incarnation of the word of God, himself the agent of creation, is both a remedy for the sin that defaces and obscures this union, and a raising of nature to new possibilities. The same Spirit of God at work in creation and the incarnation is also at work during this remaining period of human history, during which all things are being drawn into the sacrifice and victory of Christ. Above all this activity is to be seen and experienced in the church, which in the proclamation of the word and the celebration of the sacraments declares the historic triumph of God and anticipates its full manifestation in every creature. At the same time these acts of Christ in the church effect a real participation in his life and union with the Father by the members of the church today. An important distinction is to be drawn between this true church of word and sacrament, and many aspects of the empirical life of Christians who remain sinners. As a visible, historical institution the church is already the body of Christ with a real communication of grace between Head and members, and thus an inescapable task of proclamation, both in preaching and social action. In both respects the church will not be immune from criticism, and its address to the world and participation in the world's quest for unity and justice has to be marked by the humility of Christ, who was himself misunderstood. There will be occasions indeed when the word of God may be more clearly heard and the unity of the new creation more apparent outside the visible church than within it. This should not surprise the disciples of Jesus who himself directed attention to the "one alone who is good". We hear much these days about "convergence" and "unity by stages"; such ideas seem to Anglicans to be valuable because the confusions of our own history demonstrate their truth. I conclude with a quotation from Bishop Michael Ramsey which may reveal something of lasting truth not just about Anglicanism, but about the whole church throughout its earthly pilgrimage:

While the Anglican church is vindicated by its place in history, with a strikingly balanced witness to Gospel and Church and sound learning, its greater vindication lies in its pointing through its own history to something of which it is a fragment. Its credentials are its incompleteness, with the tension and the travail in its soul. It is clumsy and untidy, it baffles neatness and logic. For it is sent not to commend itself as "the best type of Christianity", but by its very brokenness to point to the universal Church wherein all have died.[22]

NOTES

1. "A Vindication of the Doctrine of the Trinity" (1690), in P. More and F. Cross, eds, *Anglicanism*, London, SPCK, 1951, p.40.
2. *Ibid.*
3. J. Pearson, "An Exposition of the Creed: Article IX" (1659), in More and Cross, *op. cit.*, pp.23ff.
4. *Christus Veritas*, London, Macmillan, 1925, p.238.
5. *Ibid.*, pp.167–68.
6. *The Kingdom of Christ*, II, p.363, London, SCM, 1958.
7. *The Doctrine of Sacrifice*, London, Macmillan, 1893, p.xli.
8. *Op. cit.*, p.194.
9. *Theological Essays*, London, J. Clarke, 1957, pp.276–77.
10. Cf. *Sermon on Pride*.
11. *Ecclesiastical Polity*, I, 5, 2.
12. *Op. cit.*, V, 56, 5.
13. *Op. cit.*, V, 56, 5.
14. *Report*, London, CIO Publishing, 1978, p.94.
15. Letter quoted in *Life*, II, 355.
16. Quoted in A. M. Ramsey, *The Gospel and the Catholic Church*, London, Longmans, Green & Co., 1936, p.212.
17. *Ecclesiastical Polity*, *op. cit.*, V, 67, 11.
18. *Report*, *op. cit.*, p.94.
19. B.F. Wescott, *The Gospel of Life*, p.xxi.
20. "The Necessity of Dogma", in *The Return of Christendom*, London, George Allen & Unwin, 1922, p.74
21. *Report*, *op. cit.*, p.54.
22. *The Gospel and the Catholic Church*, *op. cit.*, p.220.

THE CHURCH AS A PROPHETIC SIGN

Manas Buthelezi

Meaning of "sign"

A sign is a thing that has its own independent existence and status but which, within a given set of factors, draws attention to a purpose beyond what is ordinarily peculiar to it, or points to a thing of a higher order than itself.

In terms of this definition, creation and all the works of God are signs pointing to where God has been: they are God's footprints which are discerned as such only through the eyes of faith. Faith is a divine gift that equips us with the capacity of grasping where God is at in Jesus Christ: it creates a bridge between the sign and the divine reality; it gives theological content and focus to the sign.

Thomas Aquinas in his theory of the analogy of being developed the view that all created things image God in a certain degree. The infinite nature of God is a being which has existence of itself. While a finite thing is also a being, it is a being from another, that is, it is a caused being. Hence it follows that some things are like God first and most generally in as much as they exist; others in as much as they have life, and a third class in as much as they have mind or intelligence.

There is a sense in which the sign participates in the reality of the thing to which it points. Unlike the example of a road sign, the Bible says that a human being is a sign of God intrinsically, that is, by virtue of the peculiar fabric of his creatureliness: he was created in the image of God. Since sin has defaced the image of God in us it does not follow that our lives and what we are are true reflections of God's image. We are defective signs of God.

• Rt Rev. Dr Manas Buthelezi (Evangelical Lutheran Church in South Africa), Bishop of the Central Diocese. Member of the Standing Commission on Faith and Order.

It is in Jesus Christ that the true sign of God can be found. According to Luther, Christ's humanity is the sign in which all things are signified while the glorified Christ is the thing signified by all things. "Christ is the goal of all things and their centre, towards whom all look and towards whom all point, as if they said: Behold, He is the one who *is*, while we *are not*, but simply signify."

Sin is so pervasive that Luther observes that we are now only signs that "contradict the thing signified". "For our good is hidden and that so deeply that it is hidden under its own opposite. Thus our life is hidden under death, self-love under self-hatred, glory under shame.... strength under weakness. And generally, every yes we say to any good under a no, in order that our faith may be anchored in God, who is the negative essence and goodness and wisdom and righteousness and whom we cannot possess or attain to except by the negation of all our affirmation."

There is another angle to this. The church or believers corporately are a sign of Christ. The church is the body of Christ although it cannot be said to be all of it. To that extent the church is a sign: it is what is visible of the body of Christ. The church is an example of a sign that participates in the reality of what it signifies. It is in the world and yet not of the world. Like all true signs the church points beyond itself, that is, to its Lord. Its ministry in the world is a sign of the acts of God.

Let us then focus our attention on the church as a prophetic sign.

1. In liberating the truth

Liberation is very often associated with social, economic and political structures which are seen to oppress people. Hence we speak of social or political liberation. Yet the basic ministry of the church can be defined as also that of liberation. The liberation of God's message from its external signs is here at issue.

The Greek word for truth, *aletheia*, has etymologically the meaning of non-concealment. It is derived from the root, *letho* or *lanthano*, which means to cause to forget, to escape notice or to conceal. The prefix *a-* has the effect of negating the meaning.

Truth thus means what is unconcealed, inescapable or unforgettable: it means a state of affairs that is unconcealed or uncovered. It follows that untruth refers to what has been blurred or covered so that it is no longer seen for what it is. To tell the truth is to remove the cover of reality. In the Greek philosophical context truth pointed to reality in contrast to mere appearances. Truth is what belongs to the real world or the world of ideas in contrast to the world of appearances. One therefore arrives at truth as one uncovers appearances. It is like removing the mist in order to see the mountain outline. When it refers to revelation, truth is the word of God in contrast to falsehood that conceals the purity of the word of God.

Thus the task of theology as well as preaching is the setting loose of the truth. In other words, to theologize is to strip loose the historical and cultural accidents of truth so that it may be seen for what it is. In real life truth is never encountered in its purity. It is always mediated by the symbols of language as well as other objects that strike the senses. As we know, no language medium is perfect. Thus truth as unconcealed reality always confronts us under the cover of its vehicles. To use Paul's words: "Our knowledge is imperfect and our prophecy is imperfect, but when the perfect comes, the imperfect will pass away. . . for now we see in a mirror dimly, but then face to face. Now I know in part, then I shall understand fully, even as I have been fully understood" (1 Cor. 13:9–13).

As a steward and custodian of God's revealed truth, the church is a sign that guarantees that God will continue to speak to his people. It is a sign of assurance that someone will stand up and say "thus says the Lord". The preaching of God's word is no longer dependent on an isolated, charismatic seer or prophet since the whole community grounded in Christ is an authenitc sign of abiding prophecy. There is a voice of prophecy even under less glamorous circumstances of simple people meeting in a Sunday morning service. There is abiding prophecy wherever "two or three are gathered" in the Lord's name. To say that there is no saving truth outside the church or that sound theologizing cannot happen outside the perimeters of the church should be understood in the sense that outside the church there is no living sign that guarantees authenticity. The church is a prophetic sign of the authentic liberation to the populace of the oracles of God. This is no denial of the freedom of God to use any means for accomplishing his purposes. One can argue and establish a successful case that it is not necessary to walk in an established path in order to reach a particular destination; yet the established path is a helpful sign in the discernment of the margin of going totally astray.

To be sure, the church is an imperfect sign because, as the apostle says, "we have this treasure in earthen vessels, to show that the transcendent power belongs to God and not to us" (2 Cor. 4:7). A sign is helpful to the extent it clearly points beyond itself. For the church to point beyond itself is to admit penultimacy and finiteness concerning its rank in the order of priorities. A church that cannot tell or admit the truth about itself cannot be an authentic instrument for uncovering the truth of and about God.

A prophetic sign is a vocal and audible sign. This means that it is a sign-generating sign. To verbalize means to generate audible signs. To theologize and to proclaim God's word is to liberate and "uncover" truth through the medium of audible or language signs.

The truth of the word of God as we find it in the Bible is already couched in Greek and Jewish cultural symbols. It becomes God's truth for me the moment it is liberated from that cultural dress. The liberation takes place through the processes of exegesis, preaching and devotional reading. If we take all these as theological processes at various levels, we can rephrase the same idea as follows: Without exegesis, preaching or devotional reading, God's truth remains trapped within the pages of the Bible; God's word then appears as merely a piece of literature; there is no one to say or no occasion to experience the dimension of "thus says the Lord". What is missing is a prophetic sign attached to the word. The church is that prophetic sign.

The process of theologizing is an instance of the liberation of the Christian truth. The dilemma is that as we try to liberate or uncover the truth in the course of theologizing or preaching we have to use other signs or symbols which attach a new "cover" albeit of relative transparency.

Theology tries to uncover truth by reducing it to its basic elements as a theologian tries to employ living language symbols or signs so that truth may become usable and communicable and applicable to the ever-changing dynamics of life. When I speak of Christian truth I am not primarily referring to a body of concepts or philosophical propositions, but to a summary of God's act in Jesus Christ. This is because the God of the Bible is not and cannot be an object of discovery or research, but he is the source and author of revelation. Truth about God in himself is beyond our reach. We cannot uncover the reality of God in himself.

The object of theology for me is the summary of the faith of the church. Thus in a certain sense the term "theology" is a misnomer. Perhaps we should speak of "pistology". I am saying this because theology so-called is in practice or should be a study of the faith affirmations of the church rather than a scientific probe into the essence of God as such.

2. In living for others

The church lives for its Lord, Jesus Christ who was man for others. It is a visible sign to the world that God continues to care for it for He "so loved the world that he gave his only begotten Son . . . " The church is a prophetic sign to the world to the extent that it does not shy away from declaring God's will for the whole of life and developing for itself a style of living for others. The church must establish a Christian and prophetic presence in the world. This can take various forms.

When the church establishes physical Christian presence in moments of crisis in the lives of those who feel deserted, that can create a greater impact than a thousand sermons. Very often the church moves into situations in order to be heard rather than felt. There is more to communication than saying a lot of words. You can communicate a living message even through your silent body.

When somebody suffers and you stand by his side to the extent that you also share his suffering, you become a sign of Christ to that person and your physical presence becomes redemptive. There is nothing worse than the spiritual agony of suffering in solitude. As Jesus Christ was hanging on the cross he felt this agony as he cried: "My God, My God, why have you forsaken me?" To suffer in solidarity with others is redemptive. It tends to open a window of liberation in the granite wall of suffering.

Fellowship is a redemptive experience. It is a form of liberation from the death of solitude to the life of sharing the physical presence of the other. According to scripture to be physically present with the poor and the oppressed is to share the presence of Christ. The poor, the imprisoned and the generally oppressed cast a shadow of Christ behind them. To be physically present with them is to be present with Christ.

The church is a visible and abiding sign for the possibility and reality of a life fashioned after Christ, namely, that of living for others. It guarantees the visible continuity of Christ's life-style.

The highest form of prophetic witness is when the prophet declares the divine message not just in words but through the substance of his body. That happens when the prophet is placed in a position of dying for the sake of the message. Resurrection as was the case with Christ is the vindication of prophetic witness through death.

The church like its individual members has to lose its life in order to find it. A church whose daily pursuit is self-preservation cannot be an authentic sign of Christ's life. According to Paul, Christ "died for all, that those who live might live no longer for themselves but for him who for their sake died and was raised" (2 Cor. 5:15).

To live for Christ means to be a living Christ-sign. It is to reflect the image of Christ; it is to be a living letter of Christ. It is living a prophetic life.

Dying on the part of the church may mean suffering lack of world recognition in order that those for whom the church lives may become more prominent. People very often talk loosely about the need for the church to be relevant in society. In practice they mean that the church must distinguish itself in society so that society may be able to identify its achievements. In the modern world it means that the church must earn itself a column in the daily newspapers; its resolutions must be worth quoting in the papers. The church must be seen to be one of the news-makers.

Here we are faced with what appears to be a contradiction. If the church is a sign at all, it must be a visible sign. Otherwise it will remain a useless sign.

What constitutes the visibility of a sign? It is not its intrinsic qualities or the recognition of its artwork, but the extent it highlights the purpose for which it was meant or makes unmistakably recognizable that to which it points. If the sign in its own right becomes the centre of attraction its reason for existence is destroyed: it ceases to be a sign; it becomes the thing. It is no longer penultimate but ultimate in the order of priorities. What Luther describes as the "theology of the cross" in contrast to the "theology of glory" can help in the formulation of the right concept of "the relevance of the church". We should be cautious so that we do not become party to the quest for a neo-Constantinian era of the church.

The church must so serve the total human being that it remains relevant even at a point when it suffers at the hand of those for whom it has lived and when those it has made kings through its humble service become its Neroes at the end of the struggle for liberation. The church will then shine as an authentic sign of Christ.

The church will not be a force for the unity of humankind when it allows itself to be a sign fashioned after the images and ideologies of the world; for then "church" will just be another name for the world. Jesus Christ who is the founder of the church refused during his life-time to produce the type of sign the general public, including the religious Pharisees, expected. Jesus protested in the strongest possible language: "An evil and adulterous generation seeks for a sign; but no sign shall be given to it except the sign of the prophet Jonah" (Matt. 12:39).

It is noteworthy that John's gospel identifies miracles of Jesus as the signs of the coming of the kingdom. The miracles were not duplications of daily occurrences deriving from forces in the world. They were works which were peculiar to Christ as the Son of God. This insight was hidden to the world; it only belonged to those who had received faith.

It is the cross of Christ which is an effective sign for the unity of humankind. When the cross becomes the rallying point, there will then be unity in the whole world. Jesus said of his death: "And I, when I am lifted up from the earth, will draw all men to myself" (John 12:32).

When the church becomes a cross-sign there will be true unity; when it adopts death as its life-style there will be hope for unity. The desire for self-preservation tends to polarize; it will never be a prescription for the unity of the church. Reconciliation in Christ was a fruit of a cross-life style. The trouble is that the church wants to supervize its own unity as well as the unity of the world. It refuses to give itself up as a sacrificial medium for unity.

In simple terms, it is a suffering church which becomes a uniting and united church. I am referring to a church that poises itself for giving its life, its worldly prestige, for others; a church that is ready to become nothing so that others may become important. This is the heart of the cross as an ecclesiastical life-style. The Constantinian era culminated in the great schism of the sixteenth century. When the church became established it was tempted to live for itself and for its own glory: it was no longer a suffering church. It became dominated by the spirit of self-preservation which led to its inner polarization.

When the focus shifts from the self to the other, true reconciliation will result. The cross symbolized the self-emptying of Christ and, to use the words of Christ, all men were drawn to him. The cross became a rallying point: you were either for it or against it.

Unity, whether of the church or of humanity, should not mean levelling things up, an ecumenism of conformism. When Christ spoke of being lifted up and all men drawn to himself, he was not predicting some kind of universalism. He was rather setting himself up as the centre of the desirable unity of humankind. He was pointing to the way of the cross as the new medium for the healing of the divisions of humankind. His followers were to be prophetic signs to that way of the cross, God's chosen way of reconciliation. Hence for the church to be a prophetic sign means to die by pointing away from itself, but to Christ as the rallying point.

A RESPONSE TO
"THE CHURCH AS A PROPHETIC SIGN"

Hervé Legrand

Pentecost and the church's prophetic vocation for the unity of humankind

1. Pentecost is a *Leitbild* (image/guide) for the life of the church throughout history and throughout human cultures.

Vatican II saw Pentecost as a *Leitbild* for the life of the church throughout time and space. This is what it says in *Ad Gentes*, §4:

> On the day of Pentecost the union of peoples in the catholicity of the faith was prefigured by the Church of the New Covenant which speaks all tongues, includes and embraces in its charity all tongues and so overcomes the dispersion of Babel.

What is said here about Pentecost in the indicative must be understood in the imperative and applied to. This direction given by Pentecost is an imperative for the mission of the church, in the first place as *it goes through history*. Between Genesis and Revelation, Pentecost represents the mid-point of history. That is the concern of both the Greek and Latin fathers. The confusion of tongues at the building of Babel (Deut. 4:2) is met at the mid-point of time by Pentecost; from that point the movement of dispersion is changed into a movement towards unity which will be completed only at the apocalypse when "a huge crowd which as one could not count, from every nation and race, people and tongue, stand before the throne and the Lamb" (Rev. 7:9). On the day of Pentecost the church speaks all tongues because, prophetically, the Holy Spirit has given to it all the peoples of the earth, in that moment of calling it and fitting it for the immense missionary effort by which it is to attain its full

---

•Rev. Prof. Hervé Legrand (Roman Catholic Church), Dominican priest, professor of dogmatics, Catholic Institute, Paris, France.

stature. So St Augustine says, when the church will finally speak *all*
tongues then the End will come!

What is said in the indicative about Pentecost is to be understood
as an imperative for the church not only throughout history but
throughout *human cultures*. The text of Acts stresses the fact that each
of the peoples represented at Jerusalem: "Jews, Medes, Elamites,
Cretans and Arabs", each hears the good news "in his own tongue".
Here according to both Greek and Latin fathers "tongue" is to be
understood in the sense of the diversity of cultures. Unity in the
Spirit is a unity in diversity; because the mission is universal the
churches must be particular.

There you have, as you know, a decisive redressing of the
balance by Vatican II. For this last Council, the church universal
exists "in and begins from the particular churches".[1] "Sent to all
peoples of all times the Church can enter into communion with
the different civilizations, whence comes an enrichment for it and for
the different cultures." In the local churches "the Good News of
Christ constantly renews the life and the culture of all
humankind, . . . it gives fruitfulness, as it were from within, to the
spiritual qualities and gifts forever to each people . . . Its action, including that of the liturgy, contributes to form the interior liberty of
man and woman".[2] In conclusion, the Spirit of Pentecost demands
that the unity of the church be made up of particular churches in
which there must be recognized "a legitimate diversity in the matter
of worship and discipline which must apply also to the formulation
of doctrine".[3]

Such is the unity which exists in germ since Pentecost — a unity
which goes through human history, a unity which brings together
diversity and communication and calls the particular churches to live
in communion with each other.

2. Pentecost establishes the prophetic vocation of all Christians and
of all Christians in the church.

To make clear to his hearers what was happening on the day of
Pentecost, St Peter refers to the prophecy of Joel:

> It shall come to pass in the last days, says God, that I will pour out a
> portion of my Spirit on all mankind:
> Your sons and daughters shall prophesy, . . . Yes, even on my ser-
> vants and handmaids I will pour out a portion of my Spirit in those days
> and they shall prophesy (Acts 2: 12—18).

In the repetition entailed in "sons and daughters", "servants and
handmaids", this prophecy indicates that all the members of the
people of God, without exception, have the vocation of prophecy. In
a systematic way Vatican II took up again this conviction in the

exposé of its ecclesiology of the People of God.[4] It specifies that
this quality applies also to lay people.[5]

It is worthwhile noting that the code of Canon Law of 1983 explicitly receives this doctrine in Canon 204: "By baptism Christ's
faithful people are made sharers in the priestly, prophetic and royal
function of Christ."

3. From vision to practice — how can the church be prophetic for
the unity of humankind?

Let me sum up. The vocation of the church is prophetic; each of
its members is called to share the prophetic attitude, according to St
Peter, according to the texts taken up by Vatican II and by the new
Code of Canon Law.

How is this prophecy exercised with regard to the unity of the
church and the unity of humankind? I would reply: to the extent in
which the church stays in the permanent dynamism, since the new
creation pushes it ceaselessly to rebuild what Babel does not cease to
destroy.

Let me be more concrete. There is here a challenge for Christians,
a challenge with regard to the unity of humankind; there is here a
challenge for Christians as being responsible for church unity.

(1) A prophetic challenge related to the unity of humankind.

Babel is not only a mythical tale of events which took place *in illo
tempore*. Quite the contrary, Babel is one of the great marks of our
culture; the communication between people is often broken, even
more is this true of the communication between human groups. Let
me mention only some examples which could be multiplied: racism,
exaggerated nationalism, sexism, communication solely by means of
propaganda.

If Babel is a mark of our time, so too is Pentecost. The image of
the church in its origins is also that which has most contemporary
impact. If, as Christians, we are gripped by the *Leitbild* of Pentecost
reversing Babel, then we have specific reasons, as Christians, for
working, for teaching the language to immigrants, perhaps even
learning their language. We have special reasons for struggling
against racism, against stereotypes and propaganda, and for promoting a mutual appreciation between peoples antagonistic to each other.
In this way Christians and the church can be prophets with regard to
the unity of humankind. In working to re-establish communication
between peoples Christians will also have in them something that
will give a foretaste of the unity which, in their eyes, holds all peoples
together in their diversity, and which will let them begin to feel that
the communication is calling them also to a communion which they
can receive as the promised gift from God.

(2) Christians challenged about their unity by the world.

As long as Pentecost, as antitype of Babel, has been the *Leitbild* of
the church's life, this life has been lived as a new Pentecost; think of
the cities of Alexandria, Antioch or Jerusalem in the fourth century.
There, Greeks and Copts, Greeks and Syrians, who represented such
antagonistic cultures and economic interests and divergent policies,
lived side by side. Today you see Orthodox and Catholics separating
into different liturgical assemblies according to language, nationality
and rite, although they profess the same faith. Far from doing this
those fourth century Christians kept the principle of one eucharist,
although bilingual, and of one bishop. The most eschatological vision
of the monks led them to Jerusalem, to Syria and Constantinople to
set up monasteries that were trilingual and sometimes quadrilingual.
These were the famous monasteries of Acemetes.

But what happens when this image of Pentecost reversing Babel
ceases to be a *Leitbild* of church life? Here the history of Christian
divisions is eloquent — divisions follow linguistic frontiers. This is
true from the years following Chalcedon: Orthodoxy comes to
belong to the Greek language, the churches called monophysite
identify with Coptic, Syriac, Armenian. Left face to face, Latins and
Greeks also divided in the eleventh century according to cultural and
linguistic criteria. Certainly the debate on the papacy and the filioque
explains why the one are Orthodox and the other Catholic. But these
debates certainly do not explain why during the centuries all the
Latins have remained Catholics and all the Greeks Orthodox. The
break of the sixteenth century once more followed the line of Latin
and Anglo-Saxon cultures, notable exceptions being Ireland and
Poland. And today it is said that in the USA the hour of Sunday
worship is perhaps the time of greatest racial segregation.

**In what way is the world which is becoming one a challenge
to Christians?**

As you know France and Germany made war on each other three
times in 75 years. But do you also know that there is a joint commission of German and French historians who together examine all
the manuals for the teaching of history in France and in Germany? I
shall be content with this one example. In this are not "the children
of darkness" ahead of "the children of light"? I do not know of anything comparable between our churches for the inspection of manuals
of religion. Let me very seriously make a suggestion to the staff
of Faith and Order. What is said about Luther in the manuals of the
local Catholic church in a given place? What is said about the papacy
in a particular Orthodox or Protestant manual? Here humankind as it
searches for its unity can awaken in us a holy jealousy. On this topic

Dr Buthelezi has every reason to write: "A church that cannot tell or admit the truth about itself cannot be an authentic instrument for uncovering the truth of and about God." It is the same for a church that cannot admit the truth about a sister church.

Conclusion

So the unity of the church and the unity of humankind are linked. Since Pentecost, thanks to the energies of the new creation, the church is called to remake what Babel does not cease to undo; in that event it can be prophetic for the unity of the world. But at the same time the church is challenged in its unity by the unity which humankind finds itself. Perhaps the explanation for why it is left to do this alone is a moral one — laziness, lack of imagination, on the part of the church, but it is also theological because it means there is a lack of love for unity among Christians, too little of the awareness given in the Spirit who reverses Babel.

I do not know if I have understood well enough the methodology proposed by Faith and Order for this consultation. To be sure I propose another example. It is the way in which the relation between men and women, presented by the church, can contribute to the renewal of humanity, just as certain changes in society can be a source of renewal for the church.

(1) Changes in society can contribute to the renewal of the church beginning with its very faith.

The changes in relations between women and men in Western society are not the result of ideological movements such as feminism. Rather they stem much more from objective changes in medicine or in the ways of work. For the first time in the history of humanity the control at once of fecundity and infant mortality has freed women's physical and psychic energies which until now were taken up in an overwhelming way by the generation and education of children. On an average the European woman is 32 years old when she sends her last child to school. She has 40 years of life left. In our industrial society where muscle hardly counts any more, she is able simultaneously to work and to gain her financial independence.

It is then no mystery if in Western society men and women more and more become partners in public life, work, family life and in their life as a couple. And it is no mystery either if many Christian women are ill at ease when the language of theology and of the church remains far from that of partnership and use old male-centred language in which women are relative to men without the opposite being true at the same point.

In these new social conditions the promise of the New Creation ("In Christ there is no more Jew or Greek, slave or freeman, male or female", Gal. 3: 28) takes on a new actuality that it has probably never had.

Yes, the changes in society can be a challenge to ecclesial attitudes and an occasion for laying hold of the eschatalogical promises at an unsuspected depth.

(2) At the same time the renewed Christian tradition can contribute to the renewal of humanity.

The church in its tradition, its liturgy, its pastoral care, its communitarian reflection, can help Christian couples, men and women, to live in partnership. Doing so it helps society renew itself.

To be concrete, the married couples in the West are threatened, not in the first instance by ideological factors, but by accelerated urbanization and emotional immaturity. There are very disquieting signs of this:

In France in 1970 there was one divorce for every ten marriages: in 1980 the figure was 1 divorce for 4 marriages. In 1982 only 36 percent of French couples cohabiting entered into a formal marriage; in Sweden the figure was 48 per cent. There has been increase in abortion, increase in the number of people who live alone, e.g. in Paris one household out of two consists of a person living alone.

In this situation the church's efforts to uphold the value of the couple can contribute to the renewal of society.

(3) But note: that lays an obligation on the church to "renew" the very idea of the Christian couple, a couple in partnership.

General conclusion

Tradition is change in continuity. So as regards the couple tradition presupposes a threefold operation going on simultaneously.

— Reference: What has been handed down in scripture, Old and
  New Testaments? There can be no other foundation than Christ.
— Critique: In what context do we live in the past? In what context
  must it be said today?
— Creation: It can't be a repetition. The newness of the gospel must
  be declared, not simply as being unusual, but through the difference which the good news always introduces.
  No reference without critique in creation: otherwise there is a
  dead letter.
  No critique without reference in creation: that would bring
  destruction.
  No creation without reference in critique: that would produce only a
  temporary illusion.

The living Tradition is a manifestation of the process of Pentecost;
It is turned towards the future, until the coming of Christ. It sup-

poses also that Christians know how to reverse Babel, that is, that they know how to translate the message linked to an ancient culture, without betrayal, into a new culture.

So that the church may serve the unity of humankind and serve also its renewal, it is urgent that it develops a people who can interpret:
1) between the different cultures;
2) between the different stages of tradition;
3) between the churches.
I want to add a suggestion for our discussion. From a systematic point of view would it not be good to relate the concept of the kingdom of God and Pentecost with a view to finding a way ahead in the discussion of our theme?

NOTES

1. *Lumen Gentium,* 23.
2. *Gaudium et Spes* 58, Nos 3 and 4.
3. *Unitatis Redintegratio,* 17.
4. *Lumen Gentium,* 12.
5. *Lumen Gentium,* 34 and 35.

Appendix 1

A SUMMARY AND SYNTHESIS

John Baker

> The wicked grocer groces
> For a mystery and a sign,
> That men should shun the grocer's shop,
> And go to inns to dine.
>
> (G. K. Chesterton)

I

If one is going to attempt anything so foolhardy as to respond by way of summary and synthesis to such "treasures of wisdom and knowledge" as have been shared with us during this past week, it may be as well to start with a very foolish, indeed simple-minded remark: to anyone ignorant of the Christian tradition, and even to many members of our own congregations, the title of this consultation would convey no meaning at all. How can anything be simultaneously a "mystery" and a "sign"?

A sign "points beyond itself" to something else; it is a medium through which we "liberate and uncover truth".[1] This is also what the world understands by "sign"; it is to do with a special kind of communication. If we talk about "prophecy" in connection with "signs", then the same holds good. A "prophetic voice", outside the religious context, is one that opens our minds to truths we have chosen to ignore because they were uncomfortable, one that shows us where the path on which we are set is leading us. Prophecy is about truer, fuller communication.[2] In normal usage, therefore, a "prophetic sign" is one that alerts us, perhaps painfully, to things present or future which have been hidden from us, but which it is vital that we should acknowledge.

• Rt Rev. John Austin Baker (Church of England), Bishop of Salisbury, England. Member of the Standing Commission on Faith and Order.

An outsider may not consider that the church fulfills this function, but the idea itself need not be particularly obscure to them.

But at the same time, we say, the church is "mystery". Oh yes, we can explain this; there is no problem. *Musterion* in the NT is not something obscure and hidden. It is a divine secret which has now been made known (Eph., Col.). So "mystery" too is about communication. The church as "mystery" is the revelation of something which it is of the utmost importance for all human beings to grasp, something that concerns their ultimate origin and destiny, and those of the whole universe. "Mystery" and "sign" do not contradict one another, as an outsider might suppose.

But if this were all we were to say, we would be disingenuous. "Mystery" is never total revelation. Because it is a *divine* secret, because its truth is about God, much always remains "mysterious". Not only does the disclosure itself, therefore, contain elements we cannot analyze, describe or explain, but it actually introduces things beyond our understanding into our account of everyday realities. We have to admit as already true that "the cosmos is a mystery, the world around us is a mystery; my own person is a mystery and my fellow human beings are a mystery".[3] To insist in addition that we can speak of all these rightly only when we see them in relation to God, "the supreme mystery", is to add a new dimension of "mysteriousness".

That existence should be essentially and ultimately mysterious is not an alien idea, so far as most human cultures are concerned. On the contrary it seems natural to them. It is not even alien to Western scientific culture, since we moved away from the over-simple worldview of the nineteenth century. "Human beings are free — at least basically";[4] but though that freedom may be an observable fact, its nature and operation remain systematically mysterious. Likewise with fundamental physics, we have learned to accept that our observations and formulas can never eliminate the factor of ourselves as the observers and thinkers. Reality, as it is, is for ever beyond us.

In some sense, therefore, secular words too, and even mathematical symbols "point beyond" themselves to realities not directly describable. We rely on them as pointing to truth, because when we act on the assumption that they do so, they do not let us down. They "work". When we doubt some account of ourselves or of the universe around us, it is because it does not "work". There is too much evidence that does not fit; experiments do not come out as they should; extrapolations are implausible. This, it seems to me, was at the heart of the fascinating and instructive debate between Boné and Watkins,[5] and emerged also in the subsequent discussion, in the comments of Calivas, Hind, Legrand and others.

It may at first seem strange to say of some accounts of the church that they too do not "work", but this is precisely what is said by outsiders concerning the church's claims for itself. These claims simply do not seem to them to match the observable facts. How does the church as it is point to those ultimate truths which are supposed to be so central for the world's existence? What are the qualities of the church's life which justify such very exalted language about its origins and about the vital principle which sustains it?

The two questions are closely related. The God who can be said to bring "salvation" or "redemption" or "liberation", to bestow a spiritual power which can transform for the better the lives of individuals and whole communities, who is proclaimed as "Lord", whose "kingdom", if not yet consummated, is nevertheless already "in the midst", so that the power of evil is already broken; this God does not seem to square with the evidence of our experience of what it means to exist in the real world. But that would perhaps not matter if this God did correspond with existence within the church, or with the effect of the community of believers on the world of which it is a part. These things would be evidence, demanding that the gospel at least be taken seriously as a possible account of human life, and revealing an inner coherence between the presentations of the church as divine mystery and prophetic sign.

It is important to grasp that this problem is not overcome by taking care in what we say not to exaggerate the qualities of love, holiness, justice, etc. to be found in the church's life. This point may be illustrated in different ways from the major papers of both Lochman and Nissiotis. Both of them unfailingly avoid any such unreal moral and spiritual triumphalism or self-indulgent fantasy. The former explicitly warns against these temptations. [6] By basing his presentation on the categories of promise and continuing judgment, by stressing conversion as the first and unending response to the proclamation of the kingdom of God, and the total dependence of the church on the power of the Spirit, Lochman systematically keeps these temptations at bay. But at the same time he presents the church as the carrier of the truth that God's reign is a real possibility for humankind: " . . . we should and can pray: *Thy Kingdom Come!* This is a 'word of defiance'. Certainly not one which wipes out as if by magic the oppressive circumstances we have referred to but one which does bring them within the force field of the kingdom of God, and thereby relativizes them and robs them of their seeming ultimate validity. *Kyrios Christos* — the Risen One is Lord of "powers and authorities". This news liberates. We are no longer prisoners of an omnipotent fate . . . Our world does not have to "stay as it is'." [7] Similarly Nissiotis stresses the "catholicity of the Fall"; and the fact of "brokenness" running through church and world is a constant and fundamental theme of his presentation. But he too brings out the other side as well. In a powerful and crucially significant passage he writes: "It is very important that an ecclesiology should keep this curious and unique dialectic between unshaken communion in *essence* and brokenness in *existence* in the whole creation. This is because the *ekklesia* as sacramental communion is absolutely holy, and a sure guarantee for sharing in the full communion with God by his grace, but all men yet remain sinful and in broken relationship both in the ecclesial communion and in the world."[8]

This two-sided presentation, expressed in different idioms by both Lochman and Nissiotis is, of course, inescapable within the terms of the Christian gospel. It is the reason why any serious proclamation of that gospel must, as both of them do, underline the centrality of *repentance*, and of the transforming work of the *Holy Spirit*.[9] But though truly reflecting Christian experience, such an approach does not accurately meet the thrust of the world's difficulty.

How may we express this difficulty, this critique, in order to define it exactly? If God is indeed God, and if he behaves towards humankind in the way the gospel says that he does, then one would expect a greater effect from his saving activity than the church actually displays. It is not that the world expects perfection from the church, but it does expect something visibly better than the world's own average performance. In particular, it asks what correspondence there is between Jesus (seen simply as the Founder of the religion) and those who declare themselves his followers. Moreover, the world is well aware of the interaction of world and church. It is, for example, not overmuch impressed by contemporary Christian denunciations of war and torture, when it recalls Christian practice of or acquiescence in war and torture in past centuries, before protest against these things became part of liberal Western secular consciousness, and the fairly selective response of churches even today to the use of violence in the cause of different varieties of "righteousness". Nor should we forget that a religion of grace is more vulnerable to such questions than a religion of law. The more we emphasize, in our description of the essential nature of the church, the divine sacramental and sanctifying life within the community, the more legitimate it becomes for the world to demand discernible results.

There are replies one can make to this oversimplified critique, and I shall try to mention some of them in the second part of this paper. But we all need to remember that certain counter-arguments, however deeply they may be based on truth, are bound to be heard as unfair evasions, and that some of our cherished theological ideas only create more difficulties in this context.

Under the first of these two points I would include the tendency of some Christians to rebuff perfectly reasonable objections by saying: "You do not understand, because you do not have faith. If you had faith, you would see that all this is true" — in our present context, say, that evil has been defeated, even though, so far as anyone can see, "everything continues exactly as it has always been since the world began" (2 Pet. 3:4). Another example of the same sort is the common response that because the church is such a loving and open community it is full of sinners — indeed, it is unique in existing primarily *for* sinners — and therefore it is unfair to criticize it for being not obviously better than the world. ("OK, I agree that I'm a lazy, lying, backbiting, bad-tempered so-and-so, but how do you know what I might have been if I hadn't been a Christian?") Such arguments would be fine but for the fundamental claim of the church to be the divine community wherein by word and sacrament lives are changed. In this matter we are not dealing with unjust or misguided expectations foisted on us by others. We are simply asked to make good our own words.

Examples of theological ideas which create difficulties in this area include at least one which is central to ecclesiology, that of the church as the body of Christ. The story is told of the late Mgr Ronald Knox (and, no doubt, of many others) that as a theological student he used to head his essays with the words *Ad maiorem Dei gloriam*, until one day his tutor barked: "You don't think this is to the greater glory of God, do you?" In the same way one might ask of those who see Christ as so closely united with the church that the acts of the church are Christ's continuing action in the world: "You don't think these are the acts of Christ, do you?" The theological point is that the more strictly the image of the body of Christ is interpreted, in a concern to emphasize the underlying God-given unity, holiness and apostolicity (cf. John 20:21; Heb. 3:1) of the church, independent of the sinfulness of its members, the less plausible, from the viewpoint of the world, does the implicit claim become. The church does not look, to the world, like Christ. Nor are matters mended by making Christ the "Head", not the whole body.

Another example of this problem is the great biblical truth so rightly emphasized by Lochman:[10] "In the gospel Christ himself is the kingdom of God." To speak effectively of something so problematic in the eyes of the world as the sovereign rule of a righteous and loving God we have to point to a place where the evidence of history can be convincingly interpreted in terms of that sovereignty. Christians must see that place in Jesus, otherwise they would hardly be Christians! (Incidentally, this being so, it is easy to see what a thrust to the heart for the church it would be if certain Western theologians were able to establish their case that Jesus is historically unknowable.) But if the kingdom is found in Jesus decisively, nevertheless it must not be found in Jesus only. To rest the case for the kingdom on the life — even the life, death and resurrection — of one man in an ever-receding past would be both unconvincing to the world and a betrayal of the gospel itself. What is equally unconvincing, and equally a betrayal, is to acquiesce in a church which shows few if any more signs of the kingdom than the world at large.

The reason why I have dwelt on this aspect of our concerns is that it seems to me central to the subject of unity and renewal. If both church and human community are to move towards unity and renewal, and if the church is to be used by God to make a vital contribution to the unity and renewal of humankind (not to mention the contributions God constantly causes to flow in the other direction), then there has to be helpful communication between them. It is no use our composing in-house descriptions of the church, however faithful they may be to scripture and tradition, if within the church they have the fatal effect of giving believers a warm illusion that all is well, and when read by humankind outside the church they seem to have parted company with reality — not that spiritual reality which may properly be assumed to be accessible only to the Christian, if the faith is true, but the human reality which the plain sense of the Christian words seems to demand. "The unity of the church and the renewal of human community are thus inseparably linked not as two separate entities but as two concentric circles around the one, unique and the same pivotal event in history: God redeeming brokenness and bringing back into his communion 'all things' in order to renew them."[11] This image opens our eyes to an important truth. But at the very least it also calls for evidence of renewal and unity in the church which humanity, given reasonable goodwill, can recognize as something it might covet for itself.

II

What might be our response to such a critique as this? — for a response we must make if our concern for the renewal of human community is not to be merely comfortable fantasy. Here I would like to mention some aspects of the gospel message which have not been prominent in our material and discussions, but which can, I believe, be of help towards our concern for unity and renewal of both church and humankind.

When the Second Person of the Blessed Trinity took human nature of the Virgin Mary, and became a member of the human race, a man in history, God thereby adopted all humanity, past, present and future as his own family. Or, we may put it another way, humankind was taken into the eternal family of the Holy Trinity itself. It is hardly conceivable that, having entered into human existence, suffering and death in order to be with us as one of us, God would then have no intention of continuing that relationship, but would simply allow death to bring it to an end. The resurrection of Christ is not only the divine vindication of the Crucified (Rom. 1:4), it is also the divine declaration of the destiny opened to humankind and to the material, created order in which we men and women are organically integrated.[12]

We need to remember, however, that these works of God in the incarnation relate directly to humankind as a whole, not just to the church or to humankind through the church. Before there ever was a church in the sense of men and women filled with the Holy Spirit or baptized in the name of the Lord Jesus, God in Christ had already done these decisive things: made humankind into an "extended family" of the Holy Trinity; shared the human experience of that family, including pain, hunger, homelessness, bereavement, rejection and death; and opened to that family and its world the gateway to a transfigured, eternal life. That is why we preach gospel, not law, namely that these blessings are not conditional on the achievements of the church. It is the gift of them, in fact, which creates the church by evoking the response of loving faith.

But to say even this is unthinkingly to fall into the same old trap. For surely we must say that the intention of God in the incarnation was not simply to create the church (though this has been said in Christian tradition) but to recreate humankind — in other words, to unite and renew human persons and human community. In Israel God had prepared a particular human community in which this *musterion* might have become known, for the dominant vision in the scriptures of Israel was of a God who related consistently to the whole nation in grace and judgment, even though the effect of this might be to create a wide variety of temporary groupings within the nation, each having its particular situation vis-à-vis God. The problem for Israel was not that of the church and human community, but of their own human community (the nation) within the total human community. This was, as we know, the primal challenge to the infant church, inherited from Judaism, which they overcame with such courage and faith, and in so doing made clear once for all that the coming of God in the incarnation was to the whole global human community and for that community.

The church is, then, most faithful to its Lord when it sees itself unwaveringly as that part of the whole human community which has had its eyes and heart opened to what God has done for that whole community, and which therefore is entrusted with a special responsibility for that whole community. (It could be said, indeed, that the problem we label as "the church and politics" is nothing other than the identifying of that responsibility and of the appropriate ways of fulfilling it.) The church, too, sees its Lord as, among many other things, the true image of what men and women are to be, as individuals in relationship, if human community is to be united and renewed. That which "Adam" failed to incarnate and to pass on is found at last in its authentic glory in Jesus, "who is the true image of God" (2 Cor. 4:4), and in whose face, therefore, we see the "light of revelation — the revelation of the glory of God" (4:6). To list all the NT texts which converge on this truth would be tedious and unnecessary. All that we need is to hold constantly to the awareness that this is a truth for humankind, a treasure for the whole human community stored in our "earthen vessels", and not to slip back into a false distancing of the church as a separate entity from the human community. The church exists only as an organic and integral part of that community, for as soon as it tries to understand its own life as meaningful in independence from the total human community it betrays the only purpose which can justify its existence. Even that most central and distinctive activity of the church — worship — does not fall outside this frame of reference, because the objective of the church's life is that all creation should give glory to God, and the adoration which the church offers continually is offered on behalf of the whole created order to which we belong.

Nevertheless, there is a darker side to this picture, and it is that to which, in my concluding section, I wish to turn.

III

In her meditation at morning worship last week, Sister Evangeline said: "Christ did not speak to be interpreted, but to be understood." This was a valuable reminder of a truth, but it could also conceal another truth, namely that though Christ did indeed speak in order to be understood, he also knew well that many, perhaps even most people would not in fact understand him. His parables are not homely sermon illustrations at all, but the whole sermon — and if Mark's own example of the interpretation of the Parable of the Sower is anything to go by, Jesus did not interpret his parables even to his disciples, for it is inconceivable that anyone so diamond-clear in thought and speech could have made such a muddle of one of his own stories! Alas, we have to face the fact that even the NT church did not always understand what Jesus was saying. Nor do we — for the reason that the picture of God and his relation to the world which Jesus was presenting was, one must suspect, so radical that only those open to a major shift of consciousness could grasp his meaning — and then only fragmentarily and discontinuously. To internalize Jesus' teaching about God in the parables is no light matter. It involves a complete transformation of all one's values and of one's way of seeing the world.

From this certain things, among others, follow for the church. First, God's understanding of the way of unity and renewal for humankind is not at all any of the ways that humankind is perpetually and disastrously trying out for itself. Even though God's way is the only one that will work, it seems to the world wholly impracticable; and because the world sees it this way, it actually becomes impracticable. The more faithful the church is then, in preaching and in life, to God's way in Christ, the more hostile to the church is the world likely to become — or, to put it another way, the more Christians are tempted into the classic contrast between "church" and "world", instead of remaining faithful to their solidarity with the world as those who know that the grace of God can be received only as part of the one human community into which the Lord was incarnated.

The other temptation for the church is to abolish the "gap" between "church" and "world" by crossing over to the "world's" side and adopting the human community's own vision and practice of human life (though no doubt slightly modified in a gospel direction!). In this way, it is thought "the kingdoms of the world can become the kingdom of our Lord and of his Christ". But things do not work out that way. The more the church has been identified with the belief and life-style of the world, the more angry does the world become at any criticism or resistance on the part of the church. Solidarity in sin with the "world" actually makes it harder, not easier, to have solidarity with the human community in the church's vocation of witness to and representative of the divine life.

These points, which I have tried to make from a rather different perspective, have already been emphasized in other ways by Lochman[13] and Nissiotis.[14] Two further themes, however, in their contributions must be mentioned.

First, in Lochman, we have a radically eschatological understanding, in keeping with the primary gospel setting of the kingdom of God. For many this finds expression in such ways of speaking as the paradoxes of "already — but not yet", and of "becoming what you are". For Nissiotis the eschatological thrust is more naturally expressed in terms of entelechy, i.e. that the divine-human organism of the church has within itself a drive towards a certain goal. In both cases it is God's future which judges the church's failure in the present. It also makes that failure bearable for faith by understanding the church's existence as a process or pilgrimage which takes history and the material creation seriously as the medium which God has himself ordained for the working out of his purposes.

Secondly, and following naturally from the point just mentioned, we have in Nissiotis the fundamental principle of "sacramental vision", that "the church does not possess its own being as a self-perfected community, but it exists *from* God and *for* the world, making manifest the restored communion between them",[15] because " 'sacramental' means the self-communication of God through human realities at a specific moment".[16] In the categories of Lochman's paper, "the kingdom of God is not the kingdom of Christians" but the divine reality, for which as their goal Christians live, act and suffer, but which they also enjoy as eucharistically present.

It seems to me that there are important psychological contrasts between these two presentations, for all that we can also recognize that they are wrestling with the same divine realities. For Lochman, the church and its life seem more provisional, more radically called in question at every point, so that the believer can find security not in any existent manifestation of the church but only in the divine promise which has called the church with all its imperfections into existence. In the "theo-materialism" of Nissiotis the believer finds it more natural to draw strength from the objective ontological facts of the church's existence, through which God communicates himself, even though by so doing he also judges. To the former, the latter will always seem too "optimistic", too little aware of creation's drastic need for redemption; to the latter, the former will always seem too "pessimistic", too little aware that God has not allowed creation to escape from his grasp, but continually uses it here and now for sanctification, i.e. the process of bringing all creatures into submission to his kingdom. There is also inevitably a bias on the one side towards giving centrality to the word, on the other to the sacraments.

If, however, what we have said earlier about "mystery" and "sign" has any sound basis, then we should be able to learn to live with these differing emphases. For word and sacrament are both about God's self-communication through human realities, and are inseparably involved with each other. We unite in speaking of what was enfleshed in Christ as the eternal word; liturgically we all venerate the gospel and in its proclamation receive Christ. Words themselves can be apprehended only by matter, through matter. Eucharist is impossible without the recounting of the divine word — as Queen Elisabeth I of England expressed it:

What his Word doth make it,
That I believe and take it.

The creative divine word, in union with material water, incorporates into Christ at baptism. The word of pardon communicates to the sinner the divine remission of sins. We ourselves are a mystery in which word/thought and matter combine to form a being in the divine image.

But if all these interactions of divine word and matter do not communicate to us, and through us to the human community the *true* divine image, they are nothing, void. And since the collision between that image and the world which wants to make itself in another image always produces conflict, effective divine self-communication in word and sacrament always leads to suffering. The more thoroughly we believe in a *theologia gloriae*, the more inevitably we are driven to live out a *theologia crucis*.

The visible authentication of the church, therefore, and the experiential ground of hope, is the presence in all churches of Christ-like *martyria* and *diakonia*, various concrete expressions of which have been set out in all our papers, and movingly conveyed to us orally by Bishop Buthelezi. Only where such things are *not* found do we need to tremble with deathly fear; but where they are not found radically or widely enough — that is to say, everywhere — we need to repent and be converted. For where the Spirit of the Lord truly is, there will the life and death of the Lord also be.

Which brings me to one last thought. In all our papers and discussions one key Christian experience has been conspicuous by its absence. We have heard much of judgment, conversion, repentance, the Spirit, liberation and so forth. We have heard very little of forgiveness — and yet this is the key central term. We Christian people have hope and confidence within our sinfulness, because we are a forgiven people. Christ stands alone among the moral teachers of the world, because he alone does not make everything depend on moral success. Alongside the ideal he sets before us, he places the assurance that human community can survive, can know joy and peace even in failure, if only we will forgive one another. In the end it was for this above all that he gave his life. It is this which God proclaims at Easter, when he gives the Risen Christ back to the friends who had forsaken him.

But this insight could become the last and greatest evasion, if the fundamental contribution of the church to the human community is not to be itself a community in which the members forgive each other, and all forgive all other creatures. "Without love of enemies", said the Staretz Silouan, "there is no following of Christ." I end with this thought as perhaps the missing link between the divine presence and human failure within the church, and between the church's separation from and solidarity with the human community.

NOTES

1. Buthelezi, pp. 1, 2, 4.
2. Legrand, p. 3.
3. Staniloae, p. 1.
4. Boné, p. 5.
5. Watkins, p. 6.
6. Lochman, p. 13.
7. Lochman, p. 10.
8. Nissiotis, p. 11.
9. Limouris, p. 7.
10. Page 4.
11. Nissiotis, p. 11
12. Nissiotis, pp. 8f.
13. Pages 11 – 15.
14. "Co-belongingness", p. 24.
15. Page 13.
16. Page 12.

Appendix 2

REPORT OF THE FIRST CONSULTATION
OF THE UNITY/RENEWAL STUDY

I. Introduction

1. *Mandate and purpose of the study*

1. The Faith and Order study on "The Unity of the Church and the Renewal of Human Community" is the result of a decision of the Faith and Order Commission at Lima (1982). It continues earlier Faith and Order studies, especially on "The Unity of the Church and the Unity of Humankind" and on "The Community of Women and Men in the Church".

2. The WCC Assembly at Vancouver (1983) affirmed this project and emphasized its "strategic significance for the whole orientation of the work of the WCC". It also stated that the study should *have an ecclesiological focus* in accordance with the general ecclesiological orientation of all Faith and Order work.

3. The Standing Commission of Faith and Order in April 1984 developed a programme outline for the study. This seeks to combine and inter-relate both in content and in method, the various aspects of the study: the inter-relatedness of church and human community; what the church's struggle to bring renewal and unity out of its own brokenness might mean for the renewal of human community; and the implications of brokenness and renewal in human community for the unity and renewal of the church.

4. These aspects, therefore, will be given special prominence in the programme. On the one hand, the exploration of ecclesiology will take special account of the theological inter-relation between the church and efforts for renewal in the human community. On the other, studies of the interaction of ideological, social, cultural and economic systems in problems relating to power, peace and human rights and of movements towards or away from fuller community of women and men, will help to examine the understanding of the church's witness and service for the renewal of human community.

5. The process of work on this study, which is intended to come to a conclusion with the World Conference on Faith and Order, began with a first consultation. About 30 participants from different Christian traditions and parts of the world reflected from 3-10 January 1985 in Chantilly, France, on "The Church as Mystery and Prophetic Sign".

6. The report of this consultation which follows here was edited and revised by staff on the basis of comments from participants. It can only indicate some of the major aspects which were regarded as important for future work on the subject. The richness and depth of ideas and perspectives presented in the papers given on the occasion, and the many insights shared in the exchanges between the participants, cannot be adequately conveyed by such a report.

2. Background and context of our reflections

7. It is in the world that God calls the church to be his servant-people, the living temple of his Holy Spirit, the bride and body of his Son, Jesus Christ, in order that it may be the sign and instrument of the Triune God's work towards the salvation and renewal of all humankind. For the fulfilment of this vocation he wills the church to move towards that unity for which his Son prayed, a unity not only visible to the world but also of a spiritual authenticity which can help the world to respond to him in faith.

8. This world, with its multitude of diverse histories, cultures, situations and conditions, is marked by chances and dangers, hopes and anxieties, many related to specific areas, but many also becoming more and more global in character. Christians and churches live in the midst of these anxieties and hopes. They share in them and are challenged by them. There is a deep yearning for justice, peace, meaning and preservation of the resources of life, which is shared by millions and which is echoed by the yearnings of all creatures (Rom. 8). Furthermore, there are all the potentials of economic development, technology, communication, and international organizations as well as of individuals and groups committed to justice, peace and the conservation of the environment which, if used for the good of humanity and the rest of the created order, could help to overcome the manifold threats to life, which could even lead to its complete destruction.

9. The church of Jesus Christ, the millions of Christians who confess Jesus Christ as God, Lord and Saviour, are called and sent to be among the forces of life in a world marked by sin, suffering and death. In order to respond to this divine mandate the church is in need of constant renewal of its own life and witness. The church is not only to be allied with all other forces of renewal and life in the midst of the brokenness and ambivalences of the world. If it is to be faithful through its life and action to Jesus Christ, who is the way, truth and life for the world, active in the

world through the Holy Spirit, it must also proclaim him as the source of the world's true and decisive hope.

II. Humanity and church in the light of the kingdom

10. "Church" and "human community" in the title of the study refer to two closely inter-related realities which do not stand over against each other. Likewise the two issues of unity and renewal apply both to church as well as to human community each in a specific way. Unity and renewal of the church are intimately related. The renewal of human community must be seen, theologically, in the perspective of that unity of all humankind which is, in its full realization, our eschatological hope. In order to delineate this inter-relation of church and humanity the perspective of the kingdom of God is fundamental.

1. Jesus and the kingdom of God

11. According to Mark, the message of Jesus from Nazareth can be summarized in the proclamation: "The time is fulfilled, and the Kingdom of God is at hand, repent and believe in the Gospel" (Mark 1:15). According to Luke, in fulfilment of Old Testament promises the main thrust of his preaching was the good news to the poor, to the captives, to the blind and the oppressed: the proclamation of the acceptable year of the Lord (Luke 4:14−21,43). His parables were centred on the mystery of the kingdom. His mighty deeds were signs of the kingdom: "If I by the finger of God cast out demons then the kingdom of God has indeed come upon you" (Luke 11:20ff.).

12. The disciples and apostles recognized the presence of the kingdom not only in the words and deeds, but in the person of Jesus Christ. In his whole life from the manger to the cross and resurrection, the kingdom of God had drawn near to them.

13. The kingdom, proclaimed by Jesus, transcends all experiences, insights and wishes. It is a mystery which cannot be captured nor intellectually grasped by us. Jesus himself speaks about it in parables. They are not intended to communicate definitions of or abstract theories about the kingdom, but they point in a clear direction and intend to move us into that direction.

14. The kingdom is a dynamic reality, "for the kingdom of God is not in word, but in power" (1 Cor. 4:20). It is present in Jesus Christ and he himself promises it also as a future reality. He calls us to accept it and teaches us to pray for its coming. It is both part of the "here and now", and at the same time "not yet". It is a gift of the free grace of God and calls for the free decision of human beings.

2. Kingdom and humankind

15. Judgment, grace, challenge and promise of the kingdom are addressed to the whole of humanity and to each individual person. This

universal message comes from the Lord "who has called you into his kingdom and glory" (1 Thess. 2:12). Jesus preaches the kingdom as being like leaven in the world, which works until the whole has been leavened (cf. Matt. 13:33). The message of the kingdom is in a special way addressed as hope and promise to the poor and therefore the church is given a particular responsibility in its mission to the poor as well as in listening to their voice as a help in discerning the signs of the kingdom.

16. Through the message of the kingdom the Holy Spirit discloses to the world what sin, justice and judgment are (cf. John 16:8–11). Before God, who is just, holy and almighty, sinful humanity is under judgment. Therefore, Jesus calls all people to repentance in order to turn from a sinful self-centred life to a life in community in accordance with God's will.

17. But at the same time the coming of the kingdom is an event full of grace and offered to all human beings. It cannot be merited in any way, it is not the result or fulfilment of human activities, it is not an automatic step in the process of evolution. Rather, it is a gift of grace, beyond full comprehension, which intends to communicate eternal salvation to human beings and awaits their response of faith. With the presence of the kingdom in the person of Christ the history and destiny of all of humanity has undergone a fundamental change. And with the parousia of Jesus Christ there will be once again a radical and comprehensive transform-ation and fulfilment.

18. The message of the kingdom is a challenge to all humanity. Because it offers a unique opportunity for new life and hope, it confronts each individual and community with the choice to reject this opportunity or to make a radical and total decision and involvement, both reaching to the roots of existence and including all areas of life.

19. This message is at the same time a promise, which extends far beyond each individual to embrace the whole world. The fully accom-plished kingdom of God will be the "new heaven and the new earth" (Rev. 21:1). This promise includes the gift of radical newness and of all-embracing community: "Behold, I make all things new" (Rev. 21:5). Life under this promise will already here and now be a life full of hope.

20. Signs of the realization of this judgment, grace, challenge and promise are among us. This commits us to being attentive to them whenever we can discern them. But because of the ambiguity of all human life and history we are in special need of the gift of recognizing the Spirit and discerning those signs of the time which point to the coming of the kingdom already in our midst.

3. The kingdom and the church

21. *Note*: When we use the term "church" in this text we are aware that we have to differentiate between the church as willed by God and as a

historical and human reality. For the sake of brevity this differentiation (not separation!) is indicated only in some formulations.

22. The Lord Jesus Christ inaugurated his church by preaching the good news, that is, the coming of the kingdom of God. Whoever receives this message and affirms it in faith belongs to Christ's church and becomes through baptism a member of his body. This person will not be separated from humanity, but related to it in a deeper way and committed to it even more strongly. The church is that part of humanity which has been led to accept, affirm and gratefully acknowledge the liberating truth of the kingdom for all people. The church is the community of those who have been convinced of the presence and future of the kingdom. It unites all those who acknowledge the claim of the sovereign reign of God, which implies the necessity of constant conversion and renewal.

23. The church is therefore called to live as that force within humanity through which the renewal and community of all people is served as it seeks to live according to the message of the kingdom. The church is in all aspects oriented towards the final coming of the kingdom of which it is already a foretaste. While its members are committed to this new community in Christ, they are also aware of its provisional character. They yearn and strive for its fulfilment: "And the Spirit and the bride say: 'Come'" (Rev. 22:17), "Marana tha!" (1 Cor. 16:22).

24. The church, endowed with gifts of its founder and faithfully observing his precepts of charity, humility and self-denial, receives the mission of proclaiming among all peoples the kingdom of God, and sharing with them in witness and service the first-fruits of the kingdom. Accordingly the church is called to be and serve as that part of humanity which is prepared and empowered by the Holy Spirit to witness to and proclaim the kingdom in and for this world through word and deed, life, suffering and dying. It is the community of those willing to serve the kingdom for the sake of humanity. To the degree in which this happens the church is, through the Holy Spirit, an effective sign, an instrument of God's rule in this "aion" —an instrument created and used by God.

25. In all this the church is seed, nor harvest, a net with good and bad fishes, a community of sinners and at the same time justified, a beginning not an end, always endangered from within as from without, but preserved at the same time by the grace of God in an unendingly renewing feast of Pentecost.

4. *The relation between church and world*

26. In the perspective of the kingdom of God, church and world appear in their fundamental, or rather eschatological togetherness. This is no undifferentiated, monolithic unity. It is no premature amalgamation and confusion between church and world. There is a legitimate concern

for the inalienable identity of the church. We must take to heart what was said in Vancouver: "It is only a church which goes out from its eucharistic centre, strengthened by word and sacrament and thus strengthened in its own identity, resolved to become what it is, that can take the world on to its agenda."[1] In the course of history we must still go on making the distinction: the church is not the world and the structures of this world, though being the realm of God's action and of the church's mission, do not as such become church. The unity between them can only be recognized and practised in hope, i.e. in the light of the kingdom of God.

27. Seen in this light, however, this unity is in fact promised and thereby already now shapes the life, witness and mission of the church. "The church can go out to the edges of society, not fearful of being distorted or confused by the world's agenda, but confident and capable of recognizing that God is already there" at work.[2] For the kingdom of God is not only the church's final fulfilment but also the world's future. In God's plan of salvation, it is impossible to separate church and world. The Spirit of new creation bestowed upon the church in the Pentecost event, creating and recreating it ever since, opens our eyes and hands for the "eager expectation of the creation" (Rom. 8:19ff.).

III. The church as mystery

1. The mystery of Christ

28. A mystery is something that is veiled and made known, apparent but hidden. The supreme mystery is God. In scripture this same word is used for God's self-revelation in creation and self-communication in the plan of salvation. The climax of this revelation, which itself is a mystery, is the life, death, resurrection and glorification of Jesus Christ, the incarnate logos. All who are brought into communion with Christ, as divine-human person, become members of his body, the church.

29. In Ephesians, Paul speaks of his insight into the "mystery of Christ" who is our peace, breaking down the dividing wall of hostility, reconciling separated peoples in one body through the cross (Eph. 2:14,16; 3:4–6). The mystery of the divine-human relationship, revealed in Jesus Christ, is therefore the foundation of unity and community for God's people. The incarnation is an invitation to share in the glorified humanity of Christ, to be renewed in the image of God and to share in the suffering of Christ for the world. As people of God, we remember and celebrate the life and hope which Christ gives for the renewal and salvation of the world.

2. The mystery of the church

30. On the day of Pentecost the Holy Spirit brought the followers of Christ into a new relationship to God by imparting a share in the life of

God (Acts 2:1—21). In the same act each believer is brought into a new relation with other believers, forming a vital communion, the one mystical body of Christ. They are gathered in the church, which is sent into the world in order to be a foretaste of what the world is to become, the first-fruits of the new creation.

31. As the body of Christ, the church participates in the divine mystery. As mystery, it reveals Christ to the world, by proclaiming the gospel, manifesting the newness of life given by him, and anticipating the kingdom already present in him. The church is united with Christ in the humiliation of the cross while at the same time it experiences the victory of the resurrection, thus making present in the life of this world the reality of the kingdom—present now, yet still to come. The centre of the life of the church is the risen and reigning Christ, who is its Lord, its head, and the source of its power. By the Holy Spirit, the divine life is communicated to believers through word and sacraments, which themselves are called mysteries.

32. The core of this sacramental life embraces historical and natural reality so that the church is united with the whole of creation. The new creation (*ktisis*) will unite the whole of the created order with God's love and purpose, and with his will for its continuing renewal and perfection in Christ (2 Cor. 5:17; Col. 1:16f.). However, the new creation is not yet completed. Nature (*physis*), as we know it, has been alienated from the Creator (Rom. 1:20). The church therefore stands with creation in anticipation of renewal, groaning in travail, waiting for final redemption (Rom. 8:21—22).

3. The reality of brokenness in the life of the church and world

33. The broken relationship between creator and creature is a universal reality. The church proclaims its one Lord, one faith, one baptism, but even within its communion, it also reflects the brokenness of the world. The ecclesiological focus of this study of "The Church as Mystery and Prophetic Sign" must then recognize the challenge posed by the unshaken communion with the creator to the sinful brokenness in the life of both church and world.

34. Yet there is a difference between brokenness in the life of the church and in the life of humanity outside it. The world strives for unity on the basis of the aspirations and common humanity which God has given to it. The church strives for visible unity on the basis of the forgiveness of God accomplished in Christ, and on the basis of the unity already given by Christ in communion with the Father and the Holy Spirit. Such unity in redemption is already experienced in the deep community shared by Christians and is the basis for renewal and reconciliation among them.

4. The mystery and witness of the sacramental vision

35. The life of the church celebrates and communicates this renewal and reconciliation and witnesses to its reality in and for the world. By taking elements from creation and celebrating their being renewed and used by God to convey his saving presence through word and sacraments, the church witnesses to the restored relation between God and the cosmos as the new creation in Christ. This sacramental witness to Christ is an authentic and evangelical demonstration of the unity and renewal at the heart of the church. It proclaims the existence of the church as standing with the world. The church exists from God and for the world, to manifest this reality: God is with us and for the whole of humankind.

36. Through the church God transmits his saving and uniting grace to all creation. In its sacramental communion Christ is the vision and source of the unity of the church and of the renewal of human community. "As Jesus went out to publicans and sinners and had table-fellowship with them during his earthly ministry, so Christians are called in the eucharist to be in solidarity with the outcast and to become signs of the love of Christ who lived and sacrificed himself for all and now gives himself in the eucharist."[3] In the sacramental life of the church God continues to be in unity and communion with the human community and he calls his people to follow him in this way of communion and solidarity. Washed and liberated by Christ's suffering their witness takes the form of suffering with the world and for the world. Filled with hope by Christ's victory over death in his resurrection their witness takes the form of joyous and confident affirmation of God's reconciling and saving purpose for the world.

37. As such witness is rooted in our sacramental union with God and with each other, the renewal of sacramental communion calls for our solidarity with those who seek to recover fully human existence in the church and the world. Led by the prophetic judgment and by the reconciling love of the gospel, and strengthened by the mystery of its sacramental life in Christ, the church is called to serve humanity in the struggle for renewal and transformation.

IV. The church as prophetic sign

1. Sign and prophetic ministry

38. In Jesus' teaching and action concerning "signs" there are several diverse elements. On the one hand he refused to give signs from heaven to those who sought them as unambiguous guarantees of his place in God's purpose: "no sign shall be given . . . except the sign of Jonah"(Matt. 16:4). On the other hand, he urged an understanding of the signs of the times. This diversity was emphasized in the Bristol Faith and Order report of 1967 with reference to Luke 12 and 13.[4] In Luke 12:56,

Jesus asks: "Why do you not know how to interpret the present time?",
but in 13:1–5, he refuses a particular reading of events like Pilate's
massacre or the fall of the tower of Siloam; the victims were not specially
sinful. Nevertheless he draws from these events the general consequences
of God's universal judgment and the call to repent. In John, sign events,
beginning at the marriage feast in Cana (cf. John 2:11), are the
manifestation, to those who believe, of Jesus' glory and of new life in and
through him.

39. In the light of diverse uses of the term "sign", all talk of the church
as "prophetic sign" is only possible if it is directly connected with the
"mystery", the "open secret" of God's saving purpose to unite all things
and people in Christ on the basis of response to the Gospel (cf. Eph. 3:6).
God's footprints and the realization of his salvific purpose are discerned as
such only with the eyes of faith. The church is set in the world as a
prophetic sign witnessing to God's purpose through its ultimate relation
with Jesus Christ in the Holy Spirit. It is Christ, present and active in the
church through the Holy Spirit, who makes the church a sign of judgment and salvation to all humankind through its life, witness and service.

40. In order that this communion with and service to the Lord of the
church may be brought into renewing relation with the life of both
church and world, Christians are called to exercise within the church a
dynamic prophetic ministry as a vital part of the general task of preaching
the gospel. Such a prophetic ministry is not individualistic: it is to be
tested by the community of faith and is also a responsibility of that
community as a whole. Within and by that community it seeks to relate
the gospel to the critical events and issues of the day. Some of these events
and issues are not the subject of direct references in the scriptures; some of
them lead the Christians who are involved in them to fresh insights from
the witness of the scriptures and the tradition for our time. In exercising
this prophetic ministry the church also becomes aware of the way in
which its life and mission can be challenged from the side of the world by
contemporary events and causes.

41. It is in relation to this mutual challenging of world and church that
we recognize signs in the world and in the church, signs which are there in
order that they may be read and understood (cf. Hab. 2:2) and related to
the all-encompassing plan of salvation of the Triune God. This requires of
the church, in its vocation, to be a prophetic sign pointing to God's
judgment and salvation in Jesus Christ, a double implementation of its
witnessing task, an implementation both in the communication of God's
truth and in the sharing of God's love.

2. Sign and the communication of God's truth for faith

42. In word and sacraments and common life the church is called to
communicate by "translating" (in a more than linguistic sense) the gospel

message intended for all humankind so that it may be heard, understood and accepted in all cultures. Yet as the church communicates and translates the gospel from one culture to another, it cannot avoid becoming involved with the particularities of each culture, which must themselves be translated as the gospel is handed on. This is one aspect of the continuing Pentecost in the life of the church as the Holy Spirit enables the church to become an intelligible and effective prophetic sign to people in all cultures, summoning them to unity in Christ through repentance and faith.

43. The communication of God's truth through responsible prophetic ministry within and by the church reaching out to all cultures and situations will be grounded in this work of the Holy Spirit by faithfulness to the apostolic faith of the church. Such faithfulness, in the context of contemporary situations and events, involves taking risks in ministry; yet prophetic ministry must be tested by criteria. Faithfulness to the apostolic faith, self-criticism of our own efforts to communicate the gospel, and creative application of the gospel to contemporary issues and situations are all necessary to our prophetic ministry. Faithfulness without self-criticism and creative application would offer only a "dead letter". Self-criticism without faithfulness and creative application would prevent any convincing communication of the gospel. Creative application without faithfulness and self-criticism would produce only a spurious relevance.

44. Through Pentecost Christians begin to reverse the confusion of Babel: that is, they begin to learn how to communicate and apply the universal gospel across and to the variety and division of issues and cultures. In this living tradition of handing on and communicating the gospel as an expression of the process of Pentecost the prophetic witness of the church is turned towards the future, the coming of Christ in glory and the fulfilment of God's plan of salvation. In this twofold perspective the church is a prophetic sign pointing to the catholic as well as eschatological dimension of God's life-giving truth.

45. By serving as a prophetic sign through the communication and application of God's truth to all cultures and conditions in the world, the church is itself renewed and serves at the same time the renewal of human community: this comprehensive communication can become a reconciling communication between the churches, between the different stages of tradition, between the different cultures and social systems.

3. Sign and the sharing of God's love in Christ

46. The task, however, is not only one of communicating God's truth for reconciliation and salvation. In offering its common life in the service of God and his love for the world the church has also constantly to struggle through its presence alongside those who suffer and by its action on their behalf. In this sharing of God's love the church enables them to

perceive the suffering love of God in Jesus Christ for them and the church itself is led to a deeper experience of that love.

47. In this sharing of God's love through involvement in the world, the church is a sign of the presence of the kingdom of God in Jesus Christ. Therefore its struggle is something quite other than a mere activism and cannot expect to gain effective publicity for the churches' programmes. The sign should not become the centre of attention in its own right. Much Christian self-understanding is distorted by self-centredness and there is always a danger that teaching concerning the church itself will be misunderstood in this manner. The church should never be centred on itself but rather upon Christ and upon God's purpose of salvation of which it is a sign.

48. It is particularly important to avoid this misunderstanding when we honour the mystery of the church's being in Christ. However, this being in Christ does not protect the church from failures which is to say that the corporate life of the church is affected by those distortions and sins which affect individual Christians. The church is the body of Christ, not only a symbol of that body, and yet it is a body composed of human members. And we have also to recognize that the qualitative — and not just quantitative/geographical — catholicity of the church in sharing God's love with all of humanity involves it in grappling with and, to that extent, taking into its life the brokenness of the world. It cannot be protected from vulnerability and from suffering actual wounds in the struggle to overcome by the power of the resurrection the divisions and sins of humankind, including its own members. Therefore it is often not a sign in that unambiguous clarity which God wills for it. To put the matter positively: Those who are sent to be a prophetic sign of God's purpose and love in the world and who are "called, beloved in God the Father and kept for Jesus Christ" must also "keep" themselves "in the love of God" (Jude vv. 1 and 21).

4. Sign, renewal and unity in the Holy Spirit

49. It is in relation to the double task of communicating God's truth and of sharing God's love described above that it is possible to see the relationship between cross and resurrection in the life of the church. We carry "in the body the death of Jesus, so that the life of Jesus may also be manifested in our bodies" (2 Cor. 4:10). A church whose glory is the glory of the crucified and risen Lord will become a sign by its involvement in the world's divisions and sufferings for the sake of their being overcome by Christ. It will not be a self-protective, aloof body but a ferment, a seed, the first-fruits of harvest.

50. The sign character of the church leads directly into witness, moving at its extreme into martyrdom. The church is a community called to manifest and signify the permanence of the personal relationship

of God with the whole creation in a specific way and through a chosen human community, a relationship sustained by the Holy Spirit. The human struggles "outside" the church for justice, peace and liberation are not elements foreign to the one creation of God. Therefore the witness which is guided and filled by the Holy Spirit includes the judgment of the world (John 16:8–11), a share in its suffering (John 15:20), and a manifestation, in the world, of renewal in the form of reconciliation and new life (John 11:24–25). This witness is taken up by the Holy Spirit into the hope for the return of Christ and the final implementation of his kingly rule.

51. God the Father glorifies the Son as by death and resurrection the way is opened to new life in the Spirit. Throughout this study, as is evidenced by several references in this report, the participants in the consultation have spoken of the continuing Pentecost by which the church is renewed in the love of the Holy Trinity to find a life in unity. So renewed, the church is both a sign and an instrument of renewal in the human community, a renewal which can only find its authenticity and fullness as humankind is drawn together towards the consummation of God's creation in the perfected kingdom.

Note on further study

52. We have discussed these themes not only in general or abstract terms but in specific relation to particular evidences of renewal in the human community, e.g. the many instances of Christian witness concerning peace, justice and the preservation of natural resources; the expressions of Christian fellowship across the barriers which separate different social-political systems; positive developments in the relation of women and men in church and society; the common revision of historical descriptions of the past by historians of different nations. These reflections on the church as prophetic sign are the programmatic link between this consultation with its basic exploration of ecclesiology and the next stages of this process of study on unity and renewal, which will deal with the specific issues of the community of women and men and of the interaction of ideologies, social systems and cultures in relation to the renewal and unity of both church and human community. The church must not seek to express its life and self-understanding in isolation from such issues. Its involvement in such concerns is not something external to its life but in its authentic forms will be a sign of the good news, of the presence and promise of the kingdom, of the mystery of God's incarnate self-involvement with the world and the continuing Pentecost. It will be a witness to that glory which is expressed in Jesus' prayer: ". . . what shall I say, 'Father, save me from this hour'? No, for this purpose I have come to this hour. Father, glorify thy name" (John 12:27–28).

NOTES

1. *Gathered for Life*, report of the Sixth Assembly of the WCC, Vancouver 1983, ed. David Gill, Geneva, WCC, and Grand Rapids, Wm. B. Eerdmans, 1983, p.50.
2. *Ibid.*
3. "Baptism, Eucharist and Ministry", *Faith and Order Paper No. 111*, Geneva, WCC, 1982, Eucharist para. 24.
4. *Faith and Order Paper No. 51*, Geneva, WCC, 1967, pp.28–30.

Appendix 3

THE UNITY OF THE CHURCH
AND THE RENEWAL OF HUMAN
COMMUNITY: A HISTORICAL SURVEY

Gennadios Limouris

Aspects of the development before 1968

At Lausanne 1927, the delegates of the churches recognized the profound historical and doctrinal issues which separated the churches. The Lausanne conference was only a beginning, but a promising one:

> God wills unity. Our presence in this Conference bears testimony to our desire to bend our wills to His. However we may justify the beginnings of disunion, we lament its continuance and henceforth must labour, in penitence and faith, to build up our broken walls. God's Spirit has been in the midst of us.[1]

The crux of the problem at Lausanne was the different ways of looking at the church. Some of the churches focused their attention on the visible church in its organic unity, in some cases making the claim that their own church is the only true one. Others emphasized the idea of the church invisible, as a spiritual reality, declaring that the true unity of the invisible church is not impaired, or should not be, by the comparatively secondary divisions of the visible church. But most saw the endeavours for church unity in the perspective of the goal of common witness and service to the world.

Fifty years later, Jürgen Moltmann declared: "Fifty years ago in the early days of ecumenical rapprochement it was said 'doctrine divides — service unites'. Fellowship among the divided churches was therefore achieved rapidly and without any great problems in practical, diaconal service to the poor, to refugees and to the victims of persecution. Divided in Faith and Order, the churches spontaneously drew closer to one another in 'Life and Work'. Given this spontaneous fellowship on the practical level, the theologians in Faith and Order found themselves faced with the difficult task of overcoming the doctrinal differences dividing the churches. The feeling which accompanied their work was one of general scepticism rather than soaring hope. Today the situation is almost completely reversed. Now, after many years of patient, painstaking work it would be true to say 'theology unites — *praxis* divides'."[2]

The efforts to formulate a study on the theme go as far back as the 1920s. At that time the Faith and Order and Life and Work movements paralleled each other and moved towards their unification at Amsterdam under the comprehensive theme "Man's Disorder and God's Design". The continuing search for direction in the post-war period eventually found its programmatic place in the Uppsala Assembly in 1968. The main importance of this Assembly has been its affirmation, for the first time, of "the oneness of (hu)mankind as reality". There was a strong conviction that the churches needed a new openness to the world, its aspirations and achievements as well as its restlessness and despair. But at the same time the Assembly suggested, "in a time of which human interdependence is so evident, it is more imperative to make visible the bonds which unite Christians in universal fellowship."[3] And then, in its most famous single sentence, Uppsala gave us an important clue for study: "The Church is bold", it said, "in speaking of itself as the *sign* of the *coming unity* of (hu)mankind". Uppsala's account was more eschatological ("the coming unity . . . "), but the agreement was profound.[4]

So began a fifteen-year study. As Mary Tanner pointed out, "emerging from the reflection and documentation of these years are two dominant themes, like the two leading subjects of a symphony, through which the unity of church and renewal of human community has been explored: one is the theme of *brokenness*, the other a profoundly theological theme — that of the Church as sign of the coming unity of humanity".[5]

The pre-Louvain phase identified many of the continuing themes: the ambiguity of the term "mankind" (Adam) itself, whether it is right to speak of "unity" in referring to both church and humankind, the eschatological character of unity, the "*sign*" character of the church's unity, the "brokenness" of that sign because of sin, the mystery that God's reconciliation begins with judgment and repentance.[6]

From 1968 to 1978

This is the second period in Faith and Order's study. In Bristol (1967), the Commission proposed to study "Man in Nature and History" which was later transformed into the explicit study on "The Unity of the Church and the Unity of Humankind."[7] The story of the theme during this decade was instructive, both positively and negatively. It began with the drafting of a rather substantial study guide dealing with *biblical, historical, systematic, ecclesiological and ecumenical* considerations. John Deschner in his Lima report showed that two kinds of study then developed:

a) a large number of local groups took up the study;

b) the second main line of work was carried out internationally in the

Commission itself, and the topic became the main theme for the 1971 Commission meeting in Louvain.

Louvain 1971

The interest in Louvain gravitated towards five concrete sub-themes, and the search there for new questions, new openings, new relevance for church unity:

a) the struggle for human justice: questions such as law and gospel, church and state, history and *eschaton*, eucharistic fellowship and the principle of social justice;
b) the encounter with living faiths;
c) the struggle against racism: the question about racial identity and church identity;
d) the handicapped in society;
e) the differences in cultures.

The general debate at Louvain emphasized the need for greater care and clarity in using the "intercontextual method", and asked for more rigorous interdisciplinary studies.[8]

The post-Louvain phase

This phase was both difficult and creative. It concentrated mainly on trying to formulate a comprehensive document to represent the whole study. Then began the work on a sort of consolidating phase:

a) clarifying concepts;
b) developing a theological document;
c) publishing results.

In fairness, it should be noted that other Faith and Order studies, e.g. "Account of Hope", "Conciliar Fellowship," were claiming major attention during this period.

The *Utrecht* Working Committee (1972) asked for a summary document. The *Zagorsk* Working Committee in August 1973 went so far as to recommend a change of title: "The Unity of the Church in an Interdependent World". It criticized an attempted summary and asked for clarification of several themes: the notions of "human interdependence and mankind", the concept of the church as *mystery* and *sign*, the relation between the church's unity and diversity, the bearing of the topic on the growing theme of conciliar fellowship.[9]

The most important emphasis at Zagorsk, as John Deschner pointed out, was its protest against superficial notions of "the unity of humankind" or *triumphalist* claims about the church as "*sign*". Finally, Zagorsk asked for *sobriety* and *realism*.

Accra 1974

The Commission attempted to conclude and appraise the study after six years' work. The documentary work was gathered and brought together in summary form by Geiko Müller-Fahrenholz.[10] The main decision taken, however, was actually a *creative* step. The Commission produced a short statement entitled "Towards Unity in Tension" to be submitted as a contribution to the Nairobi Assembly of the WCC. It developed a very necessary and useful set of distinctions for the term "humankind", i.e.:

a) human inter-relatedness;
b) a more ideological term, "the just interdependence of free people" (a positive secular, utopian vision of the human possibility);
c) an eschatological *unity* of humankind, the unity not simply of the church, but of the kingdom to which all are called.[11]

Nairobi Assembly 1975

The Assembly described the goal of unity as "a conciliar fellowship of local churches which are themselves truly united". This description has been widely affirmed and has served to open new ways for churches to deepen their commitment to each other (e.g. covenant agreement). But the church-humanity topic provided the principal concept and content for the middle part of the Section II report, "What Unity Requires", where the unity of the church is viewed in relation to:

a) the handicapped;
b) the community of women and men in the church (it was this study which was to form the most significant development of the programme on unity and renewal in the years between Nairobi and Vancouver).

Bangalore 1978

The Commission identified "three requirements for visible unity":

a) full mutual recognition of baptism, the eucharist and the ministry;
b) common understanding of the apostolic faith; and
c) agreement on common ways of teaching and decision-making.

It committed the churches to keep this vision and goal: " . . . we wish to affirm that the vision of unity in such a conciliar fellowship, sharing the one apostolic faith as well as the gifts of baptism and the eucharist, is alive in us. Although it may seem to be only a distant possibility, the vision provides inspiration and guidance already in the present as we envisage the way ahead. Christ himself summons us to pursue the goal. Since He is the centre of our lives, the realization of the unity for which He prayed is a central task for us. . . "[12]

Sheffield 1981
This consultation directly touched three main points:
a) the ordination of women;
b) questions of theological anthropology;
c) the authority of scripture and its relation to women in the church.

These areas have been dealt with in the study: "The Community of Women and Men in the Church".[13]

From Lima 1982
In a real sense, the Commission realized that the world inter-relates with the church as much as the church provides a sign to the world. These insights were behind "The Unity of the Church — Unity of Humankind" and they were also the basis of a new study (proposed at Lima): "The Unity of the Church and the Renewal of Human Community".[14] It must be stressed that Faith and Order has no monopoly on this theme. In fact, "The Unity of the Church and its Relation to the Unity of Humankind" was put forward by the Review Committee in 1976 as one of the four "areas of concentration" for the WCC as a whole in the years after Nairobi.

a) In 1975, a joint consultation was organized by Faith and Order and the Programme to Combat Racism (the consultation report, *Racism in Theology — Theology Against Racism*, has been the subject of widespread discussion).[15]
b) A book entitled *Partners in Life* was published by Faith and Order in 1978 to stimulate further reflection on the role of disabled persons in the life of the church and to affirm that any future unity must include full incorporation of the disabled in the church's community.[16]
c) In 1976, Faith and Order organized a consultation with the Ecumenical Institute in Bossey. The report of this meeting was published in 1978, under the title *Church and State: Opening a New Ecumenical Discussion*.[17]

Baptism, Eucharist and Ministry (BEM)
Article 20 of the eucharist chapter claims:

> The eucharist embraces all aspects of life. It is a representative act of thanksgiving and offering on behalf of the whole world. The eucharistic celebration demands *reconciliation* and sharing among all those regarded as brothers and sisters in the one family of God and is a constant challenge in the search for appropriate relationships in *social, economic and political* life (Matt. 5:23f.; 1 Cor. 10: 16f.; 1 Cor. 11: 20–22; Gal. 3:28). All kinds of *injustice, racism, separation and lack of freedom* are radically challenged when we share in the body and blood of Christ. Through the eucharist the *all-renewing* grace of God penetrates and *restores human personality and dignity*. The eucharist

involves the believer in the central event of the world's history. As participants in the eucharist, therefore, we prove inconsistent if we are not actively participating in this *ongoing restoration* of the world's situation and the *human condition*. The eucharist shows us that our behaviour is inconsistent in face of the reconciling presence of God in human history: we are placed under continual judgment by the persistence of unjust relationships of all kinds in our society, the manifold divisions on account of human pride, material interest and power politics, and, above all, the obstinacy of unjustifiable confessional oppositions within the body of Christ.[18]

Notes for a study on "The Unity of the Church and the Renewal of Human Community" (from the Lima report)

1. The theme of the renewal of human community, as a crucial area for exploration of the means of church unity, continues to be key for the Faith and Order Commission in deepening its relationship to the other units of the World Council of Churches and in responding to the needs of member churches.

2. Both the theme and style of the study are needed to complete the continuing work on reception of "Baptism, Eucharist and Ministry" and "Towards the Common Expression of the Apostolic Faith Today". They have contextual aspects built into the next stage of their design but need this study on "unity and renewal" to remind them of the seriousness of contextualization. This study should also raise significant questions about the importance of "culture" on credal formulations and of "community" on eucharist and ministry. At the same time, "unity and renewal" includes a serious component for inductive research into theological issues, yet needs to be reminded of the depth of the work and challenged by new insights into the barriers or opportunities for church unity coming from the other two study processes.

3. Faith and Order needs to explore new theological methods in the promotion of unity, methods which seek to move beyond the dichotomies of universities-churches, deductive-inductive, doctrinal-historical, etc. The search for a "third way", and the reflection on what we are learning about methodology and hermeneutics, is an important part of the intended design for the study.

4. Along these lines, we are convinced that the study needs a "second level" methodology which seeks to deepen and expand the findings and insights of previous studies. The study will continue to be rooted in concrete *situations of engagement*. In seeking to clarify and narrow the focus of the study, the first step seems to be to begin with theological insights that have already emerged in other studies which present opportunities for further research, action and reflection. This would thus represent the second level of a continuing "hermeneutical circulation" in which the initial action/reflection materials, and the initial theological work (as in the Community study), would be subject to further critical reflection and

theological development, as well as further "situational testing" through already existing local and regional networks and programmes.

5. Faith and Order needs to learn how to utilize the gifts of all its members and to incorporate styles of theological reflection arising out of a wealth of cultures, spiritualities and pastoral responsibilities.

Specific recommendations

1. That the Faith and Order Commission in Lima recognize the study on "The Unity of the Church and the Renewal of Human Community" as one of its major studies in the period from Lima to 1987.

2. That the Faith and Order Commission in Lima appoint the nucleus of a Steering Committee that would, along with the staff, guide future work on the study.

3. That the Faith and Order Commission, through the Steering Committee, initiate reflection on the theme and methodology of this study in order to prepare a full prospectus to be submitted to the Commission at the earliest appropriate opportunity.[19]

Recommendations from Vancouver and core groups

1. In the Vancouver report of Issue Group No. 2, it is said that:

> . . . the Faith and Order Commission make a theological exploration of the Church as "sign" a central part of its programme on the Unity of the Church and the Renewal of Human Community. This recommendation implies our conviction that the Church is called to be a prophetic "sign", a prophetic community through which and by which the transformation of the world can take place. It is only a church which goes out from its eucharistic centre, strengthened by word and sacrament and thus strengthened in its own identity, resolved to become what it is, that can take the world on to its agenda. There never will be a time when the world, with all its political, social and economic issues, ceases to be the agenda of the Church. At the same time, the Church can go out to the edges of society, not fearful of being distorted or confused by the world's agenda, but confident and capable of recognizing that God is already there.[20]

2. The core groups (1984) confirmed the Vancouver recommendations:

3. *The Unity of the Church and the Renewal of Human Community*
(a) The study on "The Unity of the Church and the Renewal of Human Community" is designed to continue earlier Faith and Order studies (like the one on "The Unity of the Church and the Unity of Humankind") in a new perspective. After Vancouver we see much clearer its basic and also strategic significance for the orientation of the whole work of the WCC. The study, therefore, will have to reflect on the implications of the understanding of the church and the quest for unity for the renewal of human community as well as on the theological and practical implications which the different endeavours at renewal have for the search for unity. The whole study is to be set into the

perspective of the Triune God's purpose in creation, redemption and fulfilment.

(b) Proposals from Vancouver as well as from the discussion since indicate that for Faith and Order the vision of the church as "mystery" and "sign" of the renewal and unity of humankind should be made a focus of the study and the point of integration for relating this to specific areas of human brokenness and renewal. This ecclesiological task should include the concerns for the common witness of the churches for the renewal of humankind, the challenge posed to and within the churches by different societies, cultures and ideologies, and the church as an inclusive community.

(c) In order to investigate and clarify the *inter-relation between unity and renewal* appropriate contemporary issues have to serve as exemplary cases for such inter-relation. Two such issues are foreseen: (1) movements towards or away from fuller community of women and men in church and society in their inter-relation with the unity of the church; this would also be, in part, a follow-up of the former Community study; (2) the interaction of ideologies, social and economic systems and cultures with issues of power, human rights, justice and peace — and the implications of this interaction for the witness and unity of the church.

(d) A Steering Group (members of the Standing Commission) will guide the work on this study. Cooperation with other sub-units is foreseen, especially in view of the two issues mentioned above (especially with the Commission of the Churches on International Affairs, the Programme to Combat Racism, the Commission on the Churches' Participation in Development, Church and Society, Women). The churches will be involved through a "dialogic" process, which will ensure more than just talking to the churches. A first international consultation on the theme "The Church as Mystery and Prophetic Sign" is foreseen for the end of 1984.

(e) This study will continue and focus in a special way the Faith and Order concern to relate its particular emphasis on the unity of the church to contemporary issues in church and society. It will in this perspective develop further insights from BEM and the reception process of BEM which point in this direction, and it will be implemented in close connection with the apostolic faith study wherever common issues are tackled. The relation to all the Council-wide concerns [mentioned under III 8 above] is obvious.[21]

Conclusion

Unity and renewal are not just two poles, one referring to the church, the other to human community. We have learned in the ecumenical movement that *unity* and *renewal* of the church *go together*, and *only* together as two parallel poles. One is the condition as well as the consequence of the other. For this purpose, the renewal of human community is also related to God's purpose of the unity of all humanity which will find its fulfilment in the new heaven and the new earth which He will bring about. The unity/renewal study has to be seen in close relation to the perspective of God's overall purpose, the revelation of this purpose in history and the orientation of this purpose towards the kingdom, the first-fruits of which are already experienced in the Christian community.

Therefore this study is also related to the two other major ongoing study projects of the Faith and Order Commission, "Towards the Common Expression of the Apostolic Faith Today" and the *reception process* of the Lima document on "Baptism, Eucharist and Ministry" (BEM).

It is obvious from what has been said above that unity and renewal are concerns both for the church and for the human community. Renewal is a condition of unity, and unity is the result of renewal. This should apply both to the church and to human community. It is this unity-renewal dynamic that suggests theological perspectives of the study at the initial stage. This may lead to a reconstruction of theology of the church and human community in a fundamental way.

Our task was to give a historical overview of this. It should be clear from the outset that the concern for the whole of "unity" is not a new idea. In fact it is as old as the ecumenical movement itself. Therefore, these catchwords "unity of the church and renewal of the human community" keep occupying the ecumenical mind. This is well illustrated, for example, by the varied and confused discussions in several consultations and meetings of the WCC. It is true that the ecumenical movement is not quite clear about what it means or should mean to say when it speaks of this study. To put it more precisely, there are at present different approaches to grasp this theme which overlap and counteract each other. It is hoped that new ideas and new ways of studying will help to bring Faith and Order and the whole of the WCC to a clearer and more unified understanding.

But ecumenism, with its multilateral dialogues, is being carried away in a whirlwind of confessional discoveries. Theology is bewildered. Mentally intoxicated with all the analyses and ever-new ideas, it longs for a moment of synthesis. Without admitting it, it is conscious of the danger of confronting different traditions. But Tradition, dogma and history must not be forgotten — or separated — for together they make the unity and constitute the body of Christ which is his church under the guidance and the communion of the Holy Spirit.

NOTES

1. *A Documentary History of the Faith and Order Movement, 1927–1963*, ed. L. Vischer, St Louis, 1963, p.28.
2. J. Moltmann, "What Kind of Unity", in "Lausanne 77: Ffity Years of Faith and Order", *Faith and Order Paper No. 82*, Geneva, WCC, 1977.
3. *Uppsala 68 Speaks*, reports of the sections, Geneva, WCC, 1968, p.17, §20.

4. J. Deschner, Report, "Towards Visible Unity", *Faith and Order Paper No. 113*, Vol. II, Geneva, WCC, 1982, p.189.
5. M. Tanner, *The Unity of the Church and the Renewal of Human Community: an Assessment of the Relationship of Church and Renewal*, report to WCC Sixth Assembly, Vancouver, 1983, p.1.
6. J. Deschner, "The Unity of the Church and the Unity of Mankind", *Faith and Order Paper No. 85*, Geneva, WCC, 1978, p.85.
7. "New Directions in Faith and Order", *Faith and Order Paper No. 50*, Geneva, WCC, 1968, p.7.
8. See now "Faith and Order Louvain 1971", *Faith and Order Paper No. 59*, Geneva, WCC, 1971, pp.175−179.
9. Minutes of the Meeting of Working Committee, Zagorsk 1973, *Faith and Order Paper No. 66*, Geneva, WCC, 1973, pp.43−45.
10. See more in: "And Do Not Hinder Them: an Ecumenical Plea for the Admission of Children to the Eucharist", ed. G. Müller-Fahrenholz, *Faith and Order Paper No. 109*, Geneva, WCC, 1982.
11. Minutes of the Commission on Faith and Order, Accra 1974, *Faith and Order Paper No. 71*, Geneva, WCC, 1974, pp.87−88.
12. "Sharing in One Hope: Bangalore 1978", *Faith and Order Paper No. 92*, Geneva, WCC, 1978, pp.237−238.
13. C. Parvey, *The Community of Women and Men in the Church*, Geneva, WCC, 1983.
14. *Nairobi to Vancouver*, Geneva, WCC, 1983, pp.83−84.
15. See *Racism in Theology, Theology against Racism*, Geneva, WCC, 1975.
16. "Partners in Life: The Handicapped and the Church", ed. G. Müller-Fahrenholz, *Faith and Order Paper No. 89*, Geneva, WCC, 1979.
17. "Church and State: Opening a New Ecumenical Discussion", *Faith and Order Paper No. 85*, Geneva, WCC, 1978.
18. "Baptism, Eucharist, Ministry", *Faith and Order Paper No. 111*, Geneva, WCC, 1982, p.14, §20.
19. "Towards Visible Unity", *Faith and Order Paper No. 113*, Geneva, WCC, 1982, Vol. II, pp.229−230.
20. Cf. *Gathered for Life, op. cit.*, p.50.
21. Central Committee, WCC, Geneva, 1984, Document No. 1.1, Report of the Programme Unit on Faith and Witness.

Appendix 4

THE UNITY OF THE CHURCH AND THE RENEWAL OF HUMAN COMMUNITY: PROGRAMME OUTLINE

I. Mandate for the study

The aim of the Faith and Order Commission "to proclaim the oneness of the Church of Jesus Christ and to call the churches to the visible unity of one faith and one eucharistic fellowship" was never regarded as being a goal in itself. It was always seen in the framework of God's all-encompassing purpose for his church and his world. One aspect of this broader perspective is envisaged in the first of the seven functions of the Commission: "To study such questions of faith, order and worship as bear on this task (c.f. the first sentence above) and to examine such social, cultural, political, racial, and other factors as affect the unity of the church" (By-Laws of the Commission).

The decision of the Faith and Order Commission at Lima in 1982 to undertake the study on "The Unity of the Church and the Renewal of Human Community" as one of its major studies in the period from Lima to 1987 corresponds to and seeks to fulfill the above-mentioned broader perspective of the Faith and Order mandate. The *Vancouver Assembly* of the WCC has affirmed this decision, both specifically through the report of Issue Group II and generally through the many voices which have asked for the establishment of a clearer theological inter-relation between the two priority concerns of the WCC, the quest for the visible unity of the church and the task of common witness and service of Christians and churches for the sake of peace, justice and the integrity of creation in the world. In discussing a draft report on Faith and Order programme priorities for the post-Vancouver period the advisory *Core Groups* at their meeting in January 1984 as well as the WCC *Executive Committee* in February 1984 have welcomed and supported the proposed unity/renewal study-project as of "strategic significance for the orientation of the whole work of the WCC".

The moment, therefore, has come to initiate the implementation of this study by outlining its programme and the first activities related to it.

II. Significance and purpose of the study

The two poles in the formulation of the title of the study — unity and renewal — have been at the centre of the modern ecumenical movement ever since it began at the turn of this century. With the foundation of the WCC these emphases became decisive for the organizational structure and the specific types of activities of the Council. But their location within a common structure has not in itself effectively realized their necessary inter-relation, in theory as well as in practice.

Unity and renewal are not just two poles, one referring to the church, the other related to human community. We have learned in the ecumenical movement that unity *and* renewal of the church go together, one is the condition as well as consequence of the other. And the renewal of human community is also related to God's purpose of the unity of all humanity which will find its fulfilment in the new heaven and the new earth which He will bring about.

In responding to the desire and need for a deepened theological coherence between the concerns for unity and for renewal the study will have its significance in focusing on this necessary inter-relation between unity/renewal and renewal/unity and thereby deepen at the same time theological insights concerning the two poles which constitute this inter-relation.

In studying the relation of the church and its unity to Christian witness and service in areas in the world which are crying out for renewal, aspects of ecclesiology and of the understanding of the unity and renewal of the church are seen in a new light. And in studying Christian witness and service in areas of urgently required renewal in relation to ecclesiology and unity, theological reflection on and concrete Christian commitment in these areas will be strengthened. This concern for unity and renewal should be held closely together in the perspective of God's overall purpose, the revelation of this purpose in history and the orientation of this purpose towards the kingdom, the first-fruits of which are already experienced in the Christian community.

In this way the study would not only have a chance to render a significant contribution by deepening and broadening ecclesiological reflection and ecumenical convergence in Faith and Order and by assisting in the theological evaluation of specific conditions and challenges in our world and in the shaping of Christian responses to them. The study would also have the chance of affirming and contributing to the unity within the one God-given comprehensive mandate of unity and renewal in the church and the world — and for facing these mandates in a theologically consistent manner within the World Council of Churches. Herein consists indeed the "strategical significance" of the study, and this not only in view of the WCC, but also in terms of a fundamental task which is before all churches.

III. Unity/renewal in the context of Faith and Order work

The study on the unity of the church and the renewal of human community is not a completely new Faith and Order endeavour. It will continue earlier perspectives and studies and complement ongoing studies. Its continuity with Faith and Order work in the past is obvious. Already the founders of the Faith and Order movement envisaged the work for the unity of Christ's church as a necessary presupposition for a contribution to the need of a common witness and service of Christians and churches. Such common witness and service was called for after the First World War by a world divided by nationalistic and ideological power structures and rich and poor nations and by humankind burdened with many social, political and economic problems and yearning for the essential elements — both material and spiritual — for true human life.

Faith and Order focused its attention on the doctrinal issues of disunity and unity. But it did not lose sight of the broader perspective of its founders. This was taken up in the study on *God in Nature and History* and even more explicitly, after Bristol 1968, in the study on *The Unity of the Church and the Unity of Humankind*. Louvain 1971 and Accra 1974 put major emphasis on this study which, even though it did not lead to a formulated result, yielded many important insights presented in several publications.

In 1975 and 1976 two consultations were held with the Programme to Combat Racism and Bossey respectively. These led to reports on *Racism in Theology, Theology Against Racism* and *Church and State*. The inclusiveness of the church and its unity in terms of disabled persons was developed in the 1978 Faith and Order book on *Partners in Life*.

Bangalore 1978 with its *Account of Hope* rendered another important contribution to the theme of unity, common confession and renewal of life and community in this world. And this concern was reflected and developed in yet another study between Nairobi and Vancouver, in the study project on *The Community of Women and Men in the Church*.

It is obvious, therefore, that the new study will be set in the wider framework of the search for conciliar fellowship and will build on and integrate the insights of these and other Faith and Order studies from the past. But it will also be related to the two other ongoing major Faith and Order programmes. The convergence document on *Baptism, Eucharist and Ministry* indicates at several places its implications for Christian obedience in the world. The study on *Towards the Common Expression of the Apostolic Faith Today* has clearly to cope with those situations and conditions in our world which challenge and belong to the context of confessing the apostolic faith together in this time of history. The unity/renewal study will both make use of results of these two studies and in turn contribute to them through its own specific content focus and methodology.

IV. Implementation of the study

The implementation of the study on "The Unity of the Church and the Renewal of Human Community" may be analyzed under the following heads, recognizing that particular formulations will have to be tested within the study process.

1. *Orientation and internal structure*

The mandate of Faith and Order requires ecclesiology to be a central feature of our treatment of the unity of the church and the renewal of human community. To achieve this aim ecclesiology, like every other branch of theology, must be firmly located within the total context of the nature, activity and purpose of God.

As Christians we believe that God is both holy and loving, and will in the end achieve his purposes. This faith is reflected in the biblical message of the 'kingdom of God", that divine reality which was definitively expressed in the life, death and resurrection of Jesus. This theological approach is important and helpful for setting the unity of the church and the renewal of human community within a common perspective. The source of unity, community and new life, both for a sinful world and for a church of sinful men and women, in fact, the source of ultimate hope for all God's creatures, is this sovereign rule of God as revealed in Christ Jesus, crucified and risen. The quest for visible unity in the church, and for the renewal of that human community to which the church belongs, therefore stands always under the righteous judgment and redeeming grace of the Triune God. It is a quest never to be fully or permanently achieved in time, but conducted with trust in him for eschatological fulfilment.

The church, when open to the Spirit of God, can have the experience of being constantly renewed, and of moving towards a unity in obedient freedom which is Christ's own gift, will and prayer. This obedience demands that within the world the church offer true worship on behalf of humankind, and work for and exemplify renewal into Christ's kind of human living. As such it is "mystery", "sacrament", "sign", "instrument", "foretaste", and "pledge" of God's salvation through Christ for the world, even if it is all these things imperfectly because of the human sinfulness of its members. Furthermore, within the world there are people whose convictions are different from those of the Christian, but who also struggle for renewal of human community in ways with which the church is called by the Spirit of God to work in active partnership.

2. *Materials for the task*

The study will gather, summarize, evaluate, and draw implications from:

(a) material in which reflection on ecclesiology and the ecumenical quest for visible unity is brought to bear on specific areas of renewal in church and world; and

(b) material in which thinking and action in specific areas of renewal in church and world are brought to bear on ecclesiology and the ecumenical quest for visible unity.

Some of this material will need to be especially commissioned, but much will be drawn from the documentation of relevant experiences and insights already available in other Faith and Order projects, in the WCC as a whole, and other theological and secular studies.

It will be important to bring out the significance of the unity/renewal project within an already ongoing process of studying renewal and growth in unity and community. The project should also be seen as a focus and reference point for concrete theological/socio-ethical concerns and specific issues faced by Christians and churches living out their being within the contemporary world and not in a false detachment from it.

3. *Issues of human brokenness and human renewal*

It would be neither practicable nor profitable for the study to attempt to deal with all the aspects of any particular area of human renewal or human brokenness. Instead, as already indicated, it will concentrate on drawing out the implications of such instances for the nature and unity of the church, and for various aspects of its life, such as sacraments, ministry and mission.

It will also be important for the study to recognize and examine brokenness and renewal within the church (even within the WCC) as well as in the world. In so doing it should also focus not merely on issues of these kinds within the church on the one hand and in the world on the other.

It will also be essential to examine:

(1) cases where failures in the world create disunity and hinder renewal in the church, and where similar failures in the church adversely affect renewal and community in the world (for instance, where a local partnership or congregation has been shaped without its contributing to the healing of human dividedness of class or race within and around the partner churches); and

(2) cases where growth in unity/community in church or world assist similar developments in the other. This is not a triumphalist study of the church in its unity and the world in its brokenness but a study of the church in its need to overcome human sinfulness and division in its members and of places in the world where creative renewal has happened and challenges the church.

Practical limitations clearly demand that the study should focus on significant examples rather than attempt a comprehensive survey. We therefore propose to concentrate on two areas:

(a) movements towards or away from fuller community of women and men;

(b) the interaction of ideologies, social and economic systems and cultures with issues of power, human rights, justice and peace.

4. *Method of theological reflection*

This study (1) will include a strong biblical emphasis, (2) will take into account the tradition and history of doctrine and theological thinking on the subject, (3) will draw on "secular" competence in issues of brokenness and renewal, and (4) will consider new theological approaches to these issues and theological reflections implied in actions related to these issues of unity and renewal. This study will therefore require an *integrated* theological approach.

This question of theological style of work is not well expressed by contrasting deductive and inductive approaches. To reverse the usual form of two examples often contrasted in this manner, the formulation of the Creeds was "inductive" in that it drew on the experience of salvation found in Christ and the theology of liberation is "deductive" in that it does not only draw upon praxis but upon praxis seen in the light of God's self-revelation in Christ.

A better way of describing the methodological issue must therefore be developed as part of the unity/renewal study process but a preliminary account of it might be: The conviction that the Christian Tradition expresses revealed truth includes the conviction that the Tradition will pass the test of relevance in every context: "I will prove to you, then, that the Son of Man has authority on earth to forgive sins". So he said to the paralyzed man, "Get up, pick up your bed, and go home!" (Matt. 9: 6).

Equally, the claim to effective expression of God's saving purpose in each context, the prophetic claim that God is at work here and now, must be tested by the normative self-revelation of God in Christ: "Do not believe all who claim to have the Spirit, but test them to find out if the spirit they have comes from God" (I John 4: 1).

This dual process of testing is at the heart of an approach appropriate to this study of unity and renewal.

V. Working methods for the study

1. *Research*

The research for this study will include (1) the collation of the previous Faith and Order and WCC studies which are relevant, especially "Giving Account of the Hope Within Us" and "The Community of Women and

Men in Church and Society", and (2) work on new themes which will contribute to our ecclesiological perspectives. A bibliography of the literature on unity and renewal is also required. The staff as well as willing persons and institutions will be valuable partners in this research.

2. *International consultations*

International consultations, involving members of the Steering Committee and other representatives of various traditions and perspectives, are necessary for this study. Such meetings, held in different parts of the world, will contribute competence, insight, and experience from many different backgrounds and contexts. These consultations will focus on ecclesiology from the essential inter-relation between unity and renewal. Four or five consultations are anticipated for this study between 1984 and the World Conference on Faith and Order.

3. *Contact with people in particular local situations of brokenness and/or renewal*

Among the earlier WCC project materials to be studied those on "Giving Account of the Hope Within Us" and "The Community of Women and Men in the Church" particularly depended for their effectiveness on the participation of local groups of Christians who spoke of the pains and hopes of their situations. Similar participation will be vital for this study of unity and renewal.

The relatively brief time-line precludes an operation as widespread as that of the earlier studies (although their results and reports can be helpful). Rather a small number of groups that have continued and grown from the earlier studies or are engaged in similar sharing of experience can and must be involved in the study process. Reports of their reflections and the participation of members of these groups in the planned international consultations shall be important. To involve such groups may well require a "translation" of the terms and focus of the study in order to make clear its relevance for their direct concerns, and to convey clearly the specific questions addressed to a local group.

Each member of the Steering Group, as far as possible, will assume responsibility for establishing contact with one such local group, either through existing relationships or by assignment.

4. *Involvement of member churches and other ecumenical bodies*

The study will involve the participation of the member churches, even to the point of some aspect of "reception" of unity and renewal in their ecumenical vision and action.

The project will also benefit from collaboration with councils of churches, church union conversations, ecumenical institutes, theological seminaries, local communities, and Christian World Communions. Such collaboration will take different forms, e.g., the provision of relevant materials, participation in and contribution to specific aspects of the unity/renewal study, and reactions to the preliminary results which emerge from the study.

5. Cooperation with other sub-units in the WCC

The pursuit of the unity/renewal study will take place in various forms of partnership with those units and sub-units in the WCC which are especially concerned with these themes. For example, in consideration of the general theme of unity and renewal we anticipate a helpful dialogue with Unit II and the Commission on World Mission and Evangelism. Certain special issues bring us together: (a) justice and peace with the Churches' Commission on International Affairs (CCIA), the Programme to Combat Racism (PCR), the Churches' Commission for Participation in Development (CCPD), and the Commission on Inter-Church Aid, Refugee, and World Service (CICARWS), and Church and Society; (b) "Community of Women and Men" with the Sub-unit on Women; (c) the interaction of ideologies, social and economic systems, and cultures with issues of power, human rights, justice and peace, with Unit II, with the sub-unit on Church and Society, and Dialogue with Other Living Faiths, in the light of its past work on ideologies. Such conversation and collaboration could include a variety of relations, e.g., their involvement in the consultations, joint staff conversations on particular themes related to unity/renewal, sharing of resources, drawing on the results of studies and work done by these units and sub-units.

6. In view of the importance of this study for the whole ecumenical movement, Faith and Order must aim for as broad a participation as possible, and will seek to communicate effectively this study and its learnings. The types of contact listed in V, 3 – 5, point to the critical inter-relationship between participation and communication, between research and sharing.

VI. Steps in our time-table

1. The first and immediate step in implementing the study on the "Unity of the Church and the Renewal of Human Community" would include:
   (a) Research work aimed at collecting, summarizing and evaluating the work already done in the area of unity and renewal. It should identify those aspects and elements which are of specific importance for the new phase of this study. Undoubtedly this work would also help to clarify further the task and purpose of the study.
   (b) Communication with the churches as well as contact with local groups, study centres, theological seminaries, etc. with a view to their participation in the study.

  (c) Conversations with other units and sub-units in the WCC with a
view to establishing ways of collaboration with them on specific
aspects of the study.

2. The second step will be the preparation and convening of four or
possibly five small international consultations, in the following pattern
(see "Proposed Consultations" below for full description of each
consultation):

  (1) *First consultation*: "The church as mystery and prophetic sign", 3 –
10 January 1985 (Paris).

  (2) *Second consultation*: "Visible unity, renewal and community: a
study from the perspective of the community of women and men
in church and society", 25 September – 2 October 1985
(USSR/Roumania).

  (3) *Third consultation*: "The interaction of ideologies, social systems
and cultures with issues of justice and peace: its implications for the
churches in their quest for visible unity and renewal, for the
renewal of human community, and for the relationship between
them", 18 June – 25 June 1986 (Argentina/Jamaica/
Indonesia/Thailand).

  (4) *Fourth consultation*: To prepare draft of a final report for the unity
and renewal study. While the temptation will be to consider the
consultations as focused on unity *or* renewal, each consultation
shall deal with learnings for our understanding of the church from
the point of view of unity *and* renewal. 16 – 23 September 1987
(Cambridge, England).

3. The third step involves meetings of the Plenary and Standing
Commissions as follows:

  (1) *Plenary Commission* (13 – 26 August 1985, Norway): Progress
report on the study.

    The Plenary Commission in August 1985 should take account of
the work done so far, evaluate the results of research and
consultations, contribute further experiences and theological insights from different contexts, produce a preliminary report with
results so far achieved and an outline for continuing the study. The
Plenary Commission would give greater visibility to the study and
thereby stimulate interest and collaboration in the WCC con-
stituency and beyond.

  (2) *Standing Commission* (1986): Progress report on the study.

4. The fourth step involves the Faith and Order World Conference
(1988/1989): The study on the unity of the church and the renewal of
human community will be one of the major themes of the World
Conference.

5. The fifth step involves a statement to the VIIth Assembly of the WCC.

Proposed Consultations

Proposal for the first consultation on 4he unity of the church and the renewal of human community

In our planning we were guided by the following statement from Vancouver:

> It is the implication of such Church unity for the destiny of the human community — an implication clearly contained in earlier statements but not so clearly expressed — which has impressed this Vancouver Assembly. Peace and justice, on the one hand, baptism, eucharist and ministry, on the other, have claimed our attention. They belong together. Indeed the aspect of Christian unity which has been most striking to us here in Vancouver is that of a *eucharistic vision.* Christ — the life of the world — unites heaven and earth, God and world, spiritual and secular. His body and blood, given us in the elements of bread and wine, integrate liturgy and diaconate, proclamation and acts of healing. "The remembrance of Christ is the very content of the preached word as it is of the eucharistic meal, each reinforces the other. The celebration of the eucharist properly includes the proclamation of the word" (BEM, Eucharist, 12). Our eucharistic vision thus encompasses the whole reality of Christian worship, life and witness, and tends — when truly discovered — to shed new lights on Christian unity in its full richness of diversity. It also sharpens the pain of our present division at the table of the Lord; but in bringing forth the organic unity of Christian commitment and of its unique source in the incarnate self-sacrifice of Christ, the *eucharistic vision* provides us with new and inspiring guidance on our journey towards a full and credible realization of our given unity.[1]

and by this specific proposal:

> [that] the Faith and Order Commission make a theological exploration of the Church as "sign" a central part of its programme on the Unity of the Church and the Renewal of Human Community . . This recommendation implies our conviction that the Church is called to be a prophetic "sign", a prophetic community through which and by which the transformation of the world can take place. It is only a church, which goes out from its eucharistic centre, strengthened by word and sacrament and thus strengthened in its own identity, resolved to become what it is, that can take the world on to its agenda. There never will be a time when the world, with all its political, social and economic issues, ceases to be the agenda of the Church. At the same time, the Church can go out to the edges of society, not fearful of being distorted or confused by the world's agenda but confident and capable of recognizing that God is already there.[2]

I. Theme

The church as mystery and prophetic sign.

II. Focus

An ecclesiological study of the unity and renewal of the church in relation to the unity and renewal of human community.

III. Method

1. Presentations

(1) *The church and the world in light of the kingdom of God*

A biblical and theological exploration of the teaching concerning the kingdom of God in light of the church's mission in the world. This would use insights and perhaps a presenter involved in the Melbourne conference on evangelism. In any case he or she would be a biblical scholar or theologian sensitive both to Christian tradition *and* the contemporary world.

(2) *The church as a sacramental vision and challenge of Christian witness*

The theme of the church as mystery (*mysterion*) in relation to the mission of the church in the world (including a study of this theme in the tradition of the church). This would be presented by an Orthodox theologian, with a *response* given by a representative of another tradition.

(3) *The church as prophetic sign*

The mission of the church as grounded in the dynamics of the Holy Spirit and related to the hope of a "new creation". This would also address the church as a prophetic challenge to the world — at the same time being *itself* challenged by the "signs of the times" being experienced in contemporary life. The presentation would be given by a Protestant theologian, with a *response* by a representative of another tradition.

(4) *The church as eucharistic community and the renewal of human community*

The eucharistic nature of the church as a basis for its relation to the world, especially in relation to the Vancouver texts quoted above.

This would be presented by a Roman Catholic theologian, with a *response* by a representative of another tradition.

2. Extended discussion

A major portion of time shall be given to the discussion of papers and responses to them, and of the insights of the participants. In this sense a "testing" of the papers will be made in the light of the experience of those present and of the plans and early results of the apostolic faith study (especially for 1(2) and (3) and the responses to BEM (especially for 1(4)). This will be an essential part of the consultation.

3. Summary and synthesis

A theologian shall be invited to give a response to the consultation as a whole. He or she would have participated in the planning for the conference and have received the major papers beforehand, and would participate in the extended discussion. This would have to be a "sensitive listener" who would then creatively summarize and synthesize the insights gained up to that point. This would then lead to a common document giving the results of the conference and serving as the basis for further work in Faith and Order.

IV. Participants

There shall be 20 participants, including the following elements:

1) as many members of the Steering Committee as possible;
2) presenters of major papers (some of whom may be drawn from the Steering Committee itself);
3) representatives from different traditions and constituencies, with special efforts made to involve second and third world participants, and also participants in the BEM process;
4) a representative of the WCC Commission on World Mission and Evangelism (Programme Unit I).

V. Remarks

1. Special effort must be made to emphasize the relation of the themes of unity and renewal.

2. Special effort should be made to include, and use creatively, the experiences and insights of previous Faith and Order and other WCC studies, including the conferences at Salamanca, Uppsala and Melbourne.

VI. Communication of results

1. Publication of major papers and the lines of thought in the extended discussion. Additional documentation would include relevant resolutions from Faith and Order meetings and assembly meetings, relevant additional ecclesiological papers, etc.

2. Special attention shall be given to two additional factors, in collaboration with the Communication Department of the WCC:

a) preparation of a concise and readable volume which will effectively communicate the insights of the consultation to a broad public both inside and outside the churches;
b) creative and effective use of new audiovisual methods in communicating the results of the consultation: this might include videotapes, audio cassettes, etc.

VII. Place and time

The consultation is tentatively scheduled for 3—10 January 1985, at a conference centre near Paris.

VIII. Finances
The expenses of the consultation are already approved from the general
Faith and Order budget.

Proposal for the second consultation on unity of the church and the renewal of human community

I. Theme

Visible unity, renewal and community: a study from the perspective of
the community of women and men in church and society.

II. Focus

The results of the Community study which were gathered at the
Sheffield conference of 1981 have been widely disseminated, are being
considered in various settings and have already been the subject of
responses from churches. The aim of this consultation is not a general
evaluation or follow-up of Sheffield but a specific reflection in the light of
the Sheffield conference and responses to it on the relation between
renewal in the relationships and roles of women and men and the visible
unity of the church.

Three case studies on ecclesiological implications of the relations of
women and men will be presented in such a way as to bring out:
a) the specificity of each situation;
b) the effect on the unity and renewal of the church: internally, for that
   church and/or its Christian World Communion; externally, in its
   degree of communion with other churches; in witness and service,
   through its capacity to bring healing to human brokenness and to
   draw from the springs of human renewal.
The studies could make such analyses by examining: (a) changing male
and female roles; (b) the ministries of women and men in the church;
(c) the appropriation in each church of the witness of scripture and
Tradition.
The studies could focus on:
1) a "high feminist consciousness" situation in which women actively
   seek new roles;
2) a traditional culture in which women and men live within familiar
   cultural roles;
3) an Orthodox situation, explaining the particular positive resources of
   that tradition to which Orthodox churches have testified in responding to Sheffield.

The aim of the study in each case is that from such description and analysis the presenter should draw out implications for the understanding of the church, particularly of images and models of the church (e.g. in relation to the role of the Mother of God in the church, the new humanity in Christ, the church as pilgrim people on the way to renewal).

III. Participants

Twenty participants, ten women and ten men, representing a variety of Christian traditions, including at least 50 per cent who were involved in the Community study. Names for participants and presenters of case studies to be suggested to staff by members of the Steering Committee.

Criteria would include having some people, involved in the Community study, who have not pursued its implications for unity and some people, involved in the quest for unity, who have not pursued the implications for this quest of the Community study.

IV. Time and place

It would be very valuable to meet in the context of a mixed religious community or of a team of women and men working in a shared renewal project (e.g. monasteries, nunneries, parishes, etc.). The conference is tentatively scheduled for 25 September – 2 October 1985 (Prague, Czechoslovakia). ·

V. Method and pattern

1. Circulation as preparatory material of developments from the Community study and relevant responses to BEM.

2. Collection of information relating to the series of questions posed in the Klingenthal consultation of 1979.[3]

3. Discussion of the case studies in groups crossing the situations (1), (2) and (3) pattern to see the possibilities and limitations of tolerable and desirable diversity within unity, and ways of handling what seem to be intolerable diversities.

4. Daily opening worship leading to Bible study groups on the theme of renewing community (i.e. groups of participants using pre-circulated material on selected Bible passages, e.g. Ephesians, chapter 5).

Pattern: Wednesday: arrival

Thursday, Friday, Saturday: one case study each day with groups

Sunday: worship visits and some free time

Monday, Tuesday: drafting of report and implications for further "unity and renewal" process

Wednesday: departure

(This pattern is suggested rather than Saturday arrival with a Sunday as first full day for the group.)

Draft outline for the third consultation project on unity of the church and renewal of human community

I. Theme

The interaction of ideologies, social systems and cultures with issues of justice and peace: its implications for the churches in their quest for visible unity and renewal, for the renewal of human community, and for the relationship between them.

II. Aims and objectives

1. This is to a significant extent a new approach to the ecclesiological question, though one increasingly urged upon us by the realities of life today. It is important to stress, therefore, that this consultation is concerned to study ideological, social and cultural problems in their relation to issues of justice and peace not in order to explore the Christian mind on these problems in themselves but to investigate their effects on unity and renewal in church and world, and what lessons can be drawn from these experiences about the nature of church unity and renewal and the bearing which this has on the renewal of human community. In short, *this is strictly an ecclesiological study*; it is only the materials which are somewhat unusual. This basic fact has affected every aspect of the proposals which follow, including the design of the case studies suggested, and the nature of the participation.

2. It is proposed to set up three case studies on precisely defined topics. The general theme is so vast, and its ramifications in the world today so complex that there can be no question of a comprehensive approach. The three specific topics suggested have been chosen because in each of them, in different ways, the interaction which is our theme is currently involving the churches, with powerful effects on their own unity and renewal, now for good now for ill, and on their part in the quest for renewal of human community. Each should, therefore, evoke important insights for ecclesiology which will stimulate creative reflection in other contexts. The three case studies are as follows.

a) *Northern Ireland and the inheritance of history*: A classic example of a situation where both human community and the churches experience brokenness and stand in need of renewal because of a combination of ideological, social and cultural, as well as theological factors. Churches are divided and their life inhibited both within and between themselves, and also in their relationship with the world in which they are tragically involved. The movement towards visible unity and renewal in the churches is therefore called in question at fundamental levels, and subjected to severe strains. Nevertheless there is also creative progress in this movement, and new forms of self-understanding and unity are emerging both among Christians and in society at large.

b) *Ethnicity, churches and political power in the USA*: This topic has already been extensively studied, but not from the point of view of its lessons for ecclesiology. There are therefore rich materials and expertise available which have nevertheless much that is as yet unexplored to offer for our central concern. Its value is also that it presents something of a paradigm case in which the elements of race and class, justice and political power are all involved. The determination of the black churches to secure and exercise political power in the quest to renew the human community with greater justice is a programme which is divisive within white churches and also divides white churches from black. This in turn intensifies the trend towards churches which are almost exclusively racial in composition. All this raises profound and urgent ecclesiological issues which have real relevance also for the different but related situations in Latin America, Britain, and Southern Africa.

c) *East-West armed confrontation and the Pacific peoples*: The subject of the "arms race" between East and West, especially in the nuclear field, and of the search for peace with justice in an armed world, is immense and highly technical. Yet it raises acute questions for church unity and renewal and for its involvement with renewal of human community.

The churches have joined worldwide in the quest for peace in many different ways. This has put severe strains on visible unity within churches, and also between churches which find themselves in opposing ideological and political camps. As a worldwide fellowship the churches ought to be able to work powerfully for renewal of human community in the field of peace, but their unity in this task is seemingly broken by the greater power of ideologies, cultures and social systems — factors which also lie at the root of profound differences between Christians on the nature of true peace in God's plan for the world. Hard questions are also raised about the place of discipleship, the obedient following of Christ, in the essential nature and existence of the church.

We suggest that these issues should be examined in the context of one specific case study: the plight of the Pacific peoples in the nuclear weapons age. This particular case has other features which give it special significance. It involves major questions of justice, since many of the Pacific peoples are poor and powerless by global standards. Also many are almost wholly Christian societies, and the local churches are deeply integrated into their culture and social systems, and are of major importance for the renewal of human community there. In an environment threatened by super-power confrontation their situation poses critical questions about the nature of their visible unity in the worldwide fellowship of churches and communions whose other members are involved in and divided by the very forces which threaten them, and the shared responsibility of all for renewal in church and world.

III. Participants

1. For each case study three members with relevant expertise from the part of the world concerned, and three theological participants, whose task it will be to concentrate the study on the ecclesiological implications.

2. As many Steering Committee members as possible, recognizing that some at least of the nine theological participants in the case studies will be drawn from this group.

3. Representatives from various sub-units of the WCC as appropriate.

IV. Method

1. The case studies should be designed well in advance, in cooperation with the participants, to ensure that the questions addressed will be relevant to the central ecclesiological concern of the consultation.

2. On all three subjects treated in the case studies there is a great deal of material already available, and bibliographies and summaries of especially relevant items would be of great help to those taking part.

3. It will be important for all participants to discuss the subject matter with other qualified persons before the consultation, to ensure that as wide a range of informed opinion as possible is drawn upon.

4. Because this is to a significant extent a new approach in WCC work to the ecclesiological question, it will be necessary to devote a considerable proportion of the available time analyzing and drawing together the ecclesiological implications. Also the prominence of experiential elements in the material means that special emphasis must be given to theological reflection, and the participating theologians afforded every opportunity to contribute to this. All this, however, also demands of these theological participants that they familiarize themselves with the case material before arriving, and that papers, especially those of an informational character, be distributed well in advance.

V. Date

19–26 November 1986 (6 working days)

VI. Place

To be chosen from the following: Thailand, Indonesia, Singapore.

VII. Finance

Faith and Order budget, plus funds specially designated for the unity and renewal budget.

VIII. Communication

A report which should summarize the results of the case studies, and provide extended theological reflection, aimed at integrating new insights on the nature, purpose, visible unity and renewal of the church, and its mutual relation with the renewal of human community, into those gained from earlier consultations.

NOTES

1. *Gathered for Life*, report of the Sixth Assembly of the WCC, Vancouver 1983, ed. David Gill, Geneva, WCC, and Grand Rapids, Wm. B. Eerdmans, 1983, pp. 44–45.
2. *Ibid.*, p. 50.
3. "The Ordination of Women in Ecumenical Perspective", *Faith and Order Paper No. 105*, Geneva, WCC, 1980.

Appendix 5

THE UNITY OF THE SPIRIT: OPENING MEDITATION

John Deschner

" . . . the unity of the Spirit in the bond of peace . . . . the one hope which belongs to our call" (Eph. 4: 3 — 4).

I

Could there be a better text for beginning our work?

"The unity of the Spirit": precisely that koinonia which our consultation on the Third Article aims to explore.

"The bond of peace": *eirene, shalom,* a word for the renewed human community of which the body of Christ is the mysterious "bond" and sign.

And "the one hope which belongs to our call": the promise of the kingdom which makes both koinonia and peace real and effective powers of renewal here and now.

"The unity of the Spirit of the bond of peace . . . the one hope."

But before we meditate on this marvellous text, we need to remember who we are as we gather here.

I confess that I come to this meeting — and perhaps more than one of you does also — with an almost overwhelming sense of the magnitude of our task . . . that is, if one takes it seriously. The language of Nicea made understandable in our world? An answer to the issue of church unity and human community which has run like a chasm through every one of the modern ecumenical assemblies? And lurking behind both the question: Is Faith and Order actually relevant any more?

•Prof. John Deschner (United Methodist Church), Lehman Professor of Christian Doctrine, Perkins School of Theology, USA. Moderator of the Faith and Order Commission.

And then there are the deadlines which we face! The need to produce material of real substance — the basic substance, in fact — for the Plenary Commission next August in Stavanger. And beyond that the shortening years before the world conference in 1988 or 1989, when we shall ask the churches to sit down together around precisely the themes we are trying to formulate here, and with new insight, derived in part from our work, to examine their commitments to the visible unity of Christ's church.

And beyond all official pressures, there are the human difficulties in meetings such as this. All of us are deeply involved in other things. We have sacrificed costly time to come here and are all in one way or another a little impatient. As we look around, we rejoice at familiar faces here and there, but we also sigh a little over the debates to come. A puzzling and humbling ecumenical experience is about to take place: namely the realization that each one of us could probably sit down right now and write a better document, in our own eyes certainly and possibly in the eyes of our churches as well, than the ones we shall struggle to write together. Simply on the personal level, then, much of that patience and mutual forbearance of which Ephesians speaks will be needed. Something like a miracle is going to have to occur here if our work is to be worthy, as the apostle asks, of the calling to which we have been called.

II

And yet, we have come to these consultations, and fundamentally, I think, because we have been moved by our text's vision of a "mystery", to use its word, more powerful by far than the things we hear about in the evening newscasts: a mystery which it calls "the unity of the Spirit in the bond of peace . . . . the one hope which belongs to our call".

1. "*The bond of peace*": "Peace on earth" — so ran the first Christian proclamation, and there is no better word for the heart of the matter. Where there is estrangement and brokenness, there the cross of Jesus Christ stands making peace. Not simply among believers, but among human beings. And not simply among humans, but among all creatures. And not simply bringing conflict to an end, but recreating and renewing creaturely goodness. And not simply as a message of peace, but as a presence in efficacious "signs" of peace: signs such as those which our epistle mentions — the body of Christ with its baptism, and everyday relationships between man and woman, parent and child, slave and master which participate in and manifest that body. Peace has "bonds", signs, sinews, arteries and veins which nourish healing and growth.

We know this. We remember it. But we need to hear it again and more deeply. "He is our peace." He came making peace (2 : 11ff.), and creating the growing, increasingly visible body as the effective sign of that peace.

Our work on the church as "sign" is a quest for this bond of peace as the fundamental level of ecumenical reality.

Is there not guidance for us here? Our task is not simply to speak of *shalom* for human community, but of the *bond* of peace: the body of Christ's real presence as the effective sign of peace on earth; and note: as Christ's body it is a sign of God's judgment as well as God's hope. The task, then, of our renewal consultation is *ecclesiology* — an ecclesiology which means real hope for human community.

2. *"The unity of the Spirit"*: Our apostle knows that "in" the bond of peace there is included "the unity of the Spirit". What does he mean?

He means communion: Christian koinonia, the reason why he can address this whole letter to "you" in the plural. Communion means the Spirit making us members of Christ's body, members of the household of God, and therefore members one of another (2 : 19; 4 : 15). Communion means the spirit of wisdom and revelation in which we together can know the mystery of God's purpose to unite all things in Christ (1 : 10). Communion means knowing the power of this knowledge to create love and fellowship (1 : 19). Communion means seeing the deepest human conflict he knows — between Jew and Gentile — in the process of being healed (2 : 11ff.). The unity of the Spirit means mutually receiving the gifts which equip the saints for ministry and build up the body of Christ (4 : 12). It means receiving power to discern divisive winds of doctrine and to perceive the truth which can upbuild koinonia (4 : 14f.). The unity of the Spirit also means quite humble things, very near to our actual human need: being empowered to speak the truth in love (4 : 15); being empowered, as persons and as churches, to submit ourselves to one another out of reverence for Christ (5 : 21); being empowered to bear with one another in love (4 : 2), and simply having the power to be kind to one another, as God is kind to us (4 : 32).

This theme — the koinonia of the Spirit — is a kind of hidden treasure for our Third Article consultation. It has been increasingly remarked that at decisive points in the BEM documents, it is the epiclesis and the theme of the church's communion which opens doors to convergence. Just as the Spirit is not an addendum to the Creed, so the unity of the Spirit is not incidental but constitutive for the Third Article. And one of our large opportunities here is to show how true this is.

3. *"The one hope which belongs to our call"*: It is *one* hope which we share in the unity of the Spirit, not two: not one for ultimate things and another for the here and now, and especially not one hope for the church and another for human community, but one coming kingdom of judgment and mercy for all as the promise of the Father from whom every family in heaven and earth is named. *Therefore* it is hope not simply for church unity, but for the renewal of the man-woman relationship, the parent-child relationship, the relationships of the workplace. What Christ's body

signifies and the koinonia of the Spirit actualizes is a love of God whose breadth and length and height and depth surpasses everything our documents yet know how to say about hope for the human community.

And it is *real* hope, binding together the ultimate and the provisional. Therefore it generates courage and endurance, not only for the arduous tasks of reconciliation and liberation, but also for our ecumenical work in these consultations. It leads us to persist in patiently seeking out the quite modest, even provisional steps of convergence beyond the deadlocks of our debates. "Hope does not disappoint us," says Paul in Romans (5 : 5), and that can be true even here in Chantilly. In one hope, we face:

— Not just the dilemmas of pluralism, but discovering fruitful diversity in unity.
— Not just a sign pointing to unity, but an effective sign generating now what it points to.
— Not just a future conciliar event, but conciliar fellowship, koinonia, already beginning to work and becoming fruitful among us here and now.
— Not an endless repetition of false alternatives, but reciprocity, dialectic, growth towards the fullness of Christian truth.
— Not deadlock, but morale for convergence that is rooted and grounded in God's promise.

We know already from the first responses to BEM that we need to speak more clearly about precisely the realities of our text. When some see our work as too catholic, we can hope to speak more clearly about the unity, the koinonia of the Spirit. When some see our work as too protestant, we can hope to speak more clearly about the body of Christ as the bond and effective sign of peace. And when some, especially in the third world, see our work as too irrelevant to the actual world of injustice and oppression, we can hope to speak much more clearly about the kingdom, the one hope for both church and human community.

May God show us how to lead here in Chantilly a life worthy of the calling to which we have been called, with all humility and gentleness, with patience, bearing with one another in love, eager to maintain the unity of the Spirit in the bond of peace . . . just as we are called to the one hope that belongs to our call. Amen.

Appendix 6

LIST OF PARTICIPANTS

The Rt Rev. John BAKER (Church of England)
South Canonry, 71 The Close, Salisbury SP1 2ER, England

Dr George BEBAWI (Coptic Orthodox Church)
William Paton Fellow, Selly Oak Colleges, Bristol Road, Selly Oak, Birmingham B29, England

The Rev. Prof. Edouard BONE (Roman Catholic Church)
6 rue André Fauchille, 1150 Brussels, Belgium

The Rt Rev. Manas BUTHELEZI (Evangelical Lutheran Church in South Africa)
Central Diocese, P.O. Box 32413, Braamfontein 2017, South Africa

The Rev. Dr Alkiviadis CALIVAS (Greek Orthodox Archdiocese of North and South America)
Holy Cross Greek Orthodox School of Theology, 50 Goddard Avenue, Brookline, MA 02146, USA

The Rev. Prof. Nikolai CHIVAROV (Bulgarian Orthodox Church)
4 Oborishte Str, 1090 Sofia, Bulgaria

Rev. Nancy COCKS (Presbyterian Church in Canada)
No. 204, 7162/133 A Street, Surrey, BC V3W 7Z9, Canada

The Rev. Martin CRESSEY (United Reformed Church)
The Principal's Lodge, Westminster College, Madingley Road, Cambridge CB3 0AB, England

Sr CRISTELLE (Communauté des Diaconesses)
10 rue Porte de Buc, 78000 Versailles, France

The Rev. Dr Paul A. CROW Jr (Christian Church (Disciples of Christ))
P.O. Box 1986, Indianapolis, IN 46206, USA

Mrs Mirana DIAMBAYE (Eglise protestante du Christ-Roi)
B.P. 608, Bangui, Central African Republic

Prof. André DUMAS (Reformed Church of France)
45 rue de Sèvres, 75006 Paris, France

Sr EVANGELINE (Communauté des Diaconesses)
10 rue Porte de Buc, 78000 Versailles, France

Dr Padmasini J. GALLUP (Church of South India)
The Parsonage, Church of Divine Patience, Railway Colony, Madurai 625.100 Takunada, India

The Rev. Canon John HIND (Church of England)
The Theological College, Chichester, West Sussex PO19 3ES, England

Prof. Dr L. A. HOEDEMAKER (Netherlands Reformed Church)
Wassenberghstraat 58, 9718 LN Groningen, Holland

The Rev. Prof. Hervé LEGRAND (Roman Catholic Church)
Couvent St. Jacques, 20 rue des Tanneries, 75013 Paris, France

Prof. Jan M. LOCHMAN (Swiss Protestant Church Federation)
Heuberg 33, 4051 Basel, Switzerland

Mgr Basil MEEKING (Roman Catholic Church)
Secretariat for Promoting Christian Unity, 00120 Vatican City, Vatican

Prof. Dr Andor MUNTAG (Lutheran Church in Hungary)
Paulay Ede U 39, 1061 Budapest, Hungary

Prof. Nikos NISSIOTIS (Church of Greece)
5 Achilles Street, P. Faliron, Athens, Greece

Dr Milan OPOCENSKY (Evangelical Church of Czech Brethren)
Nepomucka 1025, 15000 Praha 5—Kosire, CSSR

Dr Jorge PANTELIS (Methodist Church)
Casilla 356, La Paz, Bolivia

The Rt. Rev. P.-W. SCHEELE (Roman Catholic Church)
Kardinal-Döpfner-Platz 4, 8700 Würzburg, FRG

Ms Pirjo TYÖRINOJA (Evangelical Lutheran Church of Finland)
Myllykallionrinne 2 C 23, 00210 Helsinki, Finland

Dr Keith WATKINS (Christian Church (Disciples of Christ))
Christian Theological Seminary, 1000 West 42nd Street, Indianapolis, IN 46208, USA

Faith and Order
Dr Thomas F. BEST
Mrs Eileen CHAPMAN
Dr Gennadios LIMOURIS